HOW TO MAKE AN ENTREPRENEURIAL STATE

'Defying timeworn stereotypes of bureaucracy, Kattel, Drechsler and Karo offer a fresh perspective on the state's pivotal role in societal progress. Their pioneering book will be essential to both those who want to understand, and those who want to realize the great transformations of our time.'

Professor Caspar van den Berg, Leiden University

'Bureaucracy plays a dual role in creating innovation in society and business. On the one hand, the bureaucracy is required to be an enabler in various changes in society through various policies and activities, on the other hand the bureaucracy must also be able to change itself in the midst of various regulatory rigidities. This book is very good at telling these two things and being an inspiration for practitioners, academics and students who are deep in bureaucracy.'

Professor Eko Prasojo, University of Indonesia

HOW TO MAKE AN ENTREPRENEURIAL STATE

WHY INNOVATION NEEDS BUREAUCRACY

RAINER KATTEL, WOLFGANG DRECHSLER AND ERKKI KARO

YALE UNIVERSITY PRESS
NEW HAVEN AND LONDON

For information about this and other Yale University Press publications, please contact:
U.S. Office: sales.press@yale.edu   yalebooks.com
Europe Office: sales@yaleup.co.uk   yalebooks.co.uk

Set in Adobe Garamond Regular by IDSUK (DataConnection) Ltd
Printed in Great Britain by TJ Books, Padstow, Cornwall

Library of Congress Control Number: 2022939251

ISBN 978-0-300-22727-7

A catalogue record for this book is available from the British Library.

10 9 8 7 6 5 4 3 2 1

Bureaucrats are stabilising knowledge, keeping things running, and sometimes innovating quite radically.

Brian Eno

We always have two jobs to do at the same time. On the one hand, all the time try to jump to the next level, to advance the digital state. . . . But taking it to the next level must go hand in hand with securing what we have. We cannot just make innovation leaps. But we cannot just focus on keeping the basics in order either, even if resources are scarce because people are waiting for changes. We need to deal with two challenges at once.

Siim Sikkut,
Estonia's Government Chief Information Officer,
2017–2022

CONTENTS

CONTENTS

ABBREVIATIONS

Entries with an asterisk are *not* expressed in their full form in the text.

A*STAR	Agency for Science, Technology and Research (Singapore)*
AI	artificial intelligence
AIST	Advanced Institute of Science and Technology (Japan)
ARIA	Advanced Research and Invention Agency (UK)
ARPA	Advanced Research Projects Agency (USA)
ARPA-E	Advanced Research Projects Agency – Energy (USA)
ARPA-ED	Advanced Research Projects Agency – Education (USA)*
ARPA-H	Advanced Research Projects Agency – Health (USA)
ATP	Advanced Technology Program (USA)
BNDES	National Bank for Economic and Social Development (Brazil)*

BOST	Board of Science and Technology (Taiwan)
BRA	Brazil
CCP	Chinese Communist Party
CERN	European Organization for Nuclear Research
CIA	Central Intelligence Agency (USA)
CSTI	Council for Science, Technology and Innovation Policy (Japan)
CSTP	Council for Science and Technology Policy (Japan)
CTO	chief technology officer
DARPA	Defense Advanced Research Projects Agency (USA)
DIA	Danish Innovation Agency
DoD	Department of Defense (USA)
DoE	Department of Energy (USA)
DRAM	Dynamic random-access memory
EC	European Community
ECU	European currency unit*
EPB	Economic Planning Board (South Korea)
ERA	European Research Area
EU	European Union*
FDA	Food and Drug Administration (USA)*
FOMO	fear of missing out
GDP	gross domestic product*
GDS	Government Digital Service (UK)
GFC	Global Financial Crisis (2008)
GNH	gross national happiness
ICT	information and communications technology
IDA	Industrial Development Agency (Ireland)*

ABBREVIATIONS

ImPACT	Impulsing Paradigm Change Through Disruptive Technologies Programme (Japan)
IoT	internet of things
IRSIA	Intercommunale du réseau social d'insertion et d'accueil, Belgium
IT	information technology
ITRI	Industrial Technology Research Institute (Taiwan)
KAIS	Korean Advanced Institute of Science
KIST	Korea Institute for Science and Technology
KMT	Kuomintang (Taiwan)
LDP	Liberal Democratic Party (Japan)
METI	Ministry of Economy, Trade and Industry (Japan)
MEXT	Ministry of Education, Culture, Sports, Science and Technology (Japan)
MIT	Massachusetts Institute of Technology*
MITI	Ministry of International Trade and Industry (Japan)
MoEA	Ministry of Economic Affairs (Taiwan)
MOST	Ministry of Science and Technology (South Korea, Taiwan)
MTIP	Mission-Oriented Topsector and Innovation Policy (Netherlands)
NAFTA	North American Free Trade Agreement*
NASA	National Aeronautics and Space Administration (USA)*
NDC	National Development Council (Taiwan)
NFSR	National Fund for Scientific Research (Belgium)

NGO	non-governmental organisation*
NIH	National Institute of Health (USA)
NNI	National Nanotechnology Initiative (USA)
NPM	New Public Management
NSC	National Science Council (Taiwan)
NSF	National Science Foundation (USA)
NSS	National Security State (USA)
NSTC	National Science and Technology Council (USA); National Science and Technology Committee (Korea)
NWS	Neo-Weberian State
OECD	Organisation for Economic Co-operation and Development
PA	public administration
PTR	Physikalisch-Technische Reichsanstalt [Physical-Technical Reich Institute]
R&D	research and development*
S&T	science and technology
SARS	severe acute respiratory syndrome*
SBDA	Small Business Development Act (USA)
SBIC	Small Business Investment Company (USA)
SBIR	Small Business Innovation Research (USA)
SCI	Strategic Computing Initiative (USA)
SEUM	Society for Establishing Useful Manufactures, US
SINTEF	Stiftelsen for industriell og teknisk forskning (Norway) [Foundation for Industrial and Technical Research]
SIP	Strategic Innovation Programme (Japan)
SME	small to medium-sized enterprise*

ABBREVIATIONS

STA	Science and Technology Agency (South Korea)
STEM	science, technology, engineering and mathematics*
STPC	Science and Technology Policy Council (Finland)
SWAT	special weapons and tactics*
TNO	Netherlands Organisation for Applied Scientific Research
USDS	United States Digital Service
USSR	Union of Soviet Socialist Republics*
VC	venture capital
VLSI	very large-scale integration
WTO	World Trade Organization*

FOREWORD

Mariana Mazzucato

For too long state bureaucracies have been associated negatively with stasis, inertia, complexification and resistance to change. But in fact – as this pathbreaking book shows – bureaucracies can be shaped creatively and in doing so become key to their dynamism, innovation and creativity rather than an impediment. Indeed, it will be impossible to drive growth that is more innovation-led, inclusive and sustainable without changing the state. This requires rethinking state capacity, capabilities and institutional structures. This is the wager driving the curiosity of Kattel, Drechsler and Karo as they delve deep into the exciting emerging field of creative bureaucracies.

The book is not about defending the state, but pushing it to be as dynamic as it can be – indeed, going against many of the assumptions we have grown to accept: bureaucracies as naturally rigid and boring. As my own research shows, the state and its agencies can be incredibly innovative under the right conditions. In *The Entrepreneurial State*, I demonstrated how many of the technological innovations of the digital age, those which went into the smart phone – including GPS and the internet itself – were innovated not by private sector entrepreneurs, as common sense might have it, but by state agencies such as the US state defence R&D agency DARPA, an organisation with a highly sophisticated and complex bureaucracy which funds and produces world-changing innovations. More recently, in *Mission Economy*, I revealed how the US state's space agency NASA's Apollo programme was guided by a singular ambitious mission – to put a man on the moon. This clear purpose required NASA to refigure its internal structure, to be more agile and flexible, with constant communication between project leaders. It also used new procurement methods to stimulate bottom-up innovation which resulted in many spin-off inventions and innovations that have transformed life on earth, including camera phones, software, CAT scans, LEDs, athletic shoes, water purification systems, home insulation, wireless headsets, memory foam, artificial limbs, the computer mouse and portable computer . . . the list goes on!

And now in *How to Make an Entrepreneurial State*, Kattel, Drechsler and Karo provide us with a wealth of yet more inspiring examples of bureaucratic state institutions that are systematically catalysing, funding or directly generating innovations across multiple societal domains and economic sectors. State bureaucracies, they argue, can support the flourishing of innovation across the economy and society largely because of two extraordinary characteristics. First, they are *stable*, consisting of established, enduring and secure sets of rules, relationships and procedures for making things happen, distributing resources, directing flows of capital, arbitrating over disputes, and guaranteeing against insecurities of various nature. Second, at the same time, they are *agile* and able to shift shape and respond in reflexive and creative ways to changing contextual conditions and policy problems. Kattel, Drechsler and Karo expertly argue that it is this combination – of stability and agility – that gives state bureaucracies the unique capability to cultivate change and creativity, all the while protecting past innovation gains and embedding these into existing governance arrangements for long-term endurance.

True to its title, the book shows why innovation needs bureaucracy. Despite the great potential for bureaucratic creativity, today's governments do not actually innovate all that often; they rarely engage in or with transformative change. Rethinking capitalism requires an entirely different way of building public sector organisations, making 'bureaucratic' a word that inspires creativity, not inertia. We need bureaucracies to drive innovation, shape markets and steer inclusive green transformation. We need living, learning 'creative bureaucracies'. We also need institutional solutions for civil society to hold bureaucracy accountable, without taking away the necessary level of autonomy and creativity. This means also making sure that states build capabilities to listen, and to engage with a wide group of stakeholders – creating what the well-known artist Olafur Eliasson, in an interview with me on the topic of public spaces, called safe places to disagree.

To help get this message out there, and to fuel new economic thinking and practice around it, I founded the Institute for Innovation and Public Purpose at UCL in 2017; the lead author of *How to Make an Entrepreneurial State*, Rainer Kattel, was with me from the very beginning as the institute's deputy director. Together, we have worked to build up this leading hub of research, education, policy translation and public engagement precisely for rethinking capitalism, rethinking the innovation that drives it, and rethinking the state that catalyses and regulates this dynamic process. We have established a new curriculum for our MPA programme, where one of the key courses is called *Creative Bureaucracies* – very much built on key lessons in this book. Indeed, it is creative bureaucrats of the future – those Kattel, Drechsler and Karo describe in their book as 'bureaucracy hackers' – who can act like guerrilla fighters to revolutionise state bureaucracies from the inside.

Of all the many take-home messages from this book, the idea of the bureaucracy hacker really resonates with our times. This is the figure who can solve the intractable wicked problems facing us and build organisations fit for twenty-first-century challenges. The challenges ahead – from global pandemics to climate breakdown – are bigger than any one market or sector, corporation or state agency can tackle on its own. If we are to address these crises, we need states and their bureaucracies to work together and coordinate collective action on a planetary scale not yet seen before in human history – to raise the scale and scope of innovation to new levels. And for this momentous task we need bureaucracy hackers to re-imagine and reconfigure bureaucracies around the world to unleash collective creativity and imagination for tackling the grand global challenges. We need to think bigger – and what better book for bigger thinking?

1

AGILE STABILITY

What would a world without quantum mechanics look like? There would be no computers, no iPads, no mobile phones and certainly no satellites. Most twentieth- and twenty-first-century electronics and, obviously, all the content that runs on them, from space communication to *Ghost of Tsushima*, would not exist. Data is often portrayed as the new gold or oil and, as McKinsey has claimed, by 2016 the value of global data was larger than that of the global trade in goods.[1] This would not have happened without quantum mechanics, yet it is still possible to imagine a world without them. The 1880s are not that far from us. We continue to read and maybe even discuss Dostoyevsky and enjoy Monet and many other cultural phenomena from the pre-quantum mechanics era – in British law courts and at weddings men still more or less dress like they did in the nineteenth century – but when we think about economic development and innovation, we tend to look back only as far as the aftermath of the Second World War.

This book makes a simple argument: innovations need bureaucracy. The birth and development of quantum mechanics required scientists, entrepreneurs and innovators, but it also required bureaucrats and bureaucracies. And it was not accidental. Behind the development of quantum mechanics was a complex bureaucratic web of public and private capacities and capabilities, able to envision, plan, iterate and deliver. This book tells the story of these organisations, which we call innovation bureaucracies, public sector organisations tasked with fostering innovation by creating, funding, regulating and procuring those innovations, and we argue that 'innovation bureaucracy' is not an oxymoron.

It is a counterintuitive combination of words. Literally the rule of the office – the French *bureau* for office and the Greek *kratein* for rule – to be called a 'bureaucrat' is never a compliment for a public servant. 'Bureaucracy' is a term that has always signalled slowness, complicated and superfluous procedures, getting the run-around. In short, outside of the world of public administration academics at least, it is a negative word, an insult almost, indicating the bad aspects of public administration, the professional management of public sector affairs and the implementation of public policy. (There are often even larger bureaucracies in big private sector firms and in NGOs as well, but this is not what people primarily associate with bureaucracy and is not our topic.)

We owe a lot of what came to be known as quantum mechanics to a rather obscure public organisation, the Physikalisch-Technische Reichsanstalt (PTR), established in 1887 in a small German town of 30,000 people. Until 1920 Charlottenburg was a separate city, next to Berlin, and the main purpose of the PTR – to develop physical standards and measurement instruments – does not sound wildly exciting or innovative for today's readers. However, the PTR played an important role not only in the pioneering work of Max Planck and others in quantum physics but also as a crucial cog in the rise of German industrial leadership, particularly for the electrical industry, and it helped to create technologies and global players that still exist today, such as Siemens and AEG.[2]

It took more than fifteen years of discussions to establish the PTR, but its success was phenomenal. By the early 1900s it was the global leader in its fields and it helped to win two Nobel prizes (Wilhelm Wien in 1911 and Max Planck in 1918). According to David Cahan, 'Between 1875 and 1907 the number of factories [in Germany] increased from 88 to more than 1,000 and the number of employees from slightly less than 1,300 to more than 91,000.'[3] In other words, the PTR was one of the key drivers in shifting the global technology and innovation leadership from the UK to Germany.[4]

The establishment of the PTR – who was involved, how and why, its initial resources and its organisational evolution – offers an almost ideal-typical example of how (successful) innovation bureaucracies are established and how they evolve. The PTR was established on land donated by Werner Siemens, one of the leading industrialists of the time. Moreover, Siemens heavily lobbied for the PTR with the German government, covered initial construction costs and recruited its first leader in Hermann Helmholz, an outstanding German scientist and science organiser.[5] In fact, Siemens also provided, based on his own experiences as an industrialist, its organisational design – the departmental division, hierarchy of authority and control – and guidelines on how to develop it. His idea was to find a strong or charismatic leader for the new organisation who would then build up a 'scientific bureaucracy'[6] – a blueprint of how to move from the agile and search-driven or startup phase of an organisation to a more stable delivery-focused one.

This organisational model served as a best practice case for other German organisations financing and carrying out R&D, most notably the Kaiser-Wilhelm-Gesellschaft, founded in 1911 and renamed the Max-Planck-Gesellschaft in 1946, as well as the British National Physical Laboratory, established in 1898, and the American National Bureau of Standards, established in 1901. Particularly in Germany, the PTR blueprint of advancing cutting-edge science and at the same time working closely with and providing services to industry came to dominate innovation bureaucracy. In other words, this was not a theoretical model but almost a natural best practice that emerged and evolved through attempts to build innovation bureaucracies in the private and public spheres.

The role played by Siemens and others like him is that of a charismatic 'bureaucracy hacker': somebody, usually from outside, who is highly skilled at navigating the existing bureaucracy and political networks, with enough clout to push forward changes, who can open doors for new ideas and new ways of doing things. The term 'bureaucracy hacker' comes, of course, from Silicon Valley. In a blog post for the US government digital agency 18F, Greg Godbout and Noah Kunin argued that what 18F is doing is hacking bureaucracy: 'hackers are problem solvers. We consider ourselves hackers in that positive sense: productively disruptive and curious.'[7] 18F was created in 2014 by a group of Presidential Innovation Fellows, who were part of a programme designed to bring 'entrepreneurs in residence' to government and partner them with civil servants to get novel things done.[8] 'Hacking', solving problems and building ad hoc collaborations and teams are very much part of innovation bureaucracy dynamics, providing agility in order to adapt to a changing environment or to drive needed changes in public organisations.

What bureaucracy hackers, who become the charismatic centre points of specific change movements, are extremely good at is creating 'mission mystique', a term coined by Charles Goodsell in 2011. He analysed some US agencies with particularly tough and hopeless tasks (think of the impossibility of getting long-term weather forecasts correct, at least before the era of real-time satellite images and big data) to understand how these organisations manage to keep their employees motivated and the societal status of the organisation high.

Mission mystique is essentially a bespoke belief system, unique to the specific organisation: 'The mission mystique agency is endowed with an aura of positive institutional charisma that is derived from the nature of its mission and how well it is carried out—hence the term mission mystique. It is felt both within and outside the organization. To career employees, the mystique fosters a personal commitment to advancement of the mission. To attentive outsiders, it generates admiration and respect.'[9] Creating and sustaining mission mystique is a key part of innovation bureaucracy. It allows innovation bureaucracy to cope with the risks and uncertainties associated with innovation (failing in the public sector is always tough and draws a lot of criticism) and to lead the dynamic changes of innovation processes.

In terms of bureaucracy hacking and mission mystique, PTR is a blueprint of what we call an innovation bureaucracy organisation. Structurally as well as ideologically, PTR, as when it was established, looks to us to be a very modern and familiar set-up stemming from discussions and debates that we see again and again in today's innovation discourse:

- It was born out of an acute sense of lagging behind in terms of industrial might in emerging industries (with important military and defence implications) and in nationally funded long-term basic research that the private sector did not fund;[10]
- Parliamentary debates evolved around whether to establish the PTR on a local or federal level, to create a wholly new institution or to attach it to an existing one;[11]
- In terms of hierarchy, it was created by and accountable to the Parliament (with quite detailed and technical periodic reporting);[12]
- It was formally an (Imperial) governmental agency under the Ministry of the Interior (Reichsamt des Innern – its Staatssekretär served ex-officio as chairman of the PTR's board); its status as an agency also meant that the members of the PTR were remunerated through Imperial-agency pay scales, which in the early 1900s became a problem as university salaries increased more rapidly (and by that time universities were offering more academic freedom and prestige);[13]
- It was managed by a president who oversaw two distinct (initially even in different physical locations) sections, one for, in today's language, basic research and the other for development (industrial contracts); each section had a similar hierarchical structure (head of the section, members organised in teams, assistants);[14]

- Its funding easily outmatched those of similar organisations in the US (which invested only about half of what Germany did) and England (six times less than Germany),[15] even without Siemens' contribution in land and capital.

The key organisational features, such as being a government agency, working in teams and needing to provide services to industry, became some of the reasons for its relative decline and were why it was superseded by its own imitators, the institutes of the Kaiser-Wilhelm-Gesellschaft. However, we argue that this is actually a sign of successful innovation bureaucracies: success brings emulation and the eventual decline of the emulated as the newcomers can learn, adapt and adjust to changing contexts better than the incumbent.

The sequence of events in establishing the PTR – (private) charismatic push and networking to create an organisation for a new or emerging area of activity; discussions and conflicts with existing establishment over the directionality of the organisation; leveraging political networks for support; after the initial establishment phase the introduction of more standardised procedures and routines within the organisation; followed by emulation by others, if successful – is therefore something of a blueprint for how innovation bureaucracy organisations, and innovation bureaucracy in general, come about and evolve.

Further, as is often the case with such industrial transformations in a particular country, one organisation rarely does it alone: successful innovation bureaucracies consist of different 'types' of organisations, in terms of both core tasks and suitable organisational designs. For innovations to diffuse, spaces for knowledge creation are hardly ever enough, because innovation needs not only knowledge but also significant amounts of funding, as well as arenas for networks and interactions for innovation ecosystems to emerge. This was the case with PTR as well. Its success was as much due to its founding and organisational principles as it was to co-evolution of other innovation bureaucracy organisations alongside PTR. These organisations went through similar processes of evolution. Together, the organisational configuration of late nineteenth-century German innovation bureaucracy was able to provide highly dynamic changes and investments, but also laid the foundations for longer-term success.

Created in the same period as PTR and designed to enable long-term (patient) industrial financing by private investment banks,[16] one of the earliest and more successful central banks, the German Reichsbank, was directly under the guidance of the Imperial Chancellor, yet it was initially privately owned and followed corresponding management practices.[17] Over the course of the twentieth century, not only did central banks' functions change rather drastically, focusing on fiscal and monetary policy (and since the 1980s increasingly only on monetary policy), they also underwent rather significant organisational changes. While up to the Second World War it was typical for a central bank to be closely related to, if not situated in, the Finance Ministry (i.e. governed by normal civil service rules), today central banks are typically autonomous public bodies with their own laws and regulations.[18] In consequence, central banks have altogether ceased to be part of innovation bureaucracies, although in the beginning, this was a key feature. Thus, other financing organisations – R&D and innovation agencies, loan guarantee agencies, public and private venture funds – have emerged as new elements of innovation bureaucracies, carrying out similar functions.

Equally important to the success of German industry in the late nineteenth century were industry cartels, set up to coordinate certain elements of industrial development. While private sector business interest associations have origins in medieval guilds and later in the city management of markets (specifically limiting competition but also guaranteeing delivery and quality[19]), perhaps the most prominent case of publicly supported private cartels is also the late nineteenth- and early twentieth-century German industrialisation effort, later emulated by the UK and many other countries. Typically, the organisational configurations of these cartels were very loose in the sense that the public sector's role was to coordinate various public policy fields and organisations, from competition and intellectual property to forging linkages with research institutions and applied education institutions. While private cartels have become effectively outlawed in modern economies, during the post-Second World War era the management of competition (to provide critical mass for export competitiveness while avoiding over-investment and over-capacity) was also a crucial function of industrial and development policy agencies in East Asia. The anti-trust agencies of today deal mostly with investigating price collusion and fixing, rarely dipping into the innovation arena, although this is beginning to change with competition authorities looking at some of the practices of leading digital platform companies such as Amazon and Alphabet.[20] Today's equivalents of cartels are a variety of R&D consortia, cluster organisations, technology parks, business incubators and accelerators. In all these organisations, their public leadership and organisational resources are secondary, and private funding, initiative and management practices dominate, although with highly varying degrees of success.

Simply put, we are witnessing this sequence and evolution again and again over the centuries and contexts of capitalist development: new agile innovation bureaucracy organisations are established to deal with new emerging technological or socio-economic challenges, and over time these organisations, or rather the tasks they fulfil, are 'socialised' or institutional-ised into existing public sector practices.

Perhaps somewhat surprisingly, this dynamic is well described, and indeed predicted, by none other than the great sociologist Max Weber, one of the most eminent social scien-tists of the last but one turn of the century, who had his own intimate connection with the emergence of Germany as indus-trial leader. Often a strawman for bureaucratic, legalistic and rigid organisations, Weber in fact described a variety of ways in which authority, or legitimacy, is generated and exercised, as well as how one type of authority (charismatic) becomes another type (legal-rational or bureaucratic), only to be chal-lenged again by the initial type (charismatic). Innovation is an area where these Weberian dynamics play out rather well.

In this book, we argue that these Weberian notions reveal themselves in the context of innovation bureaucracies through two ideal-typical categories of organisations – *charismatic networks* and *expert organisations* – and that their evolution is often an oscillation between the two extremes, within the same organisation, or leads to the emergence of new ones.[21] These two ideal-types of organisations possess rather different capabilities and skill sets, and they perform different functions. As we show, the charismatic networks provide agility and dynamism for innovation bureaucracies to search for new directions and ways of doing things, while expert organisations bring long-term focus, predictability and stability to deliver needed policies and results. Both are key to the success of capitalist systems. Indeed, we propose to call this symbiosis agile stability. It is this contradictory, once-again counterintuitive combination that creates the success of the entrepreneurial state.

We argue that genuinely entrepreneurial states have capacities and capabilities for 'agile stability' – that is, they are entrepreneurial not in the sense of go-getter startuppery but oriented towards *overall* success in context. This requires both agility- and stability-oriented mindsets and for organisations to be able to go along with, support and sometimes even lead the economic and societal transformations. In the public sector, this may be more difficult to ascertain than in a simple business framework where the bottom line matters, because public value is not easy to agree on.

In the pre-COVID-19 world, governments were increasingly turning their attention to how to tackle 'grand challenges' or 'wicked issues' such as climate change, demographic challenges and the promotion of health and well-being.[22] This 'normative turn' in economic and especially in innovation policy making – meaning a focus on the realisation of values towards which successful innovation systems must bend – has shown how innovation and public leadership of innovation have become increasingly crucial.

This book is, we think, the first to address the 'how' question head on. How do governments actually organise their efforts in relation to innovation? How do they achieve agile stability? What makes governments succeed or fail at this? If economic success in the place where we live is crucial for a happy, meaningful and successful life, if innovation is crucial for economic success (except in a few resource-rich places, for a while) and if innovation needs to be scaffolded and indeed organised by the state, as is demonstrably the case, then not only does the right innovation policy matter but it needs to be implemented successfully and that means it has to be made real. This book tells you how, and we do that by taking a fresh look at theory, as well as examining various success cases in time and space, resulting in a narrative that raises awareness of the need for innovation bureaucracies and may help shape their future.

This book is not about innovation policy and why and how government should design it better; there are plenty of those, including many good ones. Rather, it is about how state and public organisations develop capacities (or capacity, i.e. the space, the option to do something in an intended way) and dynamic capabilities (the skills to do so) for maintaining the stability *and* agility necessary for innovation. Indeed, we offer to redefine what entrepreneurial states are: these are states that are capable of supporting and unleashing necessary innovations in society to tackle important societal challenges (including growth and development) and maintaining broader socio-political stability at the same time.

The Innovator's Dilemma in the Public Sector

Nothing exemplifies the idea of agile stability better than the COVID-19 crisis, when governments had to find quick solutions in public health, labour markets and helping out businesses. One of the biggest lessons of the global responses to the pandemic is that governments need both long-term policy and administrative capacities (e.g. in healthcare), but also dynamic capabilities (e.g. in rapidly building track and trace systems and revising and adjusting long-term plans and strategies) in order to handle the crisis. While the pandemic is serious for all, it is especially a challenge for countries that have ignored needed investments in public sector agile stability.

For instance, countries such as the US and the UK have realised how vulnerable their production and public health systems are and how difficult it is to ramp up production and coordinate supply chains for food, medicine, ventilators, protective equipment and test kits.[23] Other countries, such as Germany and South Korea, have shown much more resilience in their production and health systems, thanks to the capacities and capabilities of their governments to coordinate private sector activity and largely public ownership of critical health system elements. Impressive test capacity in both countries was made possible by the existence of public laboratories and the presence of industries that could supply the required safety equipment and chemicals. Neither could be built in a matter of weeks or even months; these are long-term developments that require investment, planning and coordination with the private sector. When the UK government opted in late 2020 to roll out a cross-country mass-testing programme by ramping up rapid testing from 800,000 daily tests to 10 million, which included the development of new technologies (more reliable rapid tests, real-time databases, etc.) and building up seamless logistics chains, this was described as a 'moonshot' challenge, as it was considered as ambitious as any space adventure.[24]

Countries in Southeast Asia with relatively recent experience in tackling SARS were much quicker to respond with large-scale tracking of infections and the establishment of travel limitations and social distancing rules.[25] In Germany, learning from managing floods and influenza during the last two decades had led to operational emergency plans and risk analyses for pandemics and floods being available since 2013.[26] In India, while the national response has been a failure in many ways, the state of Kerala's successful response to the crisis was also the result of long-term investment in the health sector (including the protocols put in place after the Nipah virus outbreak) and a successful public-private partnership model.[27] In Vietnam, the government was quick to recognise the complexity of the problem, closed its borders early and rapidly spurred the development of low-cost test kits.[28] A similar response was found in Bhutan, formally a least developed country but with a particularly strong public sector.[29] In short, effective pandemic response governance, as well as tackling most of the wicked issues of our times (i.e. issues that cannot easily be solved without creating a host of other problems), such as inequality and climate change, requires capacities and capabilities for resilience or a functioning combination of agility and stability.[30]

If this is so obvious, why do not all countries and regions create agile stability? Well, first, it is not so obvious, and second, fashion, ideology, fear of costs and incentive systems often stand in the way. When public administrations fail, they often fail on a large scale, but when they succeed, the benefits and gains are often ascribed to others. Thus, the fact that civil servants are often risk averse should not really come as a surprise. Rather, the risk-averse behaviour indicates that there is something unique about the way public administrations deal with (the need to) change.

Perhaps not surprisingly it was Joseph A. Schumpeter (1883–1950), the most important modern innovation scholar, who captured this dilemma of government in a forceful juxtaposition. Writing in 1918 about the crisis of the tax state, a year before he became Austria's – notoriously unsuccessful – minister of finance, Schumpeter argued:

> In any case, the state has its definite limits. These are, of course, not conceptually definable limits of its field of social action, but limits to its fiscal potential. These vary considerably in each specific case according to the wealth or poverty of the country, to the concrete details of its national and social structure, and to the nature of its wealth. There is a great difference between new, active, and growing wealth and old wealth, between *entrepreneurial and rentier states*.[31] (Italics added)

Schumpeter's differentiation between entrepreneurial and rentier states – states that live from creative initiatives vs those that draw their income from previously acquired wealth or natural resources – is one of the big twentieth-century theoretical and ideological fault lines in economics and governance. On the one hand, evolutionary economists and innovation scholars are interested in a state that creates solutions for structural change in societies, for instance through bold challenge-driven and mission-oriented policies (e.g. the Manhattan and Apollo projects[32]), and invests in the long-term development of knowledge and capacities. This is a state oriented towards purposeful change to maintain and increase its competitiveness and resilience.

On the other hand, mainstream economists have been trying to understand rentier states, best embodied in the – less mainstream – public choice theories of Gordon Tullock, William Niskanen and others. This is a state where bureaucrats follow their self-interest, build ever larger organisations because this brings prestige, yet shun responsibility and curb private initiative. This is a state oriented towards permanence and status quo.

In this division, we can detect a certain loss of ambiguity. As we are arguing here, governments, and in particular public administrations, are stuck between the needs of change and permanence, and neither is necessarily evil. This ambiguity, however, cannot be resolved; it is in the nature of the public sector. We can also call it the public sector innovator's dilemma: how to provide stability and change at the same time, if both are needed, not just to make profits but to exist to begin with? The state, as Aristotle says, comes into existence so that we can survive and it stays in existence so that we can have a good life.[33]

That this ambiguity, or dilemma, has real-life consequences and is related directly to innovation is clearly expressed by John Kenneth Galbraith when he speaks about the 'bureaucratic symbiosis' that leads to industrial development *and* to inequality:

The government, we have seen, contributes notably to inequality in development. Where the industry is powerful, government responds strongly to its needs. And also to its products. It gives the automobile industry roads for its cars, the weapons industry orders for its weapons, other industries support for research and development. . . . What is done for Lockheed is sound public policy. The purchase of pictures for the National Gallery makes dubious economic sense.[34]

The balancing act between agility and stability makes public bureaucracies unique in how they work, succeed and fail. Indeed, there are innovations that were created by public officials 2,000 years ago and are still in use, such as public baths from Roman times. And some of these baths are still used for the same purposes: public health and social gathering.[35] There is nothing comparable in the private sector, at least not in the global West.

Thus, we should expect that capacities and capabilities required for agile stability are relatively unique to the public sector, but we should also be aware that this dilemma or ambiguity has both a good and a bad side. Military demand and R&D have given us not only today's digital realities, from iPhones to artificial intelligence (AI), but, as noted by Richard Nelson in the late 1970s in his classic, *The Moon and the Ghetto*,[36] ever-growing challenging social issues as well. Almost symbolically, the celebrations of fifty years of the moon landing in 2019, and parallel searches for similar 'missions' to restart our socio-economic progress globally, have been overshadowed by more critical social movements, from climate emergency to racial injustice protests.

In achieving agile stability, successful innovation bureaucracies complement private sector activities and capabilities in innovation. In other words, they co-create and sustain cross-sectoral complementarities underpinning socio-economic development.[37] This entails creating conditions, through various policy options, for the private sector and society as a whole to further explore and exploit existing technological and innovation potentials (e.g. through applied research grants for private companies or public vocational education training) to converge on and advance the (global) best practices and the socio-technological frontier. This often involves weighing competing policy subjects and their potential and needs. Policy makers ask whether they should support an existing electronics company or a new startup in services. Is one sector or economic activity more important than another? These questions tend to be oriented towards mid-term challenges and solutions, spanning a typical electoral cycle or two, and summarised in national development and innovation strategies. They are also often about using existing resources effectively and are representations of the existing political and economic landscape.

Given the constant evolution of technologies, political and economic realities and the uncertainty characterising new emerging technologies and socio-economic challenges (think of our evolving knowledge of climate change, its dynamics and impacts), the foundations of these cross-sectoral complementarities – what innovation bureaucracies and companies do and how they complement each other – are under constant pressure, particularly to change and recombine. Indeed, most economic and business elites as well as the general public seem to simultaneously criticise governments both for changing some policies and regulations too often and too fast (and thus undermining the possibilities for companies to exploit their business models and strategies) and for not changing some policies and regulations fast enough (to allow companies to explore new avenues emerging from technological and social evolutions).

Thus, and this is the focus of our book, to satisfy these conflicting expectations, successful innovation bureaucracies need to create and sustain, as their core task, this agile stability: internal dynamism and learning in policies, services, institutions and organisational formats complemented by the ability to maintain stability, patiently implement policies and deliver the services expected from the state.

On the level of innovation systems (regions and countries), successful innovation bureaucracies try to constantly balance multiple timeframes and policy cycles: on the one hand, mitigating the risks of the short- and mid-term exploitation strategies of existing industries and economic sectors and on the other hand, managing the uncertainties of radical innovation,[38] as well as the search for new competitive advantages through new directions of innovation.[39] In addition, innovation bureaucracies need to deal with a potentially 'creatively destructive' impact on existing markets, industries and institutions.

In this continuous and evolving balancing act, one of the core challenges of innovation bureaucracies emerges in its most explicit form: while risk mitigation to support the development and maximisation of rents/profits from existing industries and business institutions may require a more stability-oriented innovation bureaucracy set-up, the management of uncertainties may require different types of skills and capabilities and an innovation bureaucracy set-up that is open to change, experimentation and internal innovation. Sometimes this may even mean taking the lead in exploring new directions of technological change (e.g. through long-term funding of basic research, new institutions or regulatory frameworks). Mission-oriented innovation policies are good examples of creating not only new technological frontiers (e.g. the internet) but also entirely new markets (e.g. digital services).[40] This often involves choosing between different potential directions of long-term technological development, diverging from current trends and overcoming political and economic resistance to change.[41] Policy makers ask and make informed bets on which new renewable energy system entails the largest future potential, how much should we risk on funding nanotechnology research in universities, and so forth. Such policy questions tend to have long-term horizons and also wider moral connotations.

The evolutionary nature of this balancing act is revealed in several situations. For example, recent political debates in South Korea and Taiwan have focused on how to shift from amazingly successful catching-up and technological emulation-based development models to 'true' innovation-based development to sustain similar economic growth and development in the future.[42] Once the economies are at the techno-economic frontier (such as the US, Germany, Japan), this challenge is about never being satisfied with current levels of development, policy and institutional approaches and constantly searching for new horizons, better policies and ways to organise these, even if current institutions and living conditions seem fine. In a sense, this is the attempt to beat the certainty of the rise and fall of great powers (or any state, civilisation or group) commonly associated with Oswald Spengler,[43] through self-reinvention, along the lines of Giuseppe Tomasi di Lampedusa's idea that 'If everything should remain the same, everything must change',[44] just as big firms can reinvent themselves through rethinking how they innovate.

On the level of specific industries or sectors, these challenges exist on a somewhat more comprehensible level. While in the late nineteenth century, cars were an open-ended new technology competing with horse-drawn carriages and trains, the industry matured considerably over the twentieth century, only to face in the twenty-first century the new challenge of electric and self-driving cars. Throughout the evolution of the car industry over the past 150 years, public organisations have played diverse roles, from regulator (of safety and standards) to educator (from technical production skills to public safety awareness), to infrastructure builder (streets, highways), to research funder (electric and self-driving cars). These roles have been played by diverse organisations with diverse political and economic networks, administrative cultures, funding mechanisms and evaluation criteria. Yet without these organisations, it is safe to say, cars would not be as ubiquitous, relatively reliable and safe as they are today. In other words, the mid- and long-range questions policy makers face are answered by diverse organisations that often work in parallel, compete for political and financial resources and go through internal management reforms. What is interesting is that even studies specifically discussing the transformation of the car industry from horse-driven to electric do not discuss how public organisations have changed – or not – along the way.[45] Yet it seems far-fetched to assume that public organisations do not change over the course of 150 years. Rather, public administration histories have shown how public sector organisations go through waves or even cycles of reforms based on different political, administrative, cultural and even technological logics,[46] even if they often stay remarkably stable across several decades.[47]

However, the fluid and ambidextrous nature of innovation bureaucracy also tells us that quite different kinds of organisation are dealing with diverse tasks: regulating seat belt safety is not the same as investing in the development of self-driving cars. (Ambidexterity means being able to work with both hands equally well; in organisation theory, it means being able to both manage current strengths and capture the future.[48]) Equally important is the fact that in different cultural and political settings, different types of organisation might attempt to tackle similar challenges – and be successful. While Barack Obama may have bemoaned that 'we live and do business in the Information Age, but the last major reorganisation of the government happened in the age of black-and-white TV',[49] nobody would readily 'accuse' China of having a bureaucracy fit for the information age, and yet China has been growing rapidly through the past decades and continues to do so today, as well as taking increasing state-led control of the information age itself.

Plan of the Book

What follows is based on two sets of chapters. First, Chapters 2 and 3 offer a bird's-eye view of the history of and debates on innovation bureaucracy, mostly in a Western and predominantly European context; this extremely condensed historical narrative allows us to explore the key concepts underlying innovation bureaucracies, such as mission mystique and bureaucracy hacking, but also more traditional concepts, such as public sector capacities and capabilities. These chapters further pursue the main theoretical foundation of innovation bureaucracies, from Weber and Schumpeter to developmental and entrepreneurial state debates. Second, Chapters 4 to 6 tell the history of innovation bureaucracy since the Second World War in roughly two- to three-decade periods (1950s–1960s, 1970s–1980s and 1990s–2010s). These chapters are narrated through geographic lenses: each chapter shows how innovation bureaucracies evolved in the US, Europe and Asia respectively (with the exception of China; see our brief discussion of China in Chapter 2). Finally, Chapter 7 summarises the arguments of the book through the lenses of lessons learned from COVID responses and takes a speculative look at the decades ahead.

2

STATE OF THE DEBATE

Context: Government's Expanding Innovation Brief

How do governments understand innovations and their role in supporting and fostering innovations? Since innovation as a policy arena has been continuously expanding over past decades, in particular since the Global Financial Crisis (GFC) of 2008, we need to look at this specific context first. Before the GFC, the role of governments in innovation was expanding in the sense of developing ever more complex interventions, primarily to tackle market failures, but after the GFC legitimate expectations have gradually expanded, at least rhetorically, towards governments giving direction to innovation efforts to simultaneously tackle wicked societal challenges and co-create new market opportunities.

In the US, the then incoming Obama administration responded to the GFC with a proactive innovation strategy,[1] as well as a bold stimulus programme that proposed to spend an extra US$100 billion on innovation.[2] Through these documents, the government set itself three broad tasks: to invest in the *building blocks* of American innovation, that is in basic research, education and infrastructure, including information technology (ICT); to promote *competitive markets* that spur productive entrepreneurship through export promotion, open capital markets, incentives for entrepreneurship, and public sector and social innovation; and to *catalyse breakthroughs* in clean energy, next generation vehicles, health ICT and other twenty-first-century grand challenges.

Over the years, the question of how to actually *implement* these goals became more and more important. The original 2009 strategy relied on the continued 'DARPA-fication' of US innovation policy thinking. The Defense Advanced Research Projects Agency (DARPA) organisational model, which relies on short-term recruitment of highly recognised academic and industry experts to manage lean and flexible, but well targeted and problem-oriented, R&D projects, was taken as a successful example of how government can support innovation: design novel and agile organisations to take risks that the private sector might not be willing to take and set visions and missions with public values in mind (we discuss the DARPA model in detail in Chapter 4). Thus, the Advanced Research Projects Agency – Energy (ARPA-E) for energy innovation was created in 2009 and ARPA-ED for education was proposed in 2011. The 2015 revisions of *A Strategy for American Innovation* proposed to introduce 'innovation labs' at federal agencies to build a more systemic culture of innovation within government 'by empowering and equipping agency employees and members of the public to implement their promising ideas to more effectively serve the American people'.[3] The key US digital agency, 18F, can be seen as another example of introducing new agile

25

organisations into the governance structure to speed up public sector digital transformation (see Chapter 6).

Most of these US initiatives have been closely followed and benchmarked by other leading nations, from East Asia to Europe. For some, the US approach is a 'quantity theory of innovation', that is if you throw enough money at a challenge, some innovations will emerge,[4] but whether or not one agrees with this approach, discussions on the government's role in innovation have never been as lively as they are today.

In Japan, the 'Abenomics' of 2010s included the economic revitalisation strategy 'Japan is back!', which, after two and a half 'lost decades', sought to turn the country into the global driver of economic growth and innovation that it once was. The strategy included 'structural reforms' through deregulation that supports industrial revitalisation, for example creating 'experimental zones' where drones can deliver medicine to the elderly, and government and the private sector can figure out how best to compromise between the benefits and limits of sharing-economy business models such as Airbnb and Uber. It also included a so-called 'strategic market creation plan' that focuses on pertinent socio-economic challenges, such as the energy constraints experienced by an island nation, health and medical care in an ageing society and next-generation infrastructure in an environment prone to natural disasters, and operationalised these challenges as opportunities for innovation and the creation of new domestic and global markets. The emulation and extension of the DARPA model, which for some locals was originally copied from the Japanese 1970s–1980s approach to science and technology (S&T) development, have also been as popular as in the US.

It is important to keep in mind that while today Japan and most others look at the US and its DARPA approach as global best practice for designing and implementing innovation-supporting policies, in the 1980s the learning dynamics were the opposite: the West was trying to understand how Japan had succeeded in catching up with the West after the Second World War. Chalmers Johnson's 1982 study of the Japanese Ministry of International Trade and Industry (MITI) had a huge impact on our understanding of Japanese bureaucracy, as well as on concepts of *state* or *policy capacity* and the *public-private partnerships* in policy making. Chris Freeman's 1987 study of Japanese technology policies,[5] and how technological and institutional innovations co-evolve, is considered one of the classic texts of the 'innovation systems' approach, the most influential academic and policy-level innovation policy concept of the decades around the turn of the century.

To provide a new policy discourse and to become again one of the main global innovation hot spots, the Japanese government introduced the concept of 'Super Smart Society', or 'Society 5.0', as the new umbrella concept for guiding and directing its innovation initiatives.[6] Society 5.0 tries to take the discourse beyond existing concepts such as Industry 4.0 or the Fourth Industrial Revolution to think of innovation in a much broader, societal and future-oriented way by looking at the emergence and evolution of new technologies (internet of things (IoT), big data, robotics, new materials, personalised medicine, etc.) in a holistic and society-centric (as opposed to market- or technology-centric) way. It considers issues such as how these innovations will co-evolve in modern society, what future they will offer (merger of physical and cyber spaces) and how government can support this co-evolution in a sustainable way.

In the EU, where the GFC has had the longest-lasting impact on the economy and policies, cementing the shift from the EU's original ideology of a social-market economy towards a neoliberal austerity paradigm, the European Commission explicitly recommended that member states should try to 'sustain and where possible promote growth-enhancing expenditures within overall fiscal consolidation efforts',[7] that is, to safeguard or even increase investments into research and innovation even within the overall austerity paradigm. In addition, through the Horizon 2020 programme, the European Commission itself sought to initiate EU-wide research and innovation efforts to tackle pertinent societal challenges (health and demographic changes, sustainable energy, climate, transport, safe and secure societies) and initiate the search for innovations through explicitly experimental and co-productive, or public-private cooperation-based, approaches where basic R&D, experimentation and piloting, and user feedback are included in two- to three-year research and innovation projects carried out by multi-national and multidisciplinary teams. In 2018, the European Commission proposed that tackling these societal challenges could be made (in the 2021–2027 financial framework) more effective by focusing on specific EU-wide missions (such as achieving plastic-free oceans or creating a certain number of climate-neutral cities) that rely on bold and visionary steering coordinated by the European Commission, and agile implementation through portfolios of interdisciplinary research and innovation projects.[8] The 2019 European Green Deal and ambitions for climate neutrality try to further consolidate policy efforts around a system-wide core direction for development.

These visions and policy strategies represent broader changes in the global innovation and innovation policy discourse. First, innovation policy has become *less technocratic* and *more politicised.* Innovation has become mainstream. We can also argue that between R&D and innovation policies on the one hand and public sector innovation (as perceived by government actors) on the other, delineations have become blurred. Governments all over the world have set up large-scale national and international strategies for innovation and employed chief technology officers and S&T advisors to enact national innovation agendas through high-level policy coordination bodies composed of politicians, policy makers, 'visionary' scientists and entrepreneurs, such as the National Economic Council in the US or the Council for Science, Technology and Innovation in Japan. Historians might hear the echoes of the Second World War-era glorification of science in today's rhetoric on innovation: rationality has been replaced with creativity as a potential solution to socio-economic challenges.

Second, the roles of public and private sector organisations in innovation are being debated and questioned based on *new norms and values.* The traditionally neutral and economics-based terms and justifications for innovation policy, developed in waves of innovation studies since the 1950s – such as fixing market failures, creating a level playing field or framework conditions for innovators to compete between themselves, treating innovation as a systemic phenomenon (innovation ecosystems, systems of innovation), competitiveness and so on – have been complemented, indeed it seems superseded, by much more normative, ethical and social demands and concerns.

Thus, modern innovation policies implemented by innovation bureaucracies apparently have to fulfil several tasks:

- create conditions for private sector innovators to come up with new ideas and then turn them into innovations (the most traditional role);
- steer and coordinate public and private sector actions towards tackling societal challenges;
- unleash and lead innovation in complex established legacy sectors (from energy to education) where the entrenched interests of producers and consumers are fighting against specific directions of innovation and change;
- in some countries, renew national development models by leading the change from strategies based on the exploitation of natural resources or the import of technology and innovation towards indigenous science, technology and innovation-based development;
- especially since the GFC, proactively complement private sector risk-taking by proposing alternative pathways to development and innovation and 'creating' new markets through leadership in 'high risk, high return' research and innovation activities; and
- one way or another deliver or at least demonstrate public sector transformation or innovativeness in public sector ways of working: opening the systems of government (which in most developed countries encompass 30–40 per cent of GDP) to ideas deemed innovative, new(ish) management principles (e.g. co-creation, peer-to-peer production)

and technologies, sometimes with the aim of not only improving the efficiency of existing governance arrangements but also providing additional public value.

Given this broadening of the scope of the public innovation agenda, one could spend pages on theoretical debates on whether the government should be so proactive in innovation and whether governments are actually capable of fulfilling all these tasks in terms of picking the right things to prioritise and coordinating the delivery of those priorities.[9] Yet, these broadening expectations and justifications for the role of the state in innovation are not the creation of politicians and technocrats searching for power and legitimacy, or trying to maximise the budgets of their bureaus. These new tasks of innovation policy have, by and large, been introduced to the policy discourse and legitimised by much broader innovation 'elites' that also encompass visionary scientists and entrepreneurs.

Elon Musk, probably at times both the most celebrated and the most criticised twenty-first-century innovator and Schumpeterian entrepreneur, has collaborated with the government by starting his hoped-soon-to-be self-driving Tesla car business and solar energy empire Solar City, now called Tesla Energy, (i.e. by benefitting from government loan guarantees and subsidies worth billions of dollars) and developing the space exploration capabilities of his SpaceX (i.e. by benefitting from long-term procurement contracts from NASA, again worth billions of dollars; indeed, Musk is the self-proclaimed 'biggest fan of NASA'). He has also explicitly argued that his 'Mars-shot' of making the human species multi-planetary is only feasible through some sort of 'huge public-private partnership'.[10] And then he tweets, winning 100,000 likes, 'Bureaucracy is inherently Kafkaesque',[11] but 'that's just Elon'.

While worrying about the current progress in renewable energy research and the search for carbon-free alternatives, Bill Gates has explicitly argued that the government has to be a central driver of innovation in complex legacy sectors such as energy, where markets are too risky or uncertain, especially as there is no basis to assume that private sector organisations are always better and more capable than public ones:

> Yes, the government will be somewhat inept – but the private sector is in general inept. How many companies do venture capitalists invest in that go poorly? By far most of them. And it's just that every once in a while a Google or a Microsoft comes out, and some medium-scale successes too, and so the overall return is there, and so people keep giving them money.[12]

The Bill and Melinda Gates Foundation, together with the prize-driven innovation competitions of Google and others, has been instrumental in transferring the concept of 'grand challenges' from academic vision-setting exercises to national and international science and innovation policy discourses.[13] Thus, regardless of the mainstream anti-government narratives surrounding policy debates on economic growth and development, even the leading entrepreneurs are once again recognising that public bureaucracies aren't by default anti-innovation and less capable of innovating than private organisations.

These views are also well supported by the longer history of economic and technological progress. If one looks carefully at the historical accounts of economic development,[14] technological progress,[15] and how some countries (such as South Korea, Singapore and Taiwan) have made amazing jumps from not-so-rich peripheral (in a global-Western sense) nations to global innovation leaders,[16] public bureaucracies have been in one way or another involved in most key innovations and big leaps in techno-economic development.

This applies even to the emergence of the modern Silicon Valley-type capitalism. As demonstrated by Fred Block and Matthew Keller's *State of Innovation: The US Government's Role in Technology Development* (2015), by Mariana Mazzucato in her *Entrepreneurial State* (2013) and by Linda Weiss in her *America Inc.?* (2014), the internet and many of the 'smart' technologies inside the iPhone are examples of something that few private companies have been able to achieve without the patient public investment into basic and applied R&D, government procurement contracts and regulatory nudges that have often created first customers and markets.

Further, while running the mundane daily operations and public services of cities and local municipalities has until recently, when large tech companies seeking new markets and customers kickstarted the era of 'smart cities', hardly intrigued innovation policy communities, most modern technologies and business models are now evolving in these 'places'. National and local politicians and bureaucrats have to figure out how to live with the incumbent service providers and upstart startups that refuse to fall into existing bureaucratic and organisational categories like hotels (vs Airbnb) or transport providers (vs Uber). While some have taken a conservative approach, trying to protect the incumbent institutions, systems and interests through regulations, other national and local governments are experimenting with self-driving cars, smart grids, block-chain-based public ledgers, mobility as a service and so forth. Some, like the French government, have even tried to compete with the likes of Uber by developing somewhat similar services and building public sector technology platforms and business models that search for more sustainable socio-economic compromises between incumbents and upstarts.[17] Indeed, as argued by Dan Breznitz in several of his excellent books,[18] when it comes to designing and implementing innovation policies, these actual 'places' have 'choices' to design their own models and approaches. Our argument is that the ability to make and implement these 'choices' requires specific public sector capacities and capabilities.

Bureaucracy: The Blindspot of Innovation Research and Practice

Once we recognise that there are political, economic and soci-etal pressures for public policies and public bureaucracies to increasingly participate in the innovation 'game', a layer of often-overlooked questions arises. What are these bureauc-racies like as organisations? How do they work? Are there principles common to their successes or failures? Innovation plays a crucial role in the public as well as elite imagination and it is therefore crucial to answer these questions correctly.

In 1900, Gustav von Schmoller, leader of the 'Younger' German historical school of economics, complained that Smithian economists assume that well-functioning public bureaucracy and orderly finances are always a given and that this assumption leads them to numerous mistakes.[19] Similarly, Richard Nelson and Sidney Winter, founding fathers of modern evolutionary innovation studies, reminded us almost forty years ago:

> If one views policy making as a continuing process, the organizational and institutional structures involved become critical. Public policies and programs, like private activities, are embedded in and carried out by organizations. And, in a basic sense, it is the organizations that learn, and adapt. The design of a good policy is, to a considerable extent, the design of an organizational structure capable of learning and of adjusting behavior in response to what is learned.[20]

Yet most current innovation (policy) debates have one thing in common: implementation of policies is assumed to be exogenous to policies; what matters is the *policy choice* (e.g. what kind of R&D tax breaks work? Should we have a public venture capital fund?) and not how this choice is designed and implemented and by whom.[21] Thus, there is typically an inherent *policy bias* when we talk about innovation and the state. In the recent academic stock-taking exercises,[22] as well as meta-evaluations of innovation policies,[23] implementation issues have hardly received any attention. Such evaluations discuss in detail the effectiveness of various policies and policy mixes but not whether their design and implementation play any role in their effectiveness. It is as if we all know bureaucracies too well – they are too familiar to notice – and at the same time not at all – they are too mystifying to ascribe importance to.

35

Similarly, in major (re-)conceptualisations of innovation policy – from innovation systems thinking of the early 1990s and its rethinking in the 2010s to socio-technical systems and transitions thinking and mission-oriented innovation policy[24] – organisations and bureaucracy as actors with agency, values and so on have received scant if any attention.

This is in stark contrast to the private sector innovation discourse, where innovation is often related to implementation, namely how to *explore* new opportunities and at the same time keep *exploiting* existing strengths and what kind of organisational capabilities lead to innovations.[25] Such asymmetry is also reflected in scientific research: while studying the organisation of innovation in the public sector is relatively rare, even among Schumpeterian/evolutionary economists, studying the private sector organisation of innovation is a venerable research and teaching field.

Searching for the Silver Bullet

In the few modern academic treatments that deal with the question of how to design and structure innovation bureaucracies, we find two opposite views. One is associated with the mainstream reading of Max Weber and the other with Joseph A. Schumpeter, mirroring the policy process in innovation bureaucracy reality and that of agile stability as a concept. Both views are based on the assumptions that there is one right way to build innovation bureaucracy.

The first argues that 'traditional' Weberian meritocratic and expertise-based professional organisations (i.e. bureaucracy in a neutral-positive sense) help to deliver innovations by providing the stability element of an innovation system that allows private firms and entrepreneurs to exploit existing capabilities to collect innovation rents. The second argues that small, agile and often peripheral Schumpeterian public sector organisations, or even single policy entrepreneurs, do a better job at innovation, especially to initiate searches for new functions and the rethinking of public and private roles.

At this juncture, the debate on the role of the state in innovation often gets stuck trying to find 'best practices' and a definitive answer – a silver bullet – to the question: should we stick to modernising Weberian meritocracies or move towards radically experimental startup-like Schumpeterian organisations in government? In other words, should we choose stability or agility?

This also points at a crucial chasm in our thinking and perspectives. Schumpeter, associated with innovation and business, has a cool, or at least geeky-cool, image in organisation, management, business (*The Economist* runs a column on this topic named after him) and therefore also – if derivative and watered-down – in the governance and public management discourse. We tend to privilege organisations named after him and putatively designed by him. On the other hand, Weber often stands for dullness, hierarchy and Prussian bureaucrats in grey suits filing things in triplicate, not least within the governance and public management discourse, where in recent decades Weberianism has been the bête noire of the leading paradigm, the New Public Management (NPM)[26] (in spite of the fact that Weber just named, rather than identified with, such forms of organisations; blaming him for them is like blaming Dr Alzheimer for the disease). Since 2005, developments both in reality (the GFC) and theory (the fall of NPM and the emergence of the concept of the Neo-Weberian State, or NWS) have ameliorated this somewhat, but there are still many for whom 'Weberian' means something atavistic, indeed bad, whereas Schumpeter signals progress.

However, in the field of industrial policy, Weber regained prestige much earlier. East Asian developmental state scholars in particular – Alice Amsden,[27] Peter Evans,[28] Stephan Haggard,[29] Robert Wade[30] – turned the concept of high-capacity bureaucracy providing stability and predictability for developmental investments, together with a specific notion of 'embedded autonomy' introduced by Peter Evans (the argument that bureaucracies are well linked to the development-oriented public private networks that form the non-bureaucratic elements of bureaucracy), into a crucial variable explaining the strong state-led development performance of East Asian economies and beyond. They did not usually consider that there might actually be no genuinely Weberian structures in East Asia (with the exception of Japan; see Chapters 4–6 *infra*), but if we take 'Weberian bureaucracy' as a catch-all phrase for any 'traditional' bureaucracy that is reasonably close to Weber's features, this makes considerable sense.

This view has been best captured by Chalmers Johnson and his concept of the *developmental state*:[31] a country with a policy orientation towards economic development, supported by a small and inexpensive elite bureaucracy centred around a pilot organisation (such as the MITI in Japan), with sufficient autonomy to identify and choose the best industries and the best-fitting policy instruments, while still maintaining market-conforming methods of state intervention and public-private cooperation in state–business relations.

This line of research has *assumed* that whatever the policy and institutional differences between specific economies, the policy and administrative capacities of innovation bureaucracies can be best developed, and the best talent can be recruited and motivated, via the Weberian means of *meritocratic recruitment* and *lifetime career system,* to make working for government either financially competitive or culturally even more rewarding/ prestigious than working in the private sector. Peter Evans and James Rauch cemented these ideas through a quantitative analysis that tested the importance of some of the 'Weberian' elements (merit-based recruitment and career systems) on a much broader sample of countries,[32] without explicitly looking at innovation/development bureaucracies or even single agencies as explicit cases.[33] Their original questionnaire does not in fact contain any questions about institutional or organisational structures, or about their politico-administrative position in respective systems, or about capacities.[34] Their findings still have real traction in mainstream governance research,[35] and they have entered mainstream media discussion as well.[36]

This Weberianism has, however, been challenged by some scholars, who may be best represented by Dan Breznitz and Darius Ornston and their research on smaller, more peripheral and hence less regulated and institutionalised 'Schumpeterian development agencies'.[37] In this line of argumentation, the archetypical benchmark organisation – although hardly ever fully understood or emulated – is, as we saw earlier and at least since its reforms in the late 1960s, DARPA, which has been extensively researched and discussed, for example by William B. Bonvillian and Richard Van Atta.[38]

In 2013 Breznitz and Ornston further analysed the evolution of innovation policies in Finland, Sweden, Israel, Ireland and Singapore,[39] and they argued that peripheral Schumpeterian agencies may be the sources of the policy innovations necessary for promoting rapid innovation-based competition through 'innovations' or explorations in innovation policy (driven by continuous, radical experimentation as their core mission), given that these agencies have sufficient managerial capacities (or 'slack'). Accordingly, the peripheral status accompanied by little prestige and resources is important to reduce the likelihood of political interference, to allow space for development and to create an organisational need for policy experimentation (and innovation), but also for new forms of public-private interactions (while avoiding capture by special interests), as these agencies are unable to tap into existing political, financial and institutional resources. Importantly, this research also claims that these findings contradict the earlier development and innovation policy research that emphasised nodal or central Weberian agencies as the source of industrial and innovation policy success or impact.

More recently, in 2018, Breznitz and Ornston recognised that today these peripheral organisations may deliver only 'partial success' as the increasing politicisation of innovation policy,[40] driven by either the success of these organisations in specific policy innovations or growing expectations that innovation policy will fix all socio-economic ills, as discussed above, is likely to reduce their slack and specialisation in experimental searches for novel functions or approaches that would be scaled by larger and more central organisations. In other words, such peripheral agencies tend to be either captured by political interests and brought back to the centre of politics and policy making and/or loaded with diverse sets of tasks. For example, one of the more successful peripheral agencies, the Finnish innovation fund Sitra, has seen its workload extended from supporting private sector innovation to also focusing on social and public sector innovation challenges. Thus, the recent hype about innovation labs or 'iLabs' shows that such organisations have become more public and politically visible, and their function of policy experimentation can be sustained not necessarily by their peripheral nature but by their explicit startup-like culture, mission and public rhetoric, which sells rather well and generates the needed legitimacy and autonomy for experimentation.

How fashionable – and that means dominating the public discourse – iLabs and design units are right now becomes clear from two anecdotes. First, as one of the best-known professional observers of Singaporean development and one of the leading figures in the creation of the city state's econopolitical framework have both argued,[41] *one* of the main purposes of the iLab-esque Singaporean institutions is to lure the best-performing high-potential graduates into the civil service (always a key task). This is because classical bureaucracy, as in other high-end Asian public administration countries such as Japan or Taiwan, has become less appealing and startup environments more attractive. So, the best and brightest are being socialised into a quasi-Schumpeterian agency and what that agency actually does is secondary.

Second, Brazil in December 2015 launched its own iLab, modelled after and mentored by the Danish MindLab. The purpose of this, as was clear from the opening conference,[42] was – just to have an iLab. Again, as always with this type of fashion accessory, this does not mean that people do not believe these iLabs matter, but their actual impact is not their only point. This, in turn, shows how publicly relevant and necessary this kind of institution has become. At the same time, the Danish MindLab, in operation for sixteen years, was closed in 2018 and substituted by a much more politically controlled disruption task force working under the prime minister.[43] Further, in 2021, one of the early proponents of iLabs and founder of the MindLab, Christian Bason, proposed a radical pivot by largely questioning the validity of existing 'Schumpeterian' perspectives:

> For years, I have been a proponent of innovation labs – small, dedicated teams of people that work within or across more traditional organisations to generate change. The work of labs is ambitious, difficult, and often fun. Usually, a lab is an attractive workplace with an informal environment, supportive tools, and a meaningful role. Paradoxically, then, labs espouse everything their parent company or organisation is not – while still hoping to change it. No wonder it is difficult, if nearly impossible, for labs to achieve long-term transformational impact. I have come to believe we should stop building labs in isolation. Instead, we should tear their existing parent organisations apart, and assemble them from scratch based on a new set of design principles: human, meaningful, creative, caring, collaborative, trusting, thriving. We need to make the entire organisation the lab.[44]

What both the historical Weberian and current Schumpeterian streams of research share, however, is that it is almost never explicitly defined in the above-mentioned research what an innovation or developmental agency or organisation actually is; that is, the type of organisation is not part of the discussion:

- Johnson looked at a *ministry*;[45] later analysis of South Korea and Taiwan has emphasised *planning and policy coordination boards*,[46] often set up on purpose *outside* the usual career system and examinations;
- Evans and Rauch's empirical study of 126 countries does not differentiate systematically between ministries, development boards and other government organisations;[47]
- more recent research focusing explicitly on Schumpeterian organisations has looked at organisations with different functions from *research funding agencies* (DARPA in the US, Vinnova in Sweden and A*STAR in Singapore), *industrial development agencies* (IDA in Ireland), *ministerial departments* (Office of Chief Scientist in Israel) and other *high-level bodies* (the Finnish National Fund for R&D, Sitra, which used to be a Central Bank of Finland foundation and is now supervised by parliament; Forfas, Ireland's Policy Advisory Board for Enterprise and Science);[48]
- iLabs and design units can be independent (but government-owned or funded) foundations or units within larger departments/organisations; they can have a specific policy focus or the general mission of developing skills for policy innovation across government.[49]

These organisations have highly diverse tasks and positions within broader public management and innovation policy systems, and they differ in structure, size and skill sets. For instance, a ministerial department and public (R&D) agency even within the same country are almost always rather different organisations (how and to whom they report, hiring and promotion practices and financial reporting rules are likely to be very different as well). It seems that the selection of the above-mentioned cases as crucial elements to explain the innovation policy performance of different innovation systems is determined by their role as *change agents* within specific systems that have time- and context-specific bottlenecks and failures that these agents have helped to overcome. What these organisations do, how they are set up and why they have been crucial change agents depend on the wider system characteristics sustaining institutional complementarities between public and private spheres.

As we will see in this book, both analytically and historically, the diversity of innovation bureaucracies is richer than previous research has shown, both in *function* – what these organisations do – and *organisational design* – how they work as organisations. We argue that

- the arguments in favour of central (Weberian) vs peripheral (Schumpeterian) agencies are in fact not mutually exclusive, but they highlight the complexity and variety of how government organisations need to be structured and organised (and what type of outcomes we should expect from different organisations) to support innovations in firms and industries; that is, this *organisational variety* is in fact at the basis of the entrepreneurial state as defined through agile stability;

- innovation bureaucracies are tasked with a wide range of functions carried out by layers of different organisations;
- organisational change in innovation bureaucracies is asymmetrically cyclical: technological change generates new tasks for public organisations, but, frequently, these new tasks are initially taken up by new organisational forms that later become more standardised and 'bureaucratised', and 'hack' existing bureaucratic structures and capacities to routinise new tasks and challenges – no matter in what guise; and
- within this wave-like dynamic between hacking *and* routinisations, there are a number of skills or capabilities that are crucial to engender and maintain these capacities.

Thus, solving the public sector agile stability dilemma is by no means easy. Or to put it another way, on the system level, successful innovation bureaucracies are successful because they manage to keep the ambiguity and even contradiction between agility and stability alive – whether through organisational diversity or other means, depending on context. While this is allowed and even encouraged in the case of entrepreneurs, in the case of public innovation bureaucracies, in most countries, this has been discouraged by both the realities of politics and how governments gain trust and legitimacy, as well as by general public perceptions. This is because such behaviour is likely to increase risk and government 'waste', which has become part and parcel of the anti-state, neoliberal rhetoric, but which is based originally on purely technological concepts.[50] Because of this ongoing dilemma, we have a long history of indirect debates around agile stability that can teach us quite a bit.

The History of 'Agile Stability'

Outside economics and management sciences there is, perhaps surprisingly, a long history of discussing organisational and institutional innovations in the context of what we call agile stability. Yet, this history needs to constructed as the main protagonists not only did not know each other but also lived in quite different historical periods. Perhaps the earliest 'discussion' on innovation and different capacities within public governance, namely between Alexis de Tocqueville (1805–1869) and Weber (1864–1920) on the state-level public administrations in the US, offers some of the most pertinent discussions to date of agile stability.[51] Tocqueville's analysis, and admiration, of state-level administration is famous. Weber's counter-arguments are much more scattered and less well known (Tocqueville's was published in 1835 and 1840;[52] Weber's remarks can be found in *Wirtschaft und Gesellschaft* from 1922 and elsewhere).[53]

Tocqueville's main question in looking at US state- and especially township-level administration was: how can diverse townships in New England, without central administration, still provide relatively uniform public services, especially under an administrative system where most public functions are fulfilled by elected officials?[54] He explained this with judicial oversight of administrations and called both – decentralised administration and judicial oversight – innovations.[55] In Tocqueville's view, decentralised administrations with elected officials and judicial oversight work better than centralised ones (which, he argues, was an innovation of the French revolution[56]): centralised administrations have more resources, are good at regulating business and maintaining social order and security, but also keep society equally from improvement and decline;[57] centralised administrations are good at mastering resources to combat problems, but they are poor at rejuvenating what might be called socio-political resources for change.[58] What Tocqueville describes are administrations excelling at agility and how dynamic capabilities are specific skills but also features of governance system.

When we jump two-thirds of a century further, we can see that all the ills of centralised administration described by Tocqueville become positives in Weber's view:[59] in order to keep social order, that is to retain authority and the functioning of society, centralised bureaucracy is the 'technically' better instrument over elected officials.[60] Elected officials and *'schöpferische' Betätigung der Beamten* (the 'creative' activity of civil servants) lead to unpredictability and to a bureaucracy that seeks to retain its own power, in other words to rent-seeking behaviour.[61]

While Tocqueville and Weber had different normative goals – the former describing the benefits of active civic life, the latter understanding and describing those of a well-functioning and predictable state apparatus[62] – both discuss how *authority*, to use Weber's term, is maintained in society with competitive interests via *institutional and administrative innovations* (although Weber does not use these terms). We can paraphrase Weber as follows: the modern state is defined by its authority to use coercion to uphold the very same authority. The state, in other words, should focus on providing the stability of public order and services.

Above all, Tocqueville and Weber show how such innovations lead to differing socio-political relationships and networks, institutional and organisational structures, cultures and capacities. In other words, how these innovations drive different evolutionary changes in society. However, both also show why evolutionary processes in the public sector are punctured by political, legal, institutional and administrative constraints. Constraints are intrinsic to the public sector. Thus, to use Tocqueville's example, judicial oversight in small townships acted as a constraint on elected officials, yet this same constraint led to better services for the citizens. Weber, writing later, argued that modern societies have become increasingly more complex (because of technological and related institutional progress and co-evolution) and thus require centralised administrations that can act simultaneously as constraints and enablers. What Tocqueville and Weber describe are different capacities and capabilities: capabilities for change and capacities for stability.

In the context of management thinking and research, the roots of the idea that different systems of management are suited to different tasks can be traced back at least to Ferdinand Tönnies' research into *Gemeinschaft* and *Gesellschaft* (organic and mechanistic forms of society).[63] Although Tönnies, usually regarded as the founding father of German sociology as an independent discipline, both materially and organisationally, is only concerned with society itself in this, his classic, work, and not with any form of industrial organisation or the like (Weber developed some of his categories on the matter in direct response to this), this is picked up with direct references to Tönnies by early management theorists who describe mechanistic and organic management structures: the former to manage stability, the latter to manage change.[64] These ideas, in turn, laid the foundations for the notion of ambidextrous organisation,[65] as well as the idea that organisational learning can take place in order to *exploit* existing opportunities or to *explore* new opportunities.[66] More recently, such research centres around dynamic capabilities (e.g. Teece;[67] Helfat and Martin[68]) and the previously mentioned ambidexterity (e.g. O'Reilly and Tushman[69]).

Perhaps the simplest way to summarise this line of research is as follows: businesses have *ordinary* routines and capabilities to exploit existing strengths and business opportunities, but in order to deal with deep market uncertainty, businesses should acquire *dynamic* capabilities. This can take place within the existing organisational structures, but most research suggests that establishing new, unorthodox organisations (internally or externally) is a better, certainly much easier, way to deal with ambidexterity.

Public sector organisations play almost no role in these research lines, yet there seems to be a similar, if not identical, dichotomy, at least in the case of public innovation policy organisations: one type of organisation, capturing a network of private and public actors, that is typically small, fluid and deals with new emerging issues and sectors; and another type that is larger, based on expertise and skills, more hierarchical and that aims to enhance existing capabilities in the private sector through more complex and large-scale activities (provision of public services, regulation, finance, guidance of sectors or the economy as a whole).

As we discussed above, calling these small, fluid agencies Schumpeterian is evocative but hardly justifiable through Schumpeter's own work. While Schumpeter argued that 'new men' can bring forth innovations in all walks of life (from the economy to the arts), he did not discuss organisational underpinnings (in the public sector) in any detail.[70] However, Weber's taxonomy of domination or authority (traditional, charismatic, rational) and corresponding organisational forms does offer a way to describe what Schumpeter attempted to show in an analytical way.[71] That is, Weber offers *theoretical* reasons why and how different types of organisations can deliver different policy goals.

For Weber, different forms of authority are created by and rely on different organisations in terms of their capacities and routines, internal structures and external relations, and on what these organisations can deliver. In addition, Weber argues that new organisational forms (or change from one form to another) emerge through conflicts between old and new leaders and staff,[72] implying potential conflicts over political and policy visions.

Analytical Tools for Studying Innovation Bureaucracies

We are approaching some conceptual clarity: when looking at public sector and innovation – at innovation bureaucracies – we have to pay attention to at least four fundamental factors of innovation-oriented good governance:

Authority and power: the public sector can set and change rules, and this affects the roles of other social and economic actors and also the legitimacy of its own actions.

Leadership and directionality: the state can play a crucial role for business innovations by indirectly supporting entrepreneurial activity in the economy and society or by directly leading or co-shaping the directions of economic and societal development (e.g. towards more sustainable growth).

Dynamism and change: the public sector itself can be changed by 'Schumpeterian' entrepreneurial individuals, as well as organisations and movements.

Capacities and capabilities: capabilities for change and capacities for stability often exist in different organisational and institutional constellations that enable the government to address its core missions.

Mainstream economists have predominantly argued in favour of a model where the state provides, through its authority, minimal stable institutions that fix market failures and provide the context for the private innovators to do their thing. Of course, mainstream economists also criticise the state for being too stable and not dynamic enough in cases where private innovators require a shift to a different subset of stable institutions (or bailouts following their failures) and use this argument for further reduction of the authority and role of the state. Heterodox/evolutionary economists have based their thinking on more co-evolutionary insights, but given the ideological context of Western modernity, this thinking has focused mostly on defensive strategies and fixing the perceived conceptual failures of mainstream economics, as opposed to building and advancing a more holistic model based on the four elements discussed above: setting stable rules, hacking the rules in times of need, steering socio-economic processes and building sustainable capacities and dynamic capabilities for all these functions.

Given these ideological-theoretical divides, these debates omitted one of the crucial roles of the state – innovation leadership. This has only returned to public discourse with recent societal/grand challenges and mission-oriented innovation policy ideas,[73] but it was in fact discussed and implemented in the shadow of the ideological debates in the 1960s and 1970s. Good examples are the US Cold War military-industrial complex – which was the origin of the modern US 'innovation system'[74] – and the 1971 Organisation for Economic Co-operation and Development (OECD) experts' recommendation that its member states, especially in Europe, should focus more research and innovation efforts on tackling the persistent socio-economic challenges of urbanisation, climate and so on. The current normative turn in economic and particularly innovation policies has considerably widened the debate,[75] in terms of going beyond both 'public sector innovation' and market-fixing concepts and practices, and in this opening space bureaucracy can be seen as one of the key actors in innovation through building long-term capacities for stability and dynamic capabilities for change and adaption.

Yet, in these debates and developments, public sector capacities tend to remain a static 'black box' variable that is both employed to academically explain policy success or failure and normatively highlighted as a key aspect that policy makers need to improve in order to succeed in the innovation game.[76] Furthermore, our thinking about public sector capacities needs to be complemented by the theory of *dynamic state capabilities*. While there is a rich literature about firm-level dynamic capabilities,[77] insufficient attention has been paid to where the equivalent level of public sector capabilities comes from and their dynamic evolution over time.

The answer, we propose, is as follows. Successful innovation bureaucracies (note the plural: we do not mean a single organisation but rather a set of organisations) need to have *long-term policy and implementation/delivery capacities* and *dynamic exploration and learning capabilities* to successfully organise their policy actions related to the uncertain processes of innovation. Innovation bureaucracies, as we have seen, need to provide agile stability, and that means they must have the capacities and capabilities for both – agility *and* stability – plus those required to combine the two, fluidly calibrated to what combination is required at any given point in time. Thus, we can't treat capacities and capabilities as static black box features of public sectors that can be upgraded by simple training, consultancy and policy learning projects. Long-term capacities and dynamic capabilities are not switched on or off; simply put, there is no on/off switch for capacities.

Innovation Is Political

Anybody who was watching world politics from the second half of the 2010s has to admit that politics plays an enormous role in how innovation bureaucracy works. President Obama's 'last law' was an attempt to make permanent the public sector agility-oriented Presidential Innovation Fellows Program, which had been developed from a relatively ad hoc network to a position where it was institutionalised as a routine capacity,[78] but the incoming president decided to race straight back to the NPM and neoliberal ideational setting of the 1980s. His attempts at guiding innovation policy included the decision to set up the Office of American Innovation and to 'reinvent the government' once again,[79] as well as piggybacking on the narratives of the post-Second World War space race by pushing ideas for the American Space Force.[80] We can see similarly rapid and radical changes taking place in the UK and Brazil, to mention two obvious examples.[81]

Paradoxically, neither of these approaches is wrong per se, because the role of the state in innovation is one of the trickiest things to justify and legitimise, especially in an open, deliberative democracy. Conceptually, modern governance and public policy scholars approach the question of political and policy legitimacy from two key perspectives.[82] First, political scientists often distinguish between input, throughput and output legitimacy. Following this perspective, innovation policies may be among the most difficult to directly legitimise: policy issues and challenges are often too complex to engage non-experts in policy design (to achieve input legitimacy) and implementation phases (to achieve throughput legitimacy); and the outcomes and effectiveness of policies (output legitimacy) are difficult to prove, as shown by the Manchester Institute of Innovation Research in a huge meta-study of innovation policy impacts.[83] Second, from a more institutionalist perspective and focusing on a broader context of governance, we again come back to the Weberian notion of 'legitimate domination' to better understand the different ways governments may try to impose their authority and initiatives on society. Weber distinguished between three pure types of legitimate domination based on:[84]

- Rational grounds: 'resting on a belief in the legality of enacted rules and the right of those elevated to authority under such rules to issue commands';
- Traditional grounds: 'resting on an established belief in the sanctity of immemorial traditions and the legitimacy of those exercising authority under them'; and

- Charismatic grounds: 'resting on devotion of the exceptional sanctity, heroism or exemplary character of an individual person'.[85]

Most mainstream approaches to innovation policy have been built on the assumptions of 'rational' processes of policy making – policies are designed and implemented through impersonal and impartial processes of discovering specific 'failures' in existing markets/systems that provide commonly acceptable and analytically replicable 'rationales' for government interventions. This technocratic impersonality and analytical and procedural transparency sustain the legitimacy of the system: input, throughput and output legitimacy are provided by carefully selected 'experts' following the set rules and regulations of policy making and economic analysis and/ or by international comparisons and benchmarking exercises.

The current 'normative turn' in innovation policy and the focus on mission-oriented policies and policy experimentation seem to imply that solving persistent societal challenges, which existing policies have not been able to solve, and transformative changes driven partly by non-economic interests (e.g. sustainable development) may require more radical shifts in policy directions than can perhaps be delivered by such technocratic approaches.[86] Following Weber, such economically uncertain and high-risk policy shifts may have to be legitimised on non-rational and non-economic grounds (in Weber's view, on charismatic grounds), and this should also affect the governance arrangements emerging from this context. Thus, while we can assume that institutions as socio-economic compromises are there for the function of stability, how different political systems manage to create agility in these systems is a contextual challenge of search and selection conditioned by the broader political, technological and economic context of specific time and place.[87]

A counter-example to this approach is the classical yet still crucial – if heavily contested – Chinese notion of the Mandate of Heaven, a principle that equates government success with legitimacy – Heaven as the supreme deity is not with a government that doesn't deliver peace, food and general well-being.[88] While this justifies outside and inside takeovers of government, it also forms one of the most radical performance indicators and measurements in human history, in that if one does not deliver in the public sector, one has to go, no excuse. As Weber has also shown – if indirectly – in his book on Confucianism, this approach extended from the Emperor, the Son of Heaven, down to the lowest bureaucrat, who, within the context of overall Chinese society, then and partially even now, was not that low anyway.[89] In fact, this bureaucrat participated in a prima facie ascription of competence and even a somewhat spiritual endorsement of the office that gave him the option, and the duty, to pursue the common good. This, in turn, led to a very hierarchical system in which, however, ultimate delivery and performance were crucial and even a matter of literal survival.

Assuming that innovation and innovation policy are crucial for a country's success and its people's welfare, this means that a rather hierarchical, rule-based administration like the Chinese one should have nonetheless created a highly functional innovation bureaucracy and thus innovation system. Judging from the Chinese global economic performance across the centuries and indeed millennia, this seems to be the case – of the last 1,000 years, China was economically and also technically dominant for about 750 years and arguably is again (the rise of capitalism, roughly 1750–2000, coincided with the time of relative Chinese weakness).[90]

It is important to note that this book does not provide a deep dive into the evolution and capacities of Chinese innovation bureaucracy. While it is crucial to understand how the Chinese innovation bureaucracy will influence the global trajectories of innovation during the current Asian century, detailed analysis of the complexities of Chinese innovation bureaucracy needs its own book (in addition to existing key contributions). However, some of the prior analytical accounts have convincingly shown that the Chinese innovation system has provided, at least since the 1950s and partly because of unintended outcomes, a unique politico-institutional environment, which some describe as 'experimentation under the shadow of hierarchy',[91] and others as 'structured uncertainty'.[92]

It has been generally agreed that China is too big and complex to have a clear model of governance, and to coordinate all the different agents on all the different levels of government, but the central government, or the Chinese Communist Party, has pushed for common visions and narratives of development. The first Science and Technology Plan was adopted in the 1950s and it focused on largely political missions and security concerns, creating the highly politicised routines and top-down steering of big science projects and initiatives that are still prevalent. In the 1980s, it was explicitly emphasised that economic development should be built on S&T capabilities and it was recognised that China should build basic S&T

capabilities in areas with big global potential (bio, space, information, automation, energy, new materials), while simultaneously focusing on domestic challenges and taking advantage of Chinese-specific national, geographical and human capital advantages. In 2006, the Long-Term Development of Science and Technology document explicitly stated an ambition to shift from imitator to innovator, to focus on increasing 'indigenous innovation' through science and engineering megaprojects, as well as developing frontier technologies, increasing the share of technology advantage in economic growth (to 60 per cent), reducing the dependence on foreign technologies (to 30 per cent) and becoming one of the top five patent-holder economies globally.[93]

These formal policy goals and related design of the innovation bureaucracy – from planning ministries and government research institutions and universities to state-owned enterprises – could be portrayed as a rather traditional and classic evolution of innovation policies and bureaucracies in response to feedback from global and local arenas. For example, the policy shifts in the 1980s towards technology-based development were proposed and pushed by leading visionary scholars and resulted not only in political documents but also in the design of new funding programmes and institutions; for example, on the suggestion of Tang Aoqing, the father of quantum chemistry in China, the Chinese Academy of Sciences' Science Foundation was reformed into the National Natural Science Foundation of China, modelled on the US National Science Foundation (NSF).[94]

Still, Breznitz and Murphree point out that the context of the Chinese innovation system is fundamentally different from the classic Western and developmental state models of industrial development and innovation.[95] They argue that the challenges and complexities of governing China have resulted in a system where these common national goals and direction are operationalised and implemented through different experimental approaches in different regions and economic zones, producing diverse economic specialisation and specific capacities. While central government provides specific long-term visions and broad-brush capacities (via funding, regulations, etc.), the regional units – from each region itself to the state-owned and increasingly private firms – function in principle as agile actors experimenting and searching for competitive advantages and specialisations within the overall framework and directions. Breznitz and Murphree further claim that this has allowed China, or Chinese regions, to rediscover formal top-down policy narratives, with unique specialisations in innovation chains (especially around assembly and production) providing more sustainable innovation and growth capacities than trying to become the next Silicon Valley.[96]

By now, we can witness how technological developments have brought China right to the techno-economic frontier in biotech, information and communications technology (ICT), materials and energy research. The changing context has also created new drivers for experimentation and research in the innovation system that exist in a uniquely Chinese symbiosis with central government. For example, the local maker movement is internalised into a Chinese national innovation narrative.[97] At the same time, the large ICT conglomerates and venture funds have sought to benefit from the AI-driven local 'Sputnik moments', such as a machine becoming better than humans at Go, to, together with the central government, redraw the political and economic power divisions globally.[98]

The Breznitz theses loop back to our previous discussion of Confucian public administration and especially to its Weberian interpretation. It is of course contentious whether and to what extent Confucian public administration itself is actually back in mainland China, but that Confucianism itself is, and so strongly endorsed by Xi Jinping that being anti-Confucian has become outright risky, is not.[99] In any case, what the Confucian public administration can supply is a heuristic framework that may elucidate why Chinese innovation has been policy-processed this way.

The key here is, once again, the Mandate of Heaven: in spite of their ubiquity, smaller performance indicators do not matter so much as the actual performance overall, meaning that the people, broadly speaking, are actually satisfied with their lives and therefore with the government – and expectations for this are rising. It is not at all the case that only democratically process-legitimised governments need such a consent; to the contrary, governments that lack this legitimisation need to justify themselves even more via actual results.[100] The question of the legitimacy of the Chinese Communist Party (CCP) government is a far-reaching one, but it does seem that one of the reasons it is accepted or at least tolerated is because it delivers.[101] The Mandate of Heaven means that not only is this possible (performance begets legitimacy) but that it is necessary as well, meaning that not delivering would open the regime to fundamental criticism and the emergence of potential alternatives.

If this is the case, and independently from the current regime, then what matters, once again, are achievements and progress in technology, and especially innovation, as both contribute to the well-being of the people (understood mostly in GDP terms) and to country resilience and competitiveness. The hierarchical bureaucracy and party elite derive their legitimacy not by setting precise agendas or implementing policy in a specific way, or from particular institutions, but rather by ensuring, or even guaranteeing, that techno-economic progress happens – literally no matter how. This results in maximal agility in the pursuit of that progress, but also stability in that it is the legitimising task of state and bureaucracy to make sure that this happens. Whether this is actually historical Confucianism, ancient Confucian public administration or something else is much less important than the actual phenomenon itself – and this certainly exists.

Max Weber indicated that while it was clear, for various reasons, that capitalism couldn't originate in China, once it arrived there, it would be developed to an extremely high level, and this is one of his prophecies that has been rather impressively fulfilled.[102] Again, whether China and what used to be called the 'Sinosphere' – that is other Confucian countries, which include some of our main protagonists, such as Taiwan, Korea, Vietnam, Singapore and historically even Japan – are particularly Confucian today, is difficult to pin down.[103] However, in principle, and as a heuristic argument, what this means is that in 'Confucian' countries, innovation policy can be undertaken without much rationalistic-fashionable delivery baggage, because bureaucrats are assumed to be competent enough as long as it works in the end. So, all that matters is actual, final performance (such as an increased standard of living) – and that was the assumption behind Singapore's industrial-technological success until about a decade ago.

The Chinese example also brings up another story, one much more relevant and mainstream as this book is published than it was when it was conceived a decade ago, and that is the question of whether there is also a racially ascribed, ethnic, geographic, North/South element to innovation and innovation policy. There is – and on various levels.

First, as Weber makes abundantly clear with his concept of occidental rationalism as the main story of Imperialism and Northern global ascendancy, one of the darkest aspects of innovation policy and successful innovation bureaucracy is that colonialism and genocide in the non-Northwest are premised not only on natural resources and political divides,[104] but also on the use and directionality of techno-military innovation.[105] Although many other systems, from Benin and the Mughal Empire to Imperial China, were completely self-sufficient and functioning, the system and the logic of innovation-based capitalism led to their annihilation, at a price that was and is so high that all the achievements gained through it need to be evaluated in light of these costs.

Second, as Dingxin Zhao has pointed out,[106] from today's perspective, precisely this innovation style and logic also led to the ecological disasters, environmental degradation and cultural-societal desolation that may well be the worst or second-worst legacy of Northern capitalism, so that it may be successful for a while but is completely unsustainable when looking at the Anthropocene as such.

Third, by its claim, as Ragnar Nurkse was first to emphasise, innovation, even in the strict Schumpeterian variant, is not specific to time and place (once capitalism is the context), but how it plays out very much is.[107] It is noteworthy that while some of the most successful countries in innovation and innovation policy are non-Western, all of them, and indeed all their political (mainstream) parties, emphasise innovation as the way forward. In fact, there are no fully non-Western systems anymore, and the question is only whether the Asian leaders in innovation are successes, to use Kishore Mahbubani's perspective,[108] because Asians are just the better Westerners today or whether their Asianness – especially in the Confucian form – is what makes them more competitive even in the capitalist context, as Weber implied.[109]

Needless to say, all of these are very broad brushstrokes and all of these claims refer to tendencies towards ideal types, but for the 'bright' side of our story it is noteworthy that innovation, innovation policy and the quest for innovation bureaucracy are areas in which North/West actors and South/East ones are by now again competitors, on an equal footing at least, in spite of the prevalence of disparities, postcolonial legacies and systemic racism. The 'dark' side of innovation remains regardless.

In sum, politics inherently plays a deep role in both directionality of innovation and the way innovation bureaucracies evolve. While our focus is on organisations, in specific cases discussed in the subsequent chapters, we will discuss political aspects as well.

3

ROOTS AND TYPES OF INNOVATION BUREAUCRACIES

The Roots

Modern public organisations consciously aiming to support innovation and technological advancement emerged largely during the nineteenth century. It is no coincidence that such organisations emerged during the Industrial Revolution. Five key trends, among other variables of course but apparently *conditiones sine quae non*, help to explain the birth of *modern* innovation bureaucracy in the West:

1. The evolution of knowledge networks through learned bodies – academies, royal societies, and so on – across Europe that predated the Industrial Revolution, was tightly interwoven with political structures through 'competitive patronage' of talent,[1] and played a crucial role in the nineteenth century as networks for both knowledge and

what would today be called development or applied research.[2]

2. The emergence of polytechnics and engineering education (related to both military and civilian needs) in Europe (e.g. Ecole Polytechnique[3]) and the US (mostly military engineering at West Point) that created a supply of engineers and technicians for both public and private sectors.[4]

3. The emergence of a professional managerial class both in private companies (e.g. in railways, armouries and others) and in the public sector (e.g. the military procurement practices of the Quartermaster department during the US Civil War).[5]

4. The rise and importance of various business associations (e.g. Interessenverbände in Germany) in the late nineteenth century, which enabled close networks among politics, industry and bureaucracy.[6] These associations were important particularly in the European context for the emergence and success of cartels and tariff-driven industrial policy.

5. The importance of state-owned companies for managing strategic trade roots and Imperial ambitions. While the East India Company is the best-known case, there were numerous others, such as the Hudson Bay Company and the Verenigde Oostindische Compagnie. This is also the clearest case outside the military where innovation bureaucracies impacted many lives directly, both positively and very negatively.[7]

In the Western context, the five springs mentioned above engender almost all forms of modern innovation bureaucracies: it is as difficult to think of any such organisation without engineers (technical skills) working in them as it is to imagine them without a professional level of (middle) managers. This would indicate that, historically, innovation bureaucracies resemble quite strongly the Weber thesis formalised in the 1980s by scholars trying to understand East Asian development: hierarchical rational (elite) expert organisations supporting mostly the private sector in innovations and technological change.[8]

In the non-Western context, which, regarding positive examples of innovation and innovation bureaucracy since the late nineteenth century, comprises mostly the Confucian countries of East and Southeast Asia, *this* kind of innovation bureaucracy is a child of the global-Westernised modernisation that largely happened after, and as a consequence of, the Second World War. The exception is, as one would assume, Japan, which modern-Westernised much earlier, from the late 1860s, and which has basically behaved like the Weberian-European country it administratively was and partially still is. Also, from the early twentieth century onwards the British colonies of Hong Kong and Singapore developed if not right away towards an innovation bureaucracy proper, then certainly along the five key trends just described, at least in proto-form.

However, even the Western story is not as straightforward as it would seem. In fact, while most innovation bureaucracies use technical experts/engineers and professional managers as key ingredients of their organisational DNA, the way these become fused with various technological, financial, political and administrative contexts creates a much larger and more colourful canvas on which organisational varieties emerge. Indeed, it is the relationship between private and public initiative, and how these partnerships are organised and structured, that is one of the key determinants for how types of innovation bureaucracy organisations emerge and operate. We will come back to this soon.

What is equally important is that the functions, or tasks, innovation bureaucracies have been carrying out since the Industrial Revolution vary quite significantly at different points in time. Scholars of modern innovation systems tried to systemise the key functions or 'activities' in the innovation system (i.e. related to the provision of knowledge inputs, organisation of demand-side factors, provision of constituents, supporting firms),[9] recognising that the state has a distinct role in most activities and this leads to complex policy mixes. Others have attempted to operationalise these functions/activities through institutional complementarities (also between public and private sectors) of the 'social systems of innovation and production' and argue that these institutional complementarities may be highly diverse across economies and regions of the world.[10]

As important and insightful as they are, however, there are two common limitations in these streams of research. First, they mostly have a snapshot perspective: what are the functions 'as of now' (in the best-performing or different ideal-type systems). There is relatively little discussion of why and from where these functions emerged and how they have evolved;[11] yet, as we discussed in Chapter 2, the public sector innovation brief is constantly expanding.

Second, there is no systematic organisational perspective on how these functions have been organised, that is who is actually implementing given functions. It is noteworthy that innovation scholarship centres around activities or functions and policy mixes (of public sector activities), and institutional complementarities (mixes of institutions, e.g. university–industry linkages), but rarely discusses organisational mixes or varieties in organisational designs and their complementarities. However, both the evolution of innovation tasks and the evolution of organisations fulfilling these tasks are an important part of how we understand and how we can promote innovation bureaucracies.

The Types

Innovation bureaucracies can go about fulfilling their tasks in quite different ways: some organisations can be involved in directly creating new technologies (e.g. government research institutes), others can support private companies (e.g. funding agencies through grants) and yet others can act as intermediaries of knowledge (e.g. engineering or business associations). To simplify the picture, we argue here that innovation bureaucracy can take the shape of the following ideal types according to *how* the organisations go about dealing with innovations:

1. *Creators*: organisations directly involved in creating new knowledge and technologies, often in codified form (such as scientific publications), for instance public research institutes;
2. *Doers*: organisations involved in creating and delivering actual new products or services, for instance state-owned companies or specialised agencies (e.g. for space exploration or agriculture);
3. *Funders*: organisations that fund private or public entities involved in innovations, for instance research or innovation funding agencies;

4. *Intermediaries*: organisations that act as knowledge and interest intermediaries, such as engineering or business associations or technology parks and clusters; and

5. *Rulers*: organisations that create and constrain the legitimacy and space (through politics, policy and regulations) for the others and give direction to their missions and tasks, such as ministries, cabinet offices or specialised offices for innovation.

In how they are set up and how they operate, all the five types can be remarkably different, even within a single country (as we briefly discussed earlier as part of the history of the PTR and German innovation system), let alone when we compare in time and space. However, this taxonomy offers us a rough guide to distinguishing quite different organisations within the overall innovation bureaucracy.

If we look at the country-level context, countries today typically have a number of organisations in all categories. However, the proportions – size, turnover – among the organisations can vary quite considerably over time. Thus, for instance, the number and size of creator and doer organisations grew in the West dramatically with the Second World War and its aftermath, the Cold War, as the role of public sector in basic and applied research as well as in innovation became more important. In the preceding period, Continental European countries, particularly the likes of Germany and Italy, had hundreds of intermediary organisations, such as cartels and business associations. With the 1980s, the NPM reforms and the reduction of the proactive role of the state in the economy, new types of intermediaries have again become popular in the form of public-private partnerships, such as technology parks, philan-thropic funding of knowledge dissemination and international research networks.

However, it is not just the relative proportions among inno-vation bureaucracy organisations that vary in time. The goals these organisations are tasked to pursue also change significantly over time (e.g. new technologies come into focus; different stages of economic development require different policy foci as successful countries normally evolve from emulating to creating technologies and innovations). In addition, they are also struc-tured rather differently (ministerial departments tend to have different authority, autonomy and regulatory contexts than universities and foundations financing innovation actions), even if certain fads and fashion may pressure these organisations towards similar managerial models ('You can't manage what you don't measure') and public sector innovation practices ('Everyone should run an iLab').

We summarise these generic types of innovation bureauc-racies in Table 3.1. This provides a bird's-eye view of types, evolving tasks and organisational configurations taken by different types of innovation bureaucracies. The table describes what policy tasks have been historically pursued by govern-ments and how these goals relate to types of organisations. We also add 'original' forms (organisations that emerged in the aftermath of the Industrial Revolution) and currently 'dominant' forms (organisations found in a variety of coun-tries) for each type. There can be considerable overlap between functions and organisational forms; here they are depicted in an ideal-typical way. The point is to illustrate that in all types there is oscillation and fluidity between charismatic

Table 3.1 Taxonomy of (Western) innovation bureaucracies

Type	Tasks	Original form(s) of organisation, place, approximate time, area of activity	Currently dominant form(s) of organisation, examples, country, area of activity
Creators	Furthering knowledge frontier	Althoff system of ministerial guidance (Germany, late nineteenth and early twentieth centuries); private foundations (US, first decades of the twentieth century)	Public research institutes (e.g. NIH, US; Max-Planck-Gesellschaft, Germany; basic research); public and private universities and their joint initiatives (e.g. mission-oriented research)
Doers	Management of strategic resources and allocating these to priority innovation efforts	Private trading companies with public support, gradually nationalised (e.g. UK, Netherlands, US, 1700s–1800s); overseas trade, colonisation, public revenue creation	State-owned companies (Petrobras, BRA, natural resource management), public holding companies (Singapore), public universities (e.g. Estonian Genome Project, genetic database management and related research); also tax authorities dealing with R&D tax breaks
	Deepening technology base by carrying out crucial strategic R&D and innovation actions	Public organisation with private funding (SEUM in the US, late eighteenth century); ministerial R&D departments (UK, 1920s); developmental agencies (MITI in Japan, which housed the AIST as its bureau, 1949); network of public laboratories (Fraunhofer in Germany, 1949; sectoral national laboratories in the US, post-Second World War)	Variety of public agencies with different degrees of autonomy, size, funding (e.g. DARPA, US; Fraunhofer, Germany), financing and conducting applied research in a wide variety of areas; public intellectual property rights agencies

Type	Tasks	Original form(s) of organisation, place, approximate time, area of activity	Currently dominant form(s) of organisation, examples, country, area of activity
Funders	Long-term investment	Private banks as public debt agencies (US, early nineteenth century); private industrial banks under public-private central bank (Germany, 1870s); industry; public works	Public research funding agencies (NSF, US) European Research Council; public development banks (BNDES, BRA, industry, infrastructure, regional development); public-private venture capital partnership (In-Q-Tel, US, high tech); private foundations (e.g. Gates foundation); foreign aid organisations (World Bank, European Commission; infrastructure, regional development)
	Generating demand for new products and services	Ministerial procurement departments with close linkages to inventor networks (US, mid-nineteenth century); private professional organisations for infrastructure standards (Germany, mid-nineteenth century); public insurance schemes (Germany, 1880s, health, etc.)	Ministerial departments, public regulatory agencies (e.g. FDA, SBIR, US); new products and technologies in a wide variety of areas, particularly procurement and incremental improvement of off-the-shelf technologies; international and multilateral trade treaties as access to markets, standardisation (WTO, NAFTA)

Type	Tasks	Original form(s) of organisation, place, approximate time, area of activity	Currently dominant form(s) of organisation, examples, country, area of activity
Intermediaries	Diffusion of new skills, technology	Private business interest associations, cartels, with public support and guidance (Germany, mid- to late nineteenth century)	Public-private partnerships in the form of cluster organisations, business incubators, demo centres; public competitions authorities; technology parks and similar organisations particularly focusing on high tech; competition authorities focusing on mergers and similar issues mostly in more traditional fields (market efficiency)
Rulers	Creating legitimacy, formalising direction, setting constraints	Privy councils to heads of state, offices of president/ prime minister, ministries	High-level public-private coordination bodies (national research and innovation councils, boards, etc.), offices of president/ prime minister, ministries

networks and expert organisations, between agility and stability as the primary purpose of the organisation.

The table demonstrates that in all core innovation policy tasks there is and has been a rather wide variety of organisations. Further, in different times and contexts, the constellations of these organisations have created different degrees of agile stability and the organisational configurations and complementarities that allow agile stability in the first place. We will describe and illustrate in more detail how this has worked out and evolved in Chapters 4–6 by focusing on global post-Second World War developments in more detail. For now, we can draw the following two broad lessons from our brief travels across the written history of innovation bureaucracies.

First, at the outset, most innovation policy functions emerge in some form of fluid public-private partnership, often undertaken by a relatively small private organisation or network with some form of public support that lends the network legitimacy. Such networks are led by bureaucracy 'hackers' who are very good at creating mission mystique around and within the network. In effect, innovation bureaucracy organisations seem to emerge as reactions to dynamic socio-political (e.g. wars, crises, social movements) and technological (e.g. new radical products and processes) developments. These networks respond to a need for dynamic action, for agility.

Second, however, in time, most innovation policy networks, their rules and their tasks become socialised in one form or other (the public sector role becomes more dominant than private initiative) and organisations fulfilling them become more 'bureaucratic', typically with larger specialised staff, direct public funding and more regulated and managed processes and procedures – something that is generally called 'Weberian'. The early private belief systems underlying and embodied in the mission mystique become rationalised and routinised: rules are created, processes documented, measurement systems installed, and human resource becomes a managed routine. This is for a good reason. The functions and practices are deemed important for innovation and hence need to be maintained and secured, but the organisation becomes predictable, focusing on and providing stability in the innovation system.

Based on our historical discussion above, we can further develop Weber's argument: it is typically not just a single new organisation with a charismatic leader, but rather what we argue is it is a *charismatic network* that enables new organisations to emerge.[12] Such networks involve a number of leaders from various sectors (business, academia, politics, bureaucracy) that seek to solve an emerging (socio-political and/or technological) challenge; such networks are carried by a certain naïveté or they operate under the principle of what Albert Hirschman calls *the hidden hand*: charismatic networks take on tasks they think they can solve without realising all the challenges and risks involved, which may result in unexpected learning and creativity – and in new organisations.[13] Importantly, the charismatic nature of such networks enables the creation of mission mystique, which attracts talent and is important for legitimising the new emerging organisation.

In the context of innovation, such networks coalesce around existing bureaucratic structures (e.g. military organisations, public universities) typically focused on long-term goals and stability. In this sense, we can argue that public sector structures that are expert-driven and stability-oriented are primary forms of any innovation bureaucracy. The primacy of public bureaucratic structures can be also detected in language: late nineteenth-century German firms such as Siemens used a peculiar term for their managers, calling them *Privatbeamte* or private bureaucrats.

In the history of innovation bureaucracy, we can therefore detect *two ideal-typical 'Weberian' organisations* and their cyclical evolution. First, historically most forms of innovation bureaucracy start as one type of Weberian organisation – what we can call, counterintuitively, Weber II: charismatic, dynamic, *agile* networks, often innovating in emerging policy areas via proposing new initiatives and regulations, standards or co-operation forms. Often residing outside typical government operations, and perhaps looking like public-private partner-ships (they may have high-level political support or enjoy soci-etal prestige), they often create their own agenda and rules. The networks are led and galvanised by bureaucracy 'hackers' who are skilled operators.

However, these charismatic networks utilise existing bureaucratic structures, reconfigure them and with time they move (or rather 'grow') themselves into the 'original' type of Weberian organisation – what we therefore call Weber I (because they are the 'original', well-recognised Weberian structures): professional, centrally governed, *stable* organisa-tions that are predictable, staffed with high-level experts and strong in enhancing private sector innovation capabilities through public policies during rather stable conditions of technological maturity or, conversely, during catching-up or mission-dominated periods. This means that the instrumental performance of these organisations is related to long time horizons, predictability and cost-efficiency that allow for patient regulation and public investment in the long-term and complex activities necessary for industrial development and catching up.

In a further step, with new technologies and/or ideologies emerging, innovation bureaucracy can be pushed towards a more charismatic form again. The instrumental performance of these organisations focuses on change, breaking existing routines that have become obsolete – for example, the market has found efficiencies in these processes and taken them over – or inhibit private experimentation with new production, service, marketing or other methods. As we will speculate in Chapter 7, perhaps we are witnessing today the emergence of Weber III-type organisations, namely neo-Weberian innovation agencies that attempt to combine elements of both Weber I and II in single organisations.

These dynamics play out differently among different types of innovation bureaucracies: creators, doers, funders, facilitators and rulers develop their own logics of evolution that depend on contextual factors from politics to political economy issues (such as ownership structures) to the level of technological sophistication.

We can see in Weber I and Weber II organisational archetypes of innovation bureaucracy from which the formation of hybrid forms is possible and indeed to be expected. In addition, in many cases, as we see today for instance with iLabs or public digital innovation agencies, the functionality of the set-up once they exist in parallel does not lie in one form taking over the other (although fashionable rhetoric may have to present this as the aim) but in their substantially peaceful or competitive co-existence. Indeed, the co-existence and co-evolution are what makes agile stability of entrepreneurial states possible.

It is important to note that the line between these two organisational forms can be fluid in real life. However, the ability to detect the need for such fluidity and incorporate such new forms of organisations into daily routines is fundamental to the agile stability of innovation bureaucracies. This, however, is complicated again by the above-mentioned possible, indeed probable, need to avoid a wholesale takeover of the old by the new, because older, crucial tasks may remain as well. It is, again, safe to assume that in reality there is a more complex organisational variety of hybrids, combinations and frameworks beneath the Weberian dichotomy proposed here. Weber would have been the first to agree.

There has been little systemic research in the public or private sector, however, that looks in more detail into the simple ideal-types (e.g. exploration- vs exploitation-oriented organisations) and their evolution. While this dichotomy and the evolutionary pattern seem to give us an easy way to differentiate between organisations with more stability-oriented capacities or with dynamic capabilities, as we argued above, it seems too linear to assume that organisations – or even policy arenas, let alone countries – move from charismatic networks with dynamic capabilities to Weberian professional bureaucracies and back. Indeed, there is potentially a more complex organisational variety of hybrids.

The classic and still unique work by management thinker Henry Mintzberg may offer us the best available taxonomy to unpack these issues in more detail.[14] Mintzberg differentiates between five key organisational configurations or designs

– *entrepreneurial, machine bureaucracy, diversified, professional, innovative* organisations – that can co-exist and exhibit, depending on the contextual feedback factors, tendencies for either *cooperation* (through common ideology and missions) or *competition* (intra- and interorganisational politics). He recognises that almost all organisational designs may also be present in the public sector (most commonly, though, machine bureaucratic, diversified and professional configurations, i.e. Weber II type of organisations). Crucially, he also acknowledges that different organisational designs embody different routines and capacities affecting the overall innovation capacities and capabilities of these organisations:

> The entrepreneurial organization can certainly innovate, but in relatively simple ways. The machine and professional organizations are performance, not problem-solving types, designed to perfect standardized programs, not to invent new ones. And although the diversified organization resolves some problems of strategic inflexibility found in machine organizations, as noted earlier it too is not a true innovator.[15]

We can argue that in Mintzberg's framework, entrepreneurial organisations are closer to Weber I type of organisations, and the more conscious attempts to introduce and design innovative configurations are attempts to establish what we label as Weber III type, or neo-Weberian agencies. Further, in line with our reading of Weber, Mintzberg also looks at these configurations from the perspective of organisational *life cycles*: organisations emerge in the entrepreneurial configuration and grow to other forms until potentially declining through political forces;

and organisations can make good or bad internal choices on their configurations while also being affected by feedback from the external environment (competition, emulation, regulation, etc.), technologies and other sources. Furthermore, the shifts in organisational configurations are not only automatic or evolutionary life-cycle-like but may also result from conscious *design choices* (both in the public and private sector).[16]

We can build (as shown in Table 3.2) a more elaborate analytical taxonomy that combines two aspects of the organisational variety argument: organisational configurations or designs and their specific routines, capacities and capabilities. We have extended Mintzberg's framework by adding specific organisational routines that are considered as most important in the functioning of public sector organisations, following Pollitt and Bouckaert.[17]

We propose that innovation bureaucracies that perform 'well' are organisational configurations – sets of multiple organisations, our types of creators, doers, funders, intermediaries and rulers – that possess both long-term policy and implementation capacities and dynamic exploration and learning capabilities to change. These capacities and capabilities are stored in and delivered by different organisational configurations or designs, from charismatic networks for hacking and creating mission mystique to more professional expert organisations that routinise old and new 'best' practices and maintain their stable performance. They foster the constant search for better policy ideas and practices and guarantee the implementation of these ideas and practices. Further, the variety of organisational designs in innovation bureaucracies and the overall differences of innovation bureaucracies across different systems (countries, regions, sectors) can

Table 3.2 Taxonomy of organisational configurations, capacities and capabilities

	Entrepreneurial	Machine	Diversified	Professional	Innovative
Organisational routines	Simple, informal, flexible, little staff or middle-level hierarchy	Centralised bureaucracy, formalised, specialised work, division of labour	'Divisions' loosely coupled together under headquarters	Bureaucratic, decentralised, pigeonholes for professional autonomy	Fluid, organic, selectively decentralised 'adhocracy' (multi-disciplinary task forces)
Strategic management routines	Visionary, flexible, leadership-based	Planning that is strategic programming	'Corporate' portfolio strategy and divisions with individual strategies	Stable and also many fragmented strategies by professional judgement and collective choice	Largely emergent, evolving through a variety of bottom-up processes
Personnel management routines	Limited personnel, no systemic routines, needs-based development	Standardised work and skills and recruitment processes	Divided between headquarters and autonomous divisions	Dependent on training to standardise the skills of its professionals	Variety and mix of skills, openness to learning and experimentation
Financial management routines	Flexible, emergent	Efficiency and process oriented	Autonomous divisions, output oriented	Mixed, based on professional autonomy	Flexible, not efficiency oriented

	Entrepreneurial	Machine	Diversified	Professional	Innovative
Coordination routines	Direct supervision	Standardisation of work processes	Standardisation of outputs	Standardisation of skills	Mutual adjustment
Location in the broader system of organisations	Peripheral or within machine and/or diversified organisations	Central policy implementation units with public accountability	Central/core policy units (whole policy fields)	Specialised service providers (between core and periphery)	Peripheral or in new domains, or as parts of machine/ diversified organisations
Core capacities and capabilities	Simple/initial developments and changes	Efficiency, transparency, accountability	Concentration of different foci	Professional proficiency	Learning and complex innovations
Organisational trade-offs	Responsive, with mission vs vulnerable, restrictive, unstable	Efficient, reliable vs obsession with control, no initiative, autonomy	Autonomy, diversity vs costly, reluctance to innovate, requires measurable goals	Democracy, autonomy vs professional discretion, reluctance to innovate (unless collective action)	Innovative, effective vs inefficient (communication, coordination)

Source: Authors, elaborated based on Mintzberg, *Mintzberg on Management*.

be viewed as elements of the institutional complementarities of different capitalist systems and as a potential variable explaining the dynamism of capitalist systems.[18]

In other words, public sector capacities and capabilities for innovation are best conceived as means and ways through which agile stability is generated and maintained – or not (from the search for novelty to effective implementation, and including their combination in time and space). This is unlikely to be delivered by single forms of institutional or organisational *design*. Thus, a focus on single organisations, or policies delivered by them, as key explanatory variables and best practices of effective innovation policies misses the crucial aspect that it is the mix of capacities and capabilities needed, and their fluid but *dynamic* combination and recombination, that is at the heart of innovation bureaucracies' successes and thus of the genuinely entrepreneurial state as well.

Warning to Practitioners: Why New Public Management Is Not Agile Stability

Starting in the West in the 1980s, and following the argument that governments should adopt private-sector strategies to maximise value (understood in purely monetary terms) in the public sector,[19] NPM reforms are probably the most dominant organisational reforms in (Western) government since the nineteenth century. We should therefore take a closer look at their importance for both agile stability and innovation bureaucracy. In short, we argue that – next to many other flaws – NPM overemphasised agility. Indeed, it profoundly misunderstood the idea of agility and dynamism in the public sector. This led to many public organisations losing not only their long-term capacities but also their dynamic capabilities. NPM reforms can be viewed as an attempt to hack existing stability-oriented structures and bring more charismatic agility to governance – and as a prime example that such hacking can go badly wrong.

NPM is popularly denoted by concepts such as project management, flat hierarchies, customer orientation (as opposed to citizen orientation), abolition of career civil service, depoliticisation, total quality management, and the delivery triad of privatisation, contracting out and public-private partnerships. Transparency, citizen involvement and decentralisation are not part of the original core of NPM theoretically, because NPM's focus on the apolitical rule of the expert makes them more difficult and because they do not necessarily contradict previous forms of public administration, as well as empirically.

NPM is both regional and global. Historically and functionally it comes from Anglo-America and it was strongly pushed by most of the international finance institutions, such as the World Bank and the International Monetary Fund, which are at their core Anglo-American institutions even today. Innovation policy as it is currently practised and NPM reforms burst into the (Western) policy stage at the same time in the early 1980s.[20] And while NPM reforms had a significant impact on various areas of innovation policy, such as turning academic institutions from autonomous academic beacons towards more business-like, customer-oriented and project-based organisations, or reforming NASA to rely increasingly on outsourcing and procurements as opposed to maintaining in-house technological capacities, in many parts of the world, surprisingly, the interaction between the two has not yet been systematically studied.

We argue that this was and is an abusive marriage: many of the criticisms of innovation policy, particularly – from today's perspective – its ineffectiveness in delivering greener and more inclusive growth, have to do with the NPM practices under-lying it. This is due to the overall emphasis of NPM reforms on financial cost-efficiency at the expense of long-term vision setting (extending beyond normal/accepted project and performance management frameworks) and the ability (or agility) to take on board the uncertainties and risks of innova-tion (that cannot be ex ante codified into project and perform-ance contracts). This is not incidental but due to a core principle of NPM: the well-known tendency, especially in practice, to privilege efficiency over effectiveness, often so much so that the latter is ignored altogether.[21] Yet, paradoxi-cally, these same practices and limitations have enabled innovation policy to become a relatively independent field of rather technocratic policy making, dominated by knowledge communities trained to think and talk in terms of market fail-ures, an object of academic and policy research and an area with a certain degree of professionalisation.

Further, NPM has an even better-known sibling, namely the neoliberal economic policy agenda, known as the Washington Consensus in the development context, and this agenda has played an important role in the evolution of inno-vation policy over the past four decades. While NPM is not a unified set of reforms, its main focus has been on how public organisations work (and not so much why and what they do): management practices, relevant skills, evaluation and measurement frameworks, and how relationships with stake-holders (in NPM terms, 'customers') are structured. Success has been narrowly defined via key performance indicators. There is an important overlap with the way policies evolved under the Washington Consensus, for example in the 1990s, and the focus of innovation policy shifted from industrial and vertical policies towards horizontal ones (one-size-fits-all solutions to different sectors, industries, regions, technologies), detaching policy making from setting priorities and making choices, or exercising authority and practising leadership. This was enabled by focusing on narrow project management skills in public organisations, including outsourcing much of the project evaluation through peer review.

With the advent of the NPM agenda in the 1980s, global-Western public organisations, innovation bureaucracies among them, often drastically changed their internal practices – routines – to more and more rational(-looking) ways of doing things via ever more complex measurement and evaluation practices. These reforms have come to their full fruition with the extensive use of ICT-driven data and metrics. The goal, therefore, is a slim, reduced, minimal state in which any public activity is decreased and, if at all, exercised according to business principles of efficiency.

Yet, for the last quarter of a century, we have known that NPM reforms have not led to productivity increases or welfare maximisation.[22] At best, one may say, 'Several years of attempts and experiences of public management reforms in western Europe and other OECD countries give evidence of relative failure rather than success.'[23] NPM has overwhelmingly failed to deliver on its promise to cut costs. For instance, Hood and Dixon have found that in the core NPM country of the UK, despite three decades of outsourcing and much-hyped NPM initiatives, civil service staff costs were about the same in real terms in 2012–2013 as they had been over thirty years earlier.

Empirically, the catchword promises have not been delivered. Flat hierarchies are sometimes appropriate and sometimes not; taking citizens merely as customers takes away their participatory rights and duties and thus hollows out the state; the abolition of a career civil service will usually let administrative capacity erode; depoliticisation – and thus de-democratisation – leads to the return of the nineteenth-century, Westminster-style, Imperial bureaucrat of yore (if in managerial disguise – same power, less responsibility); and contracting out has proven to be excessively expensive and often infringes on core competences of the state, as well as on the most basic standards of equity.

By the mid-1990s, concerns were growing about NPM's effectiveness.[24] Yet, the concept or part thereof remained at the front of the public reform agenda, whether in spite or because of the failures – as Lapuente and Van de Walle have recently argued,[25] 'Administrations all over the globe have taken measures in the three main themes of NPM: competition between public and private providers, incentives to public employees and the disaggregation of public organisations.'[26]

Furthermore, all countries have not been equally subsumed by NPM reforms. As Pollitt and Bouckaert argued over a decade ago, some leading OECD countries, particularly in Europe, such as the Nordic countries, have attempted to transcend NPM reforms by supplementing them via returning to key Weberian values, such as rule by law, expertise and merit.[27] They have adopted certain private sector management practices, such as a greater focus on citizens as users, but also endeavoured to restore certain long-term capacities in order to steer attempts to build dynamic capabilities and thus find a better balance between the conflicting expectations of citizens. After all, we tend to expect universalism and equal treatment of all citizens from public sector actions, but we also really like the personalised services and approaches that the data-driven public sphere is offering. Never mind that this often happens by misusing our trust and collecting more data on us than we can imagine, nor that data never drives anything but only people using and/or designing that data; data, lest we forget, does not exist unless created.[28]

Prior to the COVID-19 crisis, leading public administrations among developed economies were in essence neo-Weberian, if we understand the term generally (and then we can include e.g. countries such as New Zealand and Singapore), while many others suffered from the negative effects of NPM reforms. The COVID-19 responses show that countries tend to revert to their dominant existing routines regarding underlying capacities. For instance, while the UK sought to largely outsource its response to the pandemic, Singapore or Germany relied strongly on public actors.

But even here, since looking good – and that, both in public administration and in innovation, means fashionable – is more important than doing well, and since COVID-19 has served, by and large, the impulse to justify one's preconceived notions rather than questioning them, even in the face of dismal failures and literally mountains of corpses, successful responses to the pandemic have been classified as either ICT-driven or agile-only NPM. A good example is the successful Taiwanese response, usually associated with the name of ICT minister Audrey Tang, which is often sold as an agile response, whereas none of this would have been possible without a highly competent, classical bureaucracy, damaged but not completely wrecked by relatively late NPM reforms. Estonia, usually billed as a neoliberal success story and 'the most digital country in the world', seriously mismanaged the second wave in early 2021, at times being the worst country globally, with hardly any ICT successes and an uncomprehensive response.[29] But once again, the obverse is true as well: over-stable Germany, where much of the Weberian quality bureaucracy has been hollowed out by NPM-style reforms since the 1980s, messed up even more completely than the EU context would suggest, with a mixture of savings paranoia, reactivity rather than pre-empting, legalistic bureaucratese, and an utter lack of successful ICT-based solutions and industrial policy measures other than the development of vaccines.

In sum, in innovation policy and beyond, we have decades of lessons and empirical proof that just focusing on and over-emphasising public sector agility, entrepreneurship and innovation does not work. We need a more systemic and self-critical approach to building dynamic capabilities in the public sector in a way that does not steer the public sector away from its core public values – in tasks allocated to the public sector, effectiveness is more important than efficiency and citizens as customers are something more than just customers – and reform away from what is good and necessary about stability-oriented public sector capacities.

Erring on the Side of Stability

Businesses often evolve into something quite different to what they started out as. For instance, in 1865 Nokia was a lumber company and Marriot began in 1927 as a root beer producer. As Schumpeter argues, fear of death by competition is what drives business to innovate and explore new pastures. Companies sense opportunities and threats, seize them – or not – and reconfigure what they do.[30] The public sector is not primarily defined by competition, even if in some cases we pretend otherwise and create rankings of schools, doctors and so on, or compete with other countries, war-like or in peace. Furthermore, a department of agriculture is likely to deal with quite similar subjects – growing food – as it did say fifty or a hundred years ago, albeit on a vastly higher level of complexity driven by technological advances in pesticides, genetically modified organisms, ICT-enabling precision agriculture, and so on, but also dynamics in consumer tastes and expectations.

Thus, public organisations rarely evolve into something completely new: military procurement organisations don't deal with horses anymore, but their core tasks are roughly similar to what they were 100 or even 400 years ago. Hence, stability and resilience are what often defines public organisations. In other words, public organisations react differently to private ones to changes in their environment; they sense differently, seize differently and sometimes reconfigure what they do, sometimes radically so: military procurement can become a major driver of communications technology, a national bureau of standards can become a major resource for industrialisation, and so forth.

However, they have a uniquely all-encompassing task that they cannot usually abandon. During the twentieth century, following Wagner's Law, that task got bigger and bigger and, never mind neoliberal ideologising, it shows no signs of diminishing much and so any attempt at reinvention is limited on that side by the task at hand. Thus, as we will see in Chapters 4–6, agility is particularly challenging for public organisations.

The Road Ahead

The next chapters discuss and highlight through narrated cases how policy and implementation capacities, and dynamic exploration and learning capabilities, have been created; how they have evolved in the global West, the global East and during different phases of global development; and how the digital revolution will impact the development and maintenance of these capacities and capabilities, and agile stability.

In the following chapters we give a bird's-eye view of the emergence and evolution of modern innovation bureaucracies from after the Second World War and throughout the Cold War era to modern days. We distinguish between four periods with distinct models of how capacities and capabilities were organised:

1. Predominantly big science, national champions and developmentalism-driven *mission-oriented* research and industrial policies organised in autonomous public agencies under strong political support and directionality (Chapter 4);
2. A shift towards more *diffusion-oriented* and more collaborative forms of innovation policy from the 1970s onwards,

organised through more hybrid and networked forms (Chapter 5);

3. After a gap of a decade or two of NPM-driven erosion of innovation capacities and capabilities in the 1980s and 1990s, the emergence of the societal challenges-focused *mission-oriented* approaches from the 2000s onwards, trying to mix the best experiences of the previous two periods (Chapter 6); and

4. The emergence of what we call neo-Weberian innovation agencies that attempt to combine both agile and stability-focused capabilities and capacities in a single organisation (Chapter 7).

In these chapters, our focus will be less on the exact details of the respective research, industrial and innovation policies, which have been extensively covered,[31] and much more on how globally leading regions/systems have generated and maintained the agile stability of their innovation systems to respond to domestic and international pressures and adjusted their policy foci and strategic actions. (Admittedly, once again, mid-level countries that are not leading but still accomplish significant strides for literally hundreds of millions of people at any given time are therefore left out of this study. That this is a pattern for innovation bureaucracy studies is an old yet fully valid criticism;[32] we hope to address this issue sometime soon in another context.)

We intend to show that in this evolving global context, there are different but recurring patterns of how capacities and capabilities for agile stability have emerged and evolved:

1. The post-Second World War *mission-oriented industrial and research policy era* was characterised by the emergence of high

politics-led *hybrid public organisations* designed to create agile stability *within* the public sector. Given the stability and context of domestic political and economic feedback arenas, some of these organisations, from rulers to funders and doers, emerged within existing research and industrial bureaucracies (Japanese MITI, DARPA, the French national research institutes and planning bodies), while others emerged on top of (i.e. the Korean presidential Blue House and its committees) or outside (i.e. the international organisations created for European research collaboration such as CERN and the Korean government research institutes) existing national bureaucracies. The period focused more on providing long-term *capacities* through wide and stable organisational bases, in particular for R&D and innovation policies. This was, in many ways, the period of 'big science meets big problems'. The dynamic capabilities were often triggered by heroic individuals at the top of these organisations (the Kennedys of R&D and innovation policies).[33]

2. The *diffusion-oriented innovation policy era*, from the 1970s onwards, was characterised by the dominance of more *hybrid networks* of agile stability, as in almost all countries different forms of public-private networks were created, either as new intermediaries or doers (policy coordination bodies, public-private research associations) to complement the institutional landscapes and legacy institutions established in the previous era. Hence, next to the concern with long-term capacity and public sector internal dynamic capabilities, there was growing recognition that to improve the feedback linkages, but also to co-opt new dynamic private sector niches into the entrepreneurial state agenda, more open and

hybrid forms of co-creation and co-production might be necessary.

3. The *modern-day innovation policy era*, from the 1990s onwards, was initially characterised by the NPM-driven emphasis on financial cost-efficiency and technocratisation, which paradoxically constrained both long-term vision setting (extending beyond normal/accepted project and performance management frameworks) and the ability (or agility) to take on board the uncertainties and risks of innovation (that cannot be ex ante codified into project and performance contracts). To overcome this, since the 2000s some entrepreneurial states have sought to rebuild capacities and capabilities for innovation through societal challenge-driven entrepreneurial discovery and mission-oriented policy efforts that try to regain legitimacy for government risk-taking and directionality, while also providing contextual feedback linkages with the private and societal spheres for dynamic capabilities. We show how in recent years this has led to the emergence of what we call neo-Weberian innovation agencies – agencies consciously making efforts to build both long-term policy capacities and dynamic capabilities.

4

AGILE STABILITY IN THE POST-SECOND WORLD WAR ERA

Big Science Meets Big Problems

Our story starts here with the post-Second World War rebuilding of the war-torn countries and societies. Such conditions, created by unexpected external events, are in both Schumpeter's and Weber's writings often linked to processes and developments – from rebuilding infrastructure to rebalancing societies – that require long-term planning, large-scale investments and in general stability and patience. In modern history of management and public administration thinking, classic Weberian systems – with planning, coordination and personnel routines focusing on long-term visions, stability and merit – are considered as best arrangement for such tasks, be it in the public or private sphere. When these external events are of negative nature (wars, environmental disasters or pandemics), we normally tend to see public sector organisations taking a bigger role in leading, funding and delivering necessary actions.

As we show in this chapter, in the case of innovation bureaucracies seeking to provide qualitatively different directions for development – from turning the Second World War military lessons to civilian use to setting up new eras and directions of economic development – we notice the first glimpses of globalisation of innovation thinking through the financial and policy influence of the US on European and Asian rebuilding projects. At the same time, we also see that different regions and countries entered this rebuilding stage with different histories and political and administrative legacies that had to be taken into account in the formation of the charismatic networks and new types of public sector organisations charged with dynamic capabilities. These organisations were part of the larger science and innovation bureaucracies necessary for the rebuilding efforts, be it energy systems (by leveraging the military's nuclear experiences), industrial production capacities, transport and logistics systems, or health and education services. This challenge of balancing between globalisation and convergence vs contextualisation has been an everlasting policy challenge ever since.

American Primacy and Agile Stability

Right after the end of the Second World War in Europe, in July 1945, Vannevar Bush, director of the US Office of Scientific Research and Development, wrote in his famous report to the president, *Science, the Endless Frontier*, that 'Scientific progress on a broad front results from the free play of free intellects, working on subjects of their own choice, in the manner dictated by their curiosity for exploration of the unknown. Freedom of inquiry must be preserved under any plan for Government support of science.'[1] This was his plea for stable government funding of basic research to allow science to come up with new solutions and technologies of general public interest during peacetime (i.e. he discussed the importance of science in public welfare and the need for a war against disease). He also proposed an independent and self-organising agency to create policy for and fund (not conduct) scientific research and education. Eventually, out of this initiative a US NSF was created. This was much less powerful than what Bush had originally envisioned, but the NSF financed basic frontier research – to date it has funded about 5 per cent of US public R&D – and the world gained the mythical 'linear view' of research and innovation (that innovation stems, in specific steps, from curiosity-driven basic research), which has guided R&D policy rhetoric globally even more than in the US.[2]

Fred Block considers this to be one of the key turning points in the history and evolution of the US innovation system,[3] where the US federal government took a more central role in steering and directing, through funding and setting priorities, the historically public-private partnership-based co-creation of technological capacities and economic development. Ever since the Second World War, the US government has invested in research, development and innovation in a manner whereby about half of the public investments go into the military sector and half into the civilian sector, and of the civilian research only a small minority is funded on the basis of the linear or diffusion-oriented model, while the majority is funded to tackle the specific challenges of mission-oriented agencies (health, environment, energy, etc.).

In one of the most insightful books on the US innovation system – *America Inc.? Innovation and Enterprise in the National Security State* – Linda Weiss has argued that instead of the vision of Bush, since post-Second World War the key dominant focus of the US federal technology and innovation policies has been on technology leadership 'in order to sustain US military-political primacy, not to achieve commercial advantage'.[4] Thus, US policies and their spillovers (technological and institutional) across the world should not be assessed through technical frameworks of economics or rational public policy analysis (i.e. scientific excellence, economic competitiveness, national independence and resource dependency). Rather, these policies have been tools of specific national identity building and (geo-)politics: be the best in S&T as this can win wars, help you rule the world and excuse domestic failures such as the moon and the ghetto problems of US public policy. In other words, these policies gave the US the ability to hatch amazing technologies for space exploration and even land on the moon, even though it was unable to tackle poverty, racism, public health and similar social issues.[5]

The US's achievement in reaching the level of development where it could think about maintaining its global primacy and dominance, including in technology and innovation, has been remarkable. As Mowery and Rosenberg noted, 'The technological position of the US economy before the Second World War bore more than superficial resemblance to the situation of Japan in 1960s and 1970s.'[6] That is, the US innovation system, like most systems globally, had been mostly driven by private initiatives, and it relied extensively on borrowing new technologies and innovations from Germany and the UK and adjusting these for local context.[7]

This also means that we cannot overlook the role of the Second World War in the context of innovation system building – Daniel Sarewitz has even claimed that what President Eisenhower called the 'military-industrial complex' is what we nowadays label the national system of innovation.[8] Weiss has argued that the War Mobilization – National Defense Expenditure Act (1940) and War Powers Act (1941) were the key change events for the US innovation system,[9] as the source of technology and innovation shifted from domestic private technology-driven logics (and from emulating Europe) towards steering and leading technological development by domestic demand/procurement (the new laws allowed for fixed-fee or cost-plus-fixed-fee arrangements that allowed private risk to be socialised), collaboration with universities,[10] and the creation of an elaborate network of federal research laboratories.[11]

In principle, this has created two parallel innovation systems in the US: the more politically legitimate military *mission-oriented system* (as explored in detail by Weiss) and the less politically legitimate and more hidden generic economic growth and *diffusion-oriented* innovation system (as explored in detail by Block and Keller) which have over time become increasingly interlinked.[12]

The innovation bureaucracy of the early mission-oriented era inherited many of its elements and traits from the Second World War period. These became centralised under the control of the president and Department of Defense (DoD, created in 1949) and was supported by the so-called National Security State (NSS) – 'a particular cluster of federal agencies that collaborate closely with the private actors in pursuit of security-related objectives'[13] – covering not only the DoD, the Central Intelligence Agency (CIA) and Homeland Security systems but also elements of energy (Department of Energy, DoE), health (National Institute of Health, NIH) and science (NSF) systems. Weiss also argues that many of the civilian agencies and instruments could be analysed outside the NSS framework, but one also has to accept the reality that even highly successful instruments, such as the NIH and the Small Business Innovation Research (SBIR) programme, as well as famous universities, from Stanford in the centre of Silicon Valley to MIT in the centre of the Boston area innovation ecosystem, were, in the early post-Second World War decades, to a large extent funded by military agencies. Even NIH became a strong ally of the NSS as it inherited the responsibilities for the wartime Office of Scientific Research and Development Committee on Medical Research and 'was not permitted to grow its budget until it inherited wartime projects'.[14]

The institutions with strong wartime legacies were already radically innovated under President Eisenhower to allow for more dynamic capabilities by encouraging specific forms of public-private partnerships to improve mutual learning and feedback through the initiatives of proactive state agents tasked to '[f]irst, form partnerships and alliances with private actors throughout the national economy; second, negotiate private-sector support for state-directed projects; and third, leverage both public and private resources in pursuit of national technological objectives'.[15]

This vision underpinned the creation of different forms of *dynamic organisations* within the US innovation bureaucracy, to provide agile input and dynamic capabilities to an otherwise normally highly centralised and bureaucratic military command and planning system. In 1957 the vision was further pushed forward by the 'Sputnik effect', which triggered the Space Race and a further redesign of the US NSS/NIS. In this context, the US introduced institutions and drivers of agility on different levels of innovation bureaucracy:

1. Centralisation of DoD R&D activities through the creation of the position of deputy director of research and engineering (Defense Reorganization Act 1958) – it is a peculiarity of rulers that their agility is often increased through centralisation of power and authority, while intermediaries, doers and funders gain agility and dynamic capabilities via decentralisation and delegation from the top.

2. Pouring money into R&D across the whole system, from new agencies to expanding existing bodies (i.e. the NIH): 'Before Sputnik the nation spent roughly 1.5% of GDP on R&D with government and private sector contributing equal shares, a decade later that investment exceeded 3% of GDP, some 70% of which was provided by the federal government.'[16]

3. Establishment of public sector-led new mission-oriented agencies, mostly set up by directors/leaders with highly mixed careers combining military service and academic and/or industrial positions. These ranged from NASA (tasked with taking man to the moon and back safely) and ARPA (tasked with preventing and creating technology surprises) to the Small Business Investment Company (SBIC) within Small Business Administration, whose objective was to create and steer venture capital funds and, given the Soviet

overall technological progress, fight the 'soft-power battle for hearts and minds'.[17]

4. Maintaining dynamic capabilities across different forms of doers from ARPA and SBIC to publicly funded, but privately managed, national laboratories; for example during the 1950 nuclear and hydrogen race, the Lawrence Livermore Lab was created next to the Los Alamos Lab as it was expected that competition would foster more creativity.[18]

What were/are these dynamic capabilities? We probably know them best from the extensive studies of ARPA/DARPA, the birthplace of the internet. It was created explicitly in response to the Sputnik moment on the initiative of Secretary of Defense McElroy, a former soap salesman and brand manager at Procter & Gamble, who managed to push the idea of the agency through despite the opposition of many established NSS organisations protecting their turfs.[19] William Bonvillian has emphasised that the DARPA model did not grow out of some theory or model but was a successful case of organisational search and selection or 'learning by doing'.[20] It was originally established in 1958 as the Advanced Research Projects Agency with a mission to anticipate and pre-empt technological surprises through ahead-of-time, high-risk, exploratory R&D and by bringing together the best minds of the US (the first director came from General Electric and his scientific advisor, Herb York, from the Lawrence Livermore National Lab, where he had worked on the prior core US mission, the Manhattan Project, and the nuclear race between the US and USSR).

Given the huge impact of the Sputnik effect on the US political climate and the speed with which ARPA was established and located in the Pentagon (partly to provide a common control post for the weapons and military R&D pursuits that tended to get fragmented under NSS turf wars), it was originally probably rather overcalibrated as it enjoyed the situation of having 'more money than ideas' and entered into many different military and civilian areas,[21] including establishing overseas R&D centres in Vietnam and Thailand dealing with both conventional and non-conventional weapons R&D, as well as controversial social science research (one of the more controversial programmes, developing solutions for the Vietnam War, was called Project Agile). Given the backlash against the Vietnam War and revelations that many top universities and their researchers (including the members of ARPA's autonomous advisory group, Jasons, which provided dynamic capabilities within ARPA itself) were involved in military research, the 1969 Mansfield Amendment to the Military Authorization Acts increased public scrutiny and control of military R&D. In 1970, ARPA was moved out of the Pentagon, had its budget cut and in 1972 was renamed the Defense Advanced Research Projects Agency. This gave it a somewhat more peripheral status and more targeted focus on 'pre-mission' or 'pre-requirement' R&D.[22]

DARPA evolved into an agile funder and intermediary, rather than into a classic doer or creator. It benefits from a well-functioning 'island-bridge' model that gives access to a uniquely autonomous ruler, the DoD (and at times the president who needed to sign off on war-related research projects), which has used its powers of procurement and chain of command to diffuse the technologies DARPA has managed to facilitate. For the latter facilitator effect, DARPA has, through its unique, flexible and dynamic organisational routines, managed to forge linkages with public and private doers (universities, national laboratories, private defence contractors). Several studies have tried to study and summarise these unique routines (here we quote extensively from the excellent synthesis by William Bonvillian):[23]

- *Small and flexible* – DARPA consists of only 100 programme managers and office directors; some have referred to DARPA as 100 geniuses connected by a travel agent.
- *Flat* – a flat, non-hierarchical organisation with empowered programme managers.
- *Entrepreneurial* – an emphasis on selecting highly talented, entrepreneurial programme managers willing to press their projects towards implementation, often with both academic and industry experience. They serve for limited (three- to five-year) terms, which sets the timeframe for DARPA projects.
- *No laboratories* – research is performed entirely by outside performers, with no internal research laboratory.
- *Focus on impact not risk* – projects are selected and evaluated on what impact they could make on achieving a demanding capability or challenge.
- *Seed and scale* – initial short-term funding is provided for seed efforts that can scale to significant funding for promising concepts, but with a clear willingness to terminate non-performing projects.
- *Autonomy and freedom from bureaucratic impediments* – DARPA operates outside the civil service hiring process and standard government contracting rules, which gives it unusual access to talent, plus speed and flexibility in contracting for R&D efforts.

- *Hybrid model* – DARPA often puts small, innovative firms and university researchers together on the same project, so firms have access to breakthrough science and researchers see pathways to implementation.
- *Teams and networks* – at its best, DARPA creates and sustains highly talented teams of researchers, highly collaborative and networked to be 'great groups' around the challenge model.
- *Acceptance of failure* – at its best, DARPA pursues a high-risk model for breakthrough opportunities and is very tolerant of failure if the payoff from potential success is high.
- *Orientation to revolutionary breakthroughs in a connected approach* – DARPA is focused not on incremental but breakthrough/radical innovation. It emphasises high-risk investment, moves from fundamental technological advances to prototyping, and then attempts to hand off the production stage to the armed services or the commercial sector.

These routines, even if not all present at the same time, are normally expected to exist in the DNA of agile and dynamic organisations,[24] but the island-bridge relationship with the DoD has provided a unique balance of autonomy and embeddedness as the basis of the dynamic capabilities, linked with the more stable and classic implementational capacities of the DoD/NSS. Further, not every agile organisation gains such legitimacy and autonomy from its oversight organisation, and other organisations might face the problem of too much political scrutiny and intervention.[25]

Rebuilding Europe

While the Second World War demolished most of the European research infrastructure (although less so in the UK), it also gave a thrust for science and research as tools for reconstruction, especially the potential of using atomic power for civilian use. While national governments – most significantly Germany through its Kaiser-Wilhelm-Gesellschaft – had also funded research before the war, it had been limited to a few areas with direct government responsibilities (defence, telecommunications, agriculture, geology, civil works) and this research was mostly carried out in the laboratories of special branches of government without any real overarching policy. The majority of research, both in the US and Europe, had been funded by the private sector.[26] There were perhaps a few systemic policy exemptions, such as the Netherlands Organisation for Applied Scientific Research (TNO), which was created in 1930 to 'help enterprises and society benefit from science and technology' while other organisations, such as the Belgian National Fund for Scientific Research (NFSR), were created as hybrids (e.g. the NFSR was pushed by King Albert I but financed by industrialists, banks and private benefactors).[27]

After the end of the Second World War, US decision makers quickly realised that its Marshall Plan for Europe also needed to help rebuild European S&T capabilities. This was largely due to the advice of the (Joint) Research and Development Board of the National Military Establishment, created as a substitute for the wartime Office of Scientific Research and Development. The last head of the latter and first head of the former was Vannevar Bush. Partly driven by Bush's visions, but also significantly influenced by the CIA's concerns that investments into European S&T might fall in the hands of the Soviets, the US narrowed the focus of aid to basic/fundamental science with long-term economic impact and no quick applications, especially in military.[28]

While the Marshall Plan was built on bottom-up principles, with European countries expected to come up with their own joint developmental initiatives, including for the rebuilding of Germany, John Krige argues that it was paradoxically probably German science that gained most from the plan as other bigger players (the UK, France, Italy) had more domestic political issues and industrial legacies that inhibited new collaborative initiatives based on the US rulebook (which had a focus on basic science, mostly physics). For example, between 1950 and 1952, the German Research Council received between a quarter and a half of its funds from the Marshall Plan.[29]

In this broader political context, the European Community (EC) started to develop its own R&D routines. For example, the early treaties establishing the EC allowed for the community-level financing of R&D in the fields of coal and steel, nuclear research and agriculture (in all other areas community-wide unanimity was required until the late 1980s[30]). Overall, ever since these early post-Second World War attempts at collaboration, Europe has faced a tricky challenge: in general, all EU member states tend to agree that international R&D collaboration is necessary for global competitiveness. Nonetheless, techno-economic legacies, especially in countries with established national champions, have limited the proactiveness of key players to pool resources on the European level, and the political differences and everlasting debate on more versus less Europe have further complicated the procedures for Europe-wide research and innovation collaboration, and the development of necessary capacities and capabilities.

Thus, most progress in European-wide research and industrial policies has been pushed through thanks to the leadership of visionary European commissioners (such as Ralf Dahrendorf and Altiero Spinelli), relying on a plethora of dynamic mechanisms and often creating parallel public institutions outside the European treaties, institutions and bureaucracy. The biggest success of these early years was clearly CERN, first proposed as an international collaboration at the Conférence Européenne de la Culture meeting in Lausanne in 1949 and eventually created through an intergovernmental treaty signed in June 1953 by twelve Western European countries (including Yugoslavia). This was basically system hacking by the willing R&D and policy communities and 'CERN was the first of a series of European laboratories created through an international treaty, with its own facilities and a permanent staff possessing a specific international status'.[31] It was followed by bodies such as the European Space Agency, European Molecular Biology Laboratory and many others.

While the EC lacked a clear legitimacy and effective decision-making system, and a bureaucracy of rulers, intermediaries, doers and funders, it managed to figure out a rather unique dynamic mechanism to keep itself, at least to some extent, up to speed with the US NSS innovation machine through the high politics-led coordination of big science efforts in the form of international treaties (or even private companies jointly owned by countries and the EC) in areas with a critical community-wide user base and demand, and lack of incumbent national interests. Lack of user base and political agreement in domains with strong national interest and competition has been also one of the reasons why no real DARPA and defence R&D system had emerged on the EU level until the European Defence Agency was created in 2004.[32]

Outside the basic science arena and the emergence of some of the largest research collaborations globally, Europe did not manage to do as well, as most of the efforts remained limited to the level of national efforts driven by the diverse sets of interests and models of capitalism found across Europe. As mentioned above, Henry Ergas has argued that most developed economies can be divided between following either *mission-oriented* or *diffusion-oriented* innovation policies.[33]

Ergas characterised France and the UK as mission-oriented countries with one crucial difference. France was much more centralised, with a strong state-led planning system and elitist corporatist networks that enabled informal policy coordination and a reliance on state-owned national champions and national research centres (around the Centre National de la Recherche Scientifique) for implementing its missions. The UK was much more decentralised, with less interventionist planning culture and a reliance on the private sector and universities to actually 'do' the required R&D and innovation efforts.

Hence, economic and industrial policy failures in the UK and elsewhere in the 1960s, particularly in contrast to successes in France, were down to both low political commitment to long-term planning (and not just business cycle management) and lack of proper capacities and capabilities within planning organisations.[34] In contrast, the French planning capacities and capabilities evolved as voluntary collusion between senior civil servants and senior managers of big business, with the politicians and organised labour representatives both largely passed by,[35] and a strong focus on building capabilities within public organisations (and not farming them out to independent commissions).[36] The idea was to deliberately select a few promising firms who seemed willing and could move ahead fast and then encourage them with large contracts, financial help and other favours,[37] with modernisation commissions consisting of hand-picked members.[38] The weaknesses stemmed from resource constraints that inhibited experimentation (too few alternative designs being tested) and agency competition that led to Frankenstein effects, especially in the energy and communications sectors, as '[a]gencies have sought to expand their power bases by diversifying their operations, generally into markets for which their technological capabilities and organisational structures are totally inappropriate'.[39] Still, the French also managed to create a paradox through their industrial missions: their own Minitel programme (videotex online service) was so successful in its design and adoption that even the network effects of the global internet could not overtake it easily in its specific niche until the early 2000s.[40]

This contrasted rather strongly with the UK approach where 'average' companies were in the driving seat for planning commissions, which, accordingly, did not set ambitious plans or develop proper implementation mechanisms. So, the UK followed its more intermediate mission-oriented approach, mostly based on sectoral ministries, coordinated through the Prime Minister's Office (except for 1964–1970 when the Ministry of Technology existed) and supported by public research councils and private foundations. As argued by Ergas:

> The British system of public administration – with its emphasis on anonymity, committee decision-making, and administrative secrecy – ensures that individual public servants have little interest 'in rocking the boat'. The emphasis on internal and procedural accountability also makes government reluctant to devolve major projects to reasonably autonomous entities, so that responsibilities are tangled, decision-making cumbersome, and the organisational and cultural context is inappropriate for developing new technologies. At the same time, the propensity of British agencies to form 'clubs' with their suppliers – within which each supplier is treated on the basis of administrative equity rather than commercial efficiency – weakens whatever incentives suppliers may have to seek an early lead, while also ensuring that resources available are so thinly spread to be ineffectual.[41]

Germany, Switzerland and Sweden were described by Ergas as diffusion-oriented systems focusing on industrial competitiveness as opposed to specific (mostly military) missions. Of these countries, we probably know most about the evolution of the German system and the particularities that stem from the federal system creating a specific division of labour and feedback dynamics. The Länder are formally in charge of academic and research policy, although the federal government has tried to overtake and compete with Länder on specific issues (and structurally coordinate via bodies such as the Wissenschaftsrat). Overall, the public sector has tried to retain a rather hands-off approach in industrial development and provide generic human capital development and industry-oriented R&D services. This resulted in a decentralised system open to search and dynamism. As summarised by Reger and Kuhlmann:

> The Länder are responsible for the higher education institutes; they maintain (to a varying extent) non-university research institutions and – also to a varying extent – have their own technology policy programmes. This does lead to some redundancies in the capacities of the research and innovation system, but it also guarantees a decentral, 'autonomous' structure of research capacities, even outside the large cities.[42]

Further, while Ergas described Germany as a diffusion-oriented country, Reger and Kuhlmann also account that next to 'the (basic) university research financed by the Länder and the special area research carried out in federal and state research establishments (so-called "Ressortforschung")' Germany was also trying to launch 'big technology programmes from the mid-50s onwards, showing a marked orientation towards goals similar to those of the USA, mainly in the fields of nuclear technology, aerospace and data processing, and later microelectronics'.[43]

One of the key factors in the demise of mission-oriented policies and industrial planning in Europe was the above-mentioned emergence of the European Economic Community, where each country had rather different planning styles and capabilities.[44] Instead of a common European style of industrial planning and mission-oriented policies emerging in the late 1960s and 1970s, rather a gridlock of plans and missions, and policy cultures, remained in place.[45] The results of this could be seen in the developments of European electronics industry: individual semiconductor industries could not compete with the US companies, but a European industry could not emerge as national policy cultures remained dominant.[46] At the same time, as we show in the next chapter, the failure gave impetus to the emergence of a new layer of European innovation bureaucracy in the 1980s.

Rebuilding East Asia

The end of the Second World War and the Cold War also drove the US to enter Asian post-war rebuilding and development efforts, from Japan to the latter's recent colonies of Korea and Taiwan, which became crucial for the US in the global fight against communism. As a result, these countries received significant amounts of US financial and technological aid (see Levi-Faur on the importance of US aid in building up nimble, fast catcher-uppers and current innovation leaders Israel, South Korea and Taiwan[47]). Over the next decades, Japan, South Korea and Taiwan, as well as the small entrepôt of Singapore, gave rise to a globally unique success story of 'developmentalism' and notions of catching up and forging ahead through 'techno-nationalism', which paradoxically are not so different from the US notion of 'primacy' based on technological superiority.[48]

The key rationales of these policies were linked to national strategic efforts to maintain national security and independence through, among other things, S&T autonomy and export-oriented industrialisation (especially for South Korea and Taiwan). Thus, these policies already had strong overarching 'missions' and were not driven solely by economic rationales but also by broader values and the goals of national security and development. Next to these similarities, Japan has traditionally pursued more networked (between politicians, bureaucrats and business sector) development strategies, while South Korea, Taiwan and Singapore have built more politically led and top-down policy and planning elements to implement generally similar technological catch-up and export-driven development strategies.[49] Not surprisingly, many of the policy and bureaucracy-level proponents of the developmentalist and techno-nationalist approaches had been strongly influenced by war and military experiences – from Korean president Park Chung-hee and the Japanese MITI bureaucrats who had served in the Japanese Army in Manchuria (and later collaborated with the US military bureaucracy as part of their aid-based industrial policies) to Taiwanese military-based rule.[50]

Japan is probably the best-documented Asian story of global development. After the Second World War, the US military command abolished some of the key institutions of Japanese society – especially the military and political elite – but kept one legacy institution, namely the bureaucracy, largely intact. As Chalmers Johnson argued in his seminal book on the developmental state, *MITI and the Japanese Miracle*, the Japanese economic bureaucracy carried on the 'economic nationalism' that had underlined Japanese developmentalism since the Meiji restoration. This probably also explains the relatively quick switch from post-war recovery to the high-speed growth policy (in 1955) and the Income Doubling Plan (1960), which had the aim of overtaking the US and Europe (as well as the reluctance to liberalisation in the 1970s and 1980s), even if the political system was still in a shambles (in fact Johnson claims that the bureaucracy gained its mission from the logic of the Meiji constitution – independent responsibility to the emperor that can be interpreted as bureaucratic responsibility to themselves during times of weak politics).

It may be important to remember at this point that Japan is occasionally classified as Confucian, but that it is, probably with North Korea, the only country that was once Confucian but isn't anymore. In fact, part of the Meiji restoration meant the abolition of Confucianism on all levels and especially in bureaucracy, where, from a position of relative strength, first the German and the French system were chosen, and, after a while, only the German one was retained. German public administration at that time was largely Prussian and the model in question was exactly the one Weber talked about, so that – and this was also so in intellectual-scholarly reception – Japan is the only case of genuinely, consciously Weberian public administration in Asia in a more strict, limited sense of the word.[51]

The very center of this bureaucracy was MITI. Although formally created in 1949, Johnson traces its origins back to the Meiji restoration and creation of the Ministry of Agriculture and Commerce (1881), which was later reformed into the Ministry of Commerce and Industry (1925), Ministry of Munitions (1943) and quickly re-reformed back into the Ministry of Commerce and Industry straight after Japanese surrender in the Second World War (and before the US military administration arrived in Japan to hide the role of economic bureaucracy in the war effort). Careful reading of Johnson's study of MITI makes one realise that while the literature often emphasises MITI as a nodal Weberian agency (and consequently one of the critical ingredients of the 'developmental state' model), MITI's greatest contribution also could be interpreted as creating and sustaining agile stability in the Japanese innovation bureaucracy for designing and implementing 'industrial structure policy'.

MITI provided the stability and long-term vision in the system through several unique forms of organisational capacities and dynamic capabilities:

- The strict principles of the Weberian hierarchical career model provided a long-term common ideology or vision and planning capacities – as Johnson emphasises, bureaucrats running MITI in the 1970s entered MITI in 1930 and were first trained during the Manchurian occupation; that is, they had experienced the high days of Japanese Imperialism and learned the challenges of rebuilding places.
- The principles of Weberian recruitment and its specific blend also provided dynamic capabilities for agility – MITI, given its historical prestige, employed the best graduates from Tokyo University (created especially in Meiji times for preparing civil servants for the country): generalist law/ public administration graduates were employed for policy planning and coordination positions and engineers for substantive work of policy design in different vertical bureaus.

- The internal system – quick turnover of vice ministers (the highest level bureaucratic position) every two to three years; division of tasks between more senior colleagues (policy coordination and networks) and juniors (substantive policy thinking); willingness and mandate to carry out internal reforms and rearrangements; the existence of its own internal R&D capabilities through the Advanced Institute of Science and Technology (AIST), which was created as a MITI bureau (from 1949 to early the 2000s) to whom complex R&D tasks could be given and from where experts could be seconded to the ministry and other organisations under MITI supervision – contributed further to the agility and dynamic capabilities of the organisation.

- Externally, MITI developed an intricate system of feedback linkages and cooperation forms with different actors necessary for economic policy making and agility: for big politics and policy connections, the system of *amakudari* (early retirement of top servants due to the high turnover of the career system) allowed MITI to send its civil servants to politics (especially to the Liberal Democratic Party, LDP, which has run Japanese politics almost without interruption, except for the 1990s) and to the management of public and private organisations as well as to academia – this created in principle a system of 'corporatism without labour' that allowed for policy priorities set on economic growth and development. For more detailed policy coordination across domains, MITI strategically sent its staff to different policy coordination bodies (e.g. Economic Planning Agency), and created different platforms for policy coordination, such as public-private deliberation councils allowed by the unique legal set-up (Japanese laws tended to be rather broad and short, giving policy makers strong discretion and space for 'administrative guidance').[52]

Of course, the reality of any kind of public bureaucracy is that there are always conflicts and turf wars between different ministries (in the Japanese case especially between MITI and the Ministry of Finance), as well as successes and failures from the policy initiatives pursued,[53] but the emergence and early evolution of MITI is one version of how innovation bureaucracies can create and coordinate agile stability that seems to have worked (in the sense of the economic bureaucracy being able to initiate and lead new developments in the innovation system).

Out of the smaller developmental states, the Korean system came to resemble the Japanese system the most through the existence of pilot economic agencies, most notably the Economic Planning Board (EPB) (and Ministry of Finance to bank-roll investments into industrial policy), reliance on big family corporations, *chaebols*, for implementing government export-oriented policies and using public finances for policy loans. The crucial difference, also in terms of the agile stability system, came from the stronger political centralisation and control by President Park and his office (the Blue House). As Thurbon claims, while President Park was strongly influenced by his experience in the Japanese army and was impressed by the abilities of the Japanese bureaucratic planning system (apparently, the Japanese ambassador to Seoul called President Park at his funeral in 1979 the last soldier of Imperial Japan), the Korean policy system became much more driven by the agility and dynamism provided by the developmental visions of the presidents and the rulers and intermediaries in his or her control; that is, the Heavy and Chemical Industries Drive of South Korea was implemented under the coordination of a specific presidential committee as normal economic planning bureaucracy was against the high-risk and high-investment policy proposed by President Park.[54] Further, especially in early phases of development, the president did not shy away from challenging existing elements of innovation bureaucracy through the introduction of new elements to the system, regardless of the view of the existing bureaucracy.

For example, five-year economic planning was introduced in 1962, but the first Technology Promotion Plan emerged as a complement to the first Five Year Economic Development Plan only after the intervention of President Park, who noted that, especially in the context of declining US aid, economic development might also require an explicit focus on local technological capabilities.[55] These initiatives were further institutionalised through the Long-Term Comprehensive S&T Promotion Plan (1967–1986) for 'reaching at the upper level among industrializing countries by equipping develop-ment capabilities of self-reliable technologies'.[56] Between 1967 and 1969, the Science and Technology Agency (STA), which in the 1990s became the Ministry of Science and Technology (MOST), was set up initially as a rather flexibly organised umbrella department of the Prime Minister's Office (with freedom to hire top-level staff outside normal hiring rules) to plan and coordinate overall S&T strategies across ministries.[57]

Further, for transferring and localising foreign knowledge and supporting the selected firms, South Korea grew throughout the 1960s and 1970s to rely on an extensive network of doers in the form of government research institutes, such as the Korea Institute for Science and Technology (KIST) and the Korean Advanced Institute of Science (KAIS), established in the late 1960s as flexibly organised and formally independent foundations under the leadership of the president and with strong aid and guidance from the US.[58] Both were established as *government-funded non-profit organisations* to focus on developing specific S&T capabilities (through technology development in KIST and human capital development through teaching in KAIS), as '[e]xisting national and public research institutes could not be alternatives to support technologies required for industrialization due to limited budgets, insufficient research facilities, stiffness of research activities, poor research environment, lack of understanding of the technological demands of industries'.[59]

Thus, both KIST and KAIS were created as *new* public organisations (doers) outside the existing S&T bureaucracy with significant financial and technical assistance from the US (who saw investments through loans and grants into S&T institutions as an apolitical opportunity to compensate Korea for its participation in the Vietnam War and the normalisation of Korea–Japan diplomatic relations). KAIS was developed (with the help of the vice president of Stanford University and a Korean professor from the Polytechnic Institute of Brooklyn) within the logic of introducing a change agent into the educational landscape as both graduate schools and universities were considered to be 'pre-modern'.[60] KIST was also intentionally designed as a change agent with strong political support from President Park. Besides considering himself as the founder of most of these institutes, Park also made sure that the institutes were managed by people supportive of the approach.[61] The organisational design of KIST was unique for the South Korean context and in fact emulated from US private initiatives:[62]

> The active and unprecedented support of the government for KIST (including salaries three times higher than those for faculty members of national universities) served as momentum and stimuli for scientists to produce extraordinary outcomes and performance. By adopting a contract-based research system and attracting Korean scientists from abroad, KIST decided to concentrate its resources on studies of industrial technologies that would contribute to the national economic growth. KIST received financial support from the government, even though it was a legally independent foundation. The contract-based research system that served mainly industrial needs for technology was also different from other research organisations. KIST followed the model of Battelle Memorial Institute (BMI) in the US. However, BMI was the contract-based institute, which was established with the private fund.[63]

While the traditional accounts of East Asian development (or at least our contemporary reading of them) emphasised single organisations – nodal economic planning agencies built based on Weberian principles coordinating specific functions[64] – as key drivers of early industrial S&T policies, we can see that already in the early phases of industrial S&T policy a diverse set of bureaucratic and dynamic organisations, and more fluid public-private networks supporting these agencies, was emerging in the industrial and innovation policy arena. Thus, we can see early indications of dynamic capabilities and systems of agile stability emerging in research and industrial bureaucracies in the broader context of national security and developmentalist policy narratives.

Political Leadership of Mission-Oriented Science and Innovation

While these national and regional histories are naturally more complex, our intention here was to highlight and illustrate that the early post-Second World War evolutions of innovation bureaucracies were driven by very specific missions (national security, national development and reconstruction) that were supported by a historically rather unique, but at the time globally rather common, model of agile stability: high-level political agents created spaces for the emergence of dynamic capabilities through unconventional public agencies (mainly funders and doers but also different intermediaries) leading the mission efforts, while their work was scaled and diffused by more traditional bureaucratic implementation structures and routines evolving in their particular national contexts.

5

HYBRIDISATION OF INNOVATION BUREAUCRACIES IN THE 1970S AND 1980S

A New Paradigm for Innovation Policies and Bureaucracies

With the emergence of a multitude of full-fledged innovation bureaucracy organisations – carrying out a variety of tasks and capabilities – the 1970s can be viewed globally as a turning point in policy narrative and contexts. The collapse of the security and military narrative as the foundational legitimisation tool for innovation bureaucracies was perhaps clearest in the US, where the backlash from the Vietnam War had a bigger impact on the legitimacy of the US NSS than simply the reform of DARPA. As the war narrative lost its legitimacy, economic competitiveness and commercialisation/diffusion narratives entered the discussions.

The role of the NSS as procurer and market maker contributed significantly to the growth of the capabilities of US firms and these narratives – fuelled by the broader changes in US geopolitical priorities, especially in East Asia, as well as the global impact of the 1970s oil crises – spilled over across the globe, leading to the weakening of mission-oriented policies and organisations and the emergence of what we call hybrid innovation bureaucracies. By the latter we mean organisational configurations attempting to attain military missions, albeit weakened ones, and make domestic companies internationally competitive through public R&D and market access.

In one of its seminal works on research and innovation policies, *Science Growth and Society: A New Perspective*,[1] the OECD – an organisation originally established to administer Marshall Plan funds in Europe – distinguished between three stages of political climate for science and research policies:

1. High public faith in the efficacy of science between the end of the war and beginning of the 1960s, especially in the UK and US, related to the winning of the Second World War and the context of the Cold War; this was accompanied by largely successful economic planning exercises and bureaucracies in Europe, especially France.
2. The period 1961–1967 witnessed the gradual emergence of the economic and system analysis, with greater focus on resource allocation concerns (including a focus on broader missions, spillovers from military investments, the technology gap between developed and underdeveloped countries, and an emphasis on the goal of investing 3 per cent of GDP in research and innovation in the OECD countries).

3. Finally, gradual disenchantment with science and research (including issues of prioritisation and direction, especially the role of science and research in war, etc.). Next to the competitiveness narrative, a focus on domestic challenges (public services, poverty, health, urbanisation, etc.) also started to gradually emerge in the discourse.[2]

Importantly, this period coincides with growing criticism of the large machine bureaucracies of the welfare state in the Anglo-American countries,[3] most notably through public choice theories that laid the groundwork for NPM reforms (as discussed in Chapter 3) in the West. One of the key tenets of the reforms was the idea of decentralisation and managerial independence. This proved crucial in the formation of new innovation bureaucracy organisations and the way in which capacities and dynamic capabilities were built and maintained.

OECD meetings were vital for fostering international demand, or at least providing an international platform, for science and innovation policy rulers. The OECD had organised regular ministerial meetings since 1963, and while in the first meeting only four countries had designated ministers for science, by 1965 two-thirds of OECD members had ministers with such tasks and by 1968 science ministers were accompanied by economic ministers. The key policy debates took place between two approaches and their viability: sectoral division of the funding to defence, health and agriculture as in the US versus a centralised approach with a central allocation of resources as in other countries. At the time there was a belief that the US system looked attractive until the mid-1960s, but in the context of limited resources a more centralised approach might be more preferred. The second debate was on the appropriate balance between centralisation (of goals, priorities) and decentralisation (for implementation), and the OECD thought that traditional governance systems and bureaucracies were not equipped with sufficient dynamic capabilities (our language here) to discover and define new challenges (and change internally to tackle these). For this one would need to create:

> at ministerial level or on the periphery of government, or even outside executive altogether, a new type of institution, a sort of watchdog of political, social and economic life, which will be responsible for detecting the threats inherent in progress and for proposing means for harmonizing the course of progress with the aspirations of community [e.g. the UK's Cabinet Policy Review Group].[4]

Hybridisation and the Public-Private Networks in the US

In this broader context, the US NSS bureaucracy went through significant reforms of 'civilianisation' as it had to readjust its strategies for carrying out its missions. As the Cold War focus was shifting towards the novel tools of electronics and ICT, and as US companies became increasingly capable of forging new niches globally in these sectors, the NSS had to form more close-knit partnerships to engage these companies and their capabilities in their missions through *dual use* technology development possibilities and markets beyond simple military contracts. There were several important rearrangements of the NSS bureaucracy and integration of the mission- and diffusion-oriented policy logics towards what Weiss calls the hybridisation of NSS bureaucracy;[5] for example:

- Classic military missions (e.g. biological warfare) were transformed into commercial missions with dual use possibilities (e.g. development of biotechnology) supported by institutional readjustments (e.g. in 1972 the Frederick Cancer Research and Development Centre shifted from the DoD to the NIH as the National Cancer Institute took over people and capabilities, although physically it remained located in the defence complex);
- Given the public pressures, the DoD had to cut its direct ties with the university sector and this resulted in less direct funding to universities (with the NSF and NIH taking over that role) as well as the creation of new intermediaries: Stanford Research Institute, now a globally admired innovation engine,[6] was founded in 1970 based on the DoD-created capabilities at Stanford University and in 1973 the Draper Laboratory was formally spun out of MIT; both were created as independent not-for-profit entities that still remained largely funded by the NSS.[7]

Still, by the late 1970s, the domestic critique of the NSS had peaked as, on the one hand, Japan was making huge strides in its economic development and competitiveness, raising debates about the 'technology gap', and, on the other hand, there was a growing perception that the Soviet Union had achieved military parity and its invasion of Afghanistan created the demand for a new push for technological superiority through the Offset Strategy, which had to be based on new forms of public-private collaboration, because '[m]any of the advanced design and manufacturing capabilities for achieving the goal of the Offset Strategy were located in the commercial arena, not among the large defense contractors conventionally identified with the military industrial complex. This meant that the DoD had to explore new ways of procuring advanced technology that could also meet commercial interests if it were to access the so-called "nontraditional" suppliers.'[8]

Fred Block has argued in his 'hidden developmental state thesis' that this hybridisation of the US NSS was part of a bigger shift in the US national innovation system from the 1970s onwards as one could see similar hybridisation emerging in the area of health research and innovation,[9] especially around genetic engineering (its biggest scientific breakthroughs came in 1971 and the same year is often considered as the start date of the current ICT-based techno-economic paradigm[10]). The NIH – a rather unique mix of funder and doer – was instrumental in supporting the emergence and progress of the biotechnology field. While rather different from the ARPA/DARPA model in many crucial aspects – it relied on longer peer review-based research grants and owned its own labs[11] – its success in fighting human diseases (its formal mandate) rested on fostering dynamic public-private networks to speed up research commercialisation. For this, the NIH brought together its long-term and patient research (funding) capacities as well as political manoeuvring capacities (to balance regulatory and innovation incentives) with the dynamic innovation capabilities found among market actors. For example, Block has emphasised that:

> NIH officials in this critical period were also supportive of efforts by scientists to commercialize their discoveries. Some of his colleagues were scandalized when the UCSF scientist Herbert Boyer helped found Genentech in 1976, the first of the biotech start-ups specifically created to commercialize genetic engineering. However, NIH raised no objections when Boyer continued to use his NIH-funded lab at UCSF for Genentech's first commercial project – the development of a bacteria that would synthesize human insulin.[12]

He argues further that despite the political shift towards the rhetoric of market fundamentalism in the 1980s, there were also several broader policy initiatives introduced throughout the decade that created an arena for hybrid networks to emerge in different sectors of the economy.[13] These policy initiatives included regulatory reforms and new rules – for example the Stevenson–Wydler Technology Innovation Act and the Bayh–Dole Act in 1980 – that allowed and incentivised public organisations (from funders to doers) to collaborate with the private sector through technology transfer and innovation co-creation, as well as regulatory acts and incentive programmes to support research collaborations/consortia and commercialisation in the private sector, such as the Small Business Development Act 1982 (SBDA), National Cooperative Research Act in 1984 and the Advanced Technology Program (APT) in 1988.

As part of the SBDA, the SBIR programme (piloted by the NSF in late the 1970s) introduced an almost compulsory focus on dynamic research, but also policy capabilities, into the US federal system. All government agencies with research budgets had to allocate a few percentages (from 0.2 to 3.2 per cent, depending on years) of their R&D funds to the SBIR programme to finance private sector pre-commercial technology development. In carrying out this obligation, the agencies 'could provide funds as grants or contracts and they could solicit proposals with narrow or broad specifications of relevant research'.[14] It seems that these developments were also underlined by the need to adjust the NSS system; for example the DoD was one of the first to pilot it in 1981 as the Defense Small Business Advanced Technology programme, before it became a full programme in 1982; the DoD has always been one of the largest funders – almost the majority funder – of the SBIR programme as non-NSS agencies provide 5 per cent.[15]

Still, these broader regulatory and policy initiatives also resulted in some of the largest R&D and innovation co-creation partnerships of the 1980s and 1990s, such as the AI-focused Strategic Computing Initiative (SCI, 1983–1993; followed by other similar initiatives over the decades until the present time) and a not-for-profit R&D consortium, SEMATECH (started in 1987, still in action but without public funding). Federal seed funding (US$1 billion was invested over 1983–1993 into the former initiative and US$500 million over five years into the latter, mostly funnelled via DARPA) was able to pool significant private sector co-funding and participation to sustain US technology competitiveness (and primacy).[16]

Both of these models represented a particular idea of how the public sector can be an agent of long-term technology vision or direction setting and a demand articulation agent as well as an agile change agent with dynamic risk-taking capabilities:

> SEMATECH became a model for subsequent industrial policy efforts. Over the next 20 years, there were repeated efforts by government officials to assemble similar types of industrial consortia to accelerate technological development up and down the supply chain. The core idea was that putting some federal money into the mix gives industry participants an incentive to begin cooperating to identify shared research and logistical challenges that might be solved through joint efforts. The hope is that once industry officials see the benefits of this kind of cooperation, they will continue to finance the consortium efforts without government funds.[17]

This model of hybridisation led by dynamic public sector change agents was not fully a US invention as it emerged in the 1980s rather as a global convergent model for creating long-term capacities and dynamic capabilities in innovation systems.

Hybridisation and the Public-Private Networks in Asia

The late 1970s and early 1980s were the period when Japan entered the global innovation game and according to some provided, or at least co-created, the above-mentioned new global best practices for creating agile stability in innovation systems. If one reads the literature on key innovation policy innovations of the 1980s, one acronym – VLSI – seems to stand out as a trigger/rationale for inventing new innovation policy mechanisms and organisations. VLSI stands for very large-scale integration, or the integrated circuit technology, which in the late 1970s was considered to be the next technology for developing more reliable and smaller computers. After allegedly stealing internal IBM documents, which indicated plans for introducing new systems in Japan by 1980, the Japanese realised that to catch up and compete with the US in the new and emerging electronics sector, Japan had to improve its technological capabilities.[18] Hence, the four-year (1976–1980) VLSI project was created, and the Very Large Scale Integrated Technology Research Association was established with the support of MITI.

Indeed, technology development consortia had become one of MITI's key policy tools as industrial structure policy (including import quotas, restrictions on foreign direct investments) had become less effective or fallen under international criticism. In principle, these associations could be treated as one (more legal) form of MITI-mediated cartels (intermediaries), and Sakakibara claims that when VLSI started there were about forty consortia/associations in action.[19] The crucial innovation of the VLSI project itself was the creation of a novel doer, a joint research laboratory (between Fujitsu, Hitachi, Mitsubishi Electric, Nippon Electric Company and Toshiba) to which R&D workers and engineers were seconded to focus on common and basic technologies (while applied technologies were also collaboratively developed, but in the labs of the firms themselves). Sakakibara further claims in his original study that this innovation was not MITI's brainchild and it was not an emulation of private sector practices.[20] In fact, MITI opposed the lab and preferred to continue the old industrial structure policy by forcing these companies to merge and collaborate on their own, and the companies similarly disliked the idea of pooling capabilities outside their internal labs. Rather, it was mandated by a powerful LDP leader who argued that the Japanese market in the sector was too fragmented to compete globally.

Still, once it was given the task, MITI relied on its traditional organisational long-term capacities and routines to carry it out: the managing director of the association was selected from retired MITI bureaucrats (through the famous *amakudari* or 'descent from heaven', whereby top bureaucrats retire from their positions to other high positions in public and private sector organisations) and the manager of the co-operative lab was seconded from MITI's Electrotechnical Laboratory. In other words, MITI bureaucrats became intermediaries of a mostly private collaborative effort: the total budget was 70 billion yen – US$288 million in 1983 – of which 30 billion was provided by government, which was equal to about two to three times what the companies would have invested alone (but not significant in comparison to what Texas Instruments or Bell Labs invested in the US).

The VLSI project is in general considered a success. Callon,[21] though, claims liberalisation of the sector in the same period, as well as the fact that eventually most R&D was carried out in the firms and not in the joint lab, reduced the actual impact of the consortia (for Callon, VLSI acted as a high-tech subsidy and not a collaborative organisation). Still, in the 1980s the experience and hype around the VLSI project triggered a broader global emulation of the idea of industrial mission-oriented collaborative R&D efforts – the Japanese themselves introduced several less effective initiatives (for super computers, fifth-generation computers, etc.).

As mentioned above, the US NSS bureaucracy responded to domestic developments by emulating the Japanese VLSI model, introducing the SCI and SEMATECH Consortium, funded, of course, through DARPA. Wade argues that DARPA functioned for SEMATECH to a large extent exactly like MITI functioned for the VLSI project:

> In the early years the consortium was fragile, especially when the semiconductor price cycle was up and the companies were making good profits – then they hesitated to send top-notch people to work for the consortium. DARPA's steward-ship (funding and close collaboration at the *technical* level where its suggestions would be most appreciated) helped overcome collaborators' fears of either 'getting screwed' by other collaborators' non-reciprocity or opportunism or having their collaborators 'screw up' through incompetence. By 1994 it was sufficiently established that its board stopped further federal funding. It flourishes to this day.[22]

Among close neighbours of Japan, Korea had its own VLSI programme as a presidential Blue House initiative,[23] as well as further attempts to introduce public and private R&D capabilities in the ICT sector. In 1982, the STA initiated the long-term National R&D Program (while the Ministry of Education initiated the Academic Research Promotion Program) and tried to create incentives and frameworks for public-private research consortia between government research institutes and *chaebols*.[24] Other policy actors – especially the Ministry of the Postal Service (later the Ministry of Information and Communication) and the Ministry of Trade and Industry – entered the S&T policy arena in the late 1980s with their own Information and Communication Technology Program and Industrial Technologies Program (1987).[25] These initiatives were part of a bigger shift in the Korean innovation landscape as the 1979 assassination of President Park arguably led to a significant rethinking of the development model and a shift from 'modernisation' through export-led growth towards a crisis-based narrative of 'saving the economy' through a 'technology drive', which was 'an idea that involved a virtuous circle in the development of technology, industry, and the nation through the quick improvement of the domestic technology to the level of advanced countries'.[26] This also implied that S&T grew into a self-standing policy domain next to the EPB-led overall economic planning, which was also increasingly focused on market liberalisation.[27]

Throughout the 1980s and 1990s, Taiwan also became a big fan of collaborative research projects coordinated by the Industrial Technology Research Institute (ITRI) – Taiwan's main public sector technology development and transfer centre – and its clones.[28] The formal innovation bureaucracy was complemented by a network of 'parastatal' networks and agencies for technology testing, quality assurance and so on.[29] Similar to Korea, this was part of a larger shift in the Taiwanese innovation landscape as, by the late 1970s, the global oil crises, loss of international recognition, change of leadership and gradual Taiwanisation and technocratisation of the political elite, plus accumulating pressures from scientists and foreign advisors, led to the restructuring of the basic approach to S&T:

according to Greene,[30] politicians made bureaucratic planners not only planners but also S&T leaders. In 1976, the Council for Science Development was replaced with the Committee of Applied Technology to better coordinate national plans with a clear focus on technology development and diffusion. In 1978, national S&T conferences were initiated that combined foreign, public sector, academic and industrial expertise to discuss and coordinate these plans across organisational and sectoral borders. In 1979, the committee proposed a new long-term National S&T Plan that foresaw a more active role for state institutions (research organisations, state-owned enterprises) in supporting private industries, international technology cooperation and transfer. To implement this strategic approach, the role of key S&T policy actors was strengthened. One of the key agencies was originally created in 1979 as the Science and Technology Advisory Office, and in 1993 it became the Department of Industrial Technology of the Ministry of Economic Affairs (MOEA). Together with the Industrial Development Bureau, it sought to plan and coordinate policies and gradually move from improving industrial infrastructure (developing basic infrastructure, establishing ITRI and science parks in the 1970s) to industrial upgrading (in the 1980 and 1990s).

Hybridisation and Public-Private Networks in Europe

This wave of VLSI emulation, or the need to respond to Japan's huge innovation drive, also affected Europe. The rhetoric of innovation and competitiveness policies had already entered European debates in the 1970s,[31] but given the multi-level governance intricacies of the EU, it was mostly a rhetoric, or policy, of coordination and 'labels'. As was emphasised a decade ago by Peter Tindemans, a former Dutch science and innovation policy bureaucrat: 'No new institutions of major funding mechanisms have been created for innovation policy apart from innovation councils or platforms. These councils or platforms underline that innovation is very much about interactions between various stakeholders and more integrated approaches between various policy domains without lumping together responsibilities or funding streams for all these domains.'[32]

Further, throughout the 1980s, most European national economies were facing economic crises and the need to rethink their industrial policy models to focus on protecting existing low- and middle-tech industries based predominantly on conservative corporatist agreements (relying on state aid, protective industrial policies, strong social safety nets, etc.). As Darius Ornston argues in his detailed account of these challenges, *When Small States Make Big Leaps*,[33] most Western European countries did not truly prioritise innovation and R&D in this period of development, and they opted to respond to these challenges by attempting to either protect the corporatist agreements (especially those countries less influenced by the crises, e.g. Germany, Austria, Norway), push towards unilateral liberalisation (the UK under Thatcher; the Baltic states during the 1990s catch-up) or experiment with more competitive corporatist agreements, mostly focusing on competitive tax systems and labour market rules. The most successful in implementing these strategies were Ireland and the Netherlands (and also, in the 1990s, Central and Eastern

European economies), while the compromises achieved in Southern Europe were less competitive.

In the most innovative way, three Scandinavian countries – Finland, Denmark, Sweden – managed to forge through what Ornston labels as 'creative corporatist' agreements focusing on newer high-tech industries and the development of necessary capabilities. While Sweden and Denmark focused on reforming their labour market and educational systems, the Finnish agreement became the most focused on R&D and innovation, and its novel public-private R&D collaboration-based innovation bureaucracy became, by the 1990s, arguably one of the best practices in Europe (see more in the next chapter).

Still, the VLSI race triggered at least a partial shift away from supporting maturing or sunset industries through industrial policy towards focusing on sunrise industries through innovation projects. This happened both as national initiatives (e.g. the Alvey programme in the UK and Filière in France, as well as attempts to introduce national ICT programs in the Scandinavian countries) and as European-wide responses in the form of the European Strategic Programme for Information Technology (ESPRIT) programme (adopted in 1984 as part of the First Framework Programme) and the EUREKA initiative (1985).

These European-level initiatives focusing on pre-competitive R&D (to be in line with EU competition rules) paved a way for the emergence of the EU as a formally legitimate player in the European innovation policy scene. Before these projects, much of the EU negotiations and decision making was organised on the level of middle-level bureaucrats and, given the lack of legal mandate for European-level actions in research and innovation, this normally led to nothing much. Rather, it required political leadership, determination and proactive engagement with the industrial partners to break the European lock-in in innovation policy. Apparently, it was Étienne Davignon, the European commissioner for industrial affairs from 1977 to 1985 and also research and technological development from 1981 to 1985 (the combination of these roles was already a remarkable 'hack' of existing policy silos), who led the changes by organising a round table of top electronics industrialists representing large, politically powerful firms from the larger member states to collaborate in improving the performance and competitiveness of the European industry vis-à-vis the US and Japan.[34] From the EC side, the industry-level collaborations were supported by the ESPRIT. ESPRIT and several similar national projects (e.g. Alvey in the UK) were all designed, like VLSI, as collaborative projects between firms, universities and research institutes to promote pre-competitive and widely applicable generic research.[35]

This novel collaborative approach – co-financed projects funded under the programme had to be cross-border in nature – was initially developed as a proof-of-concept programme followed by public-private scaling (it started in 1982 with 11.5 million ECU and extended to 1.5 billion from 1984 to 1993). It also became a model for initial EU collaborations in research and innovation and the model was further extended to different areas. ESPRIT had some unique characteristics – small numbers of industrial partners with significant R&D labs and capacities, one of the larger budgets in the Framework

Programme, more granular levels of planning and coordination – that contributed to its agility. These were partly overlooked in later programmes that became more politicised (e.g. RACE in telecommunications and BRITE-EURAM in materials).[36]

Thus, while the EU finally managed to push through new formal collaborative forms of innovation support, the institutional context created its own complexities and uncertainties (especially its slow speed of decision making and funding), reducing the policy space for developing long-term capacities and dynamic capabilities. This again pushed the willing member states to seek alternative solutions outside the European institutions for maintaining competitiveness with the US and Japan, especially in near-market R&D, which was more difficult to organise and agree under the EU competition rules.

Hence, the EUREKA programme was launched 'not as an EU programme, but as a loose intergovernmental initiative designed to promote "near-market" research: that is, R&D leading to "products, processes and services having a worldwide market potential" in a relatively short period of time'.[37] It differed quite a lot from the model of ESPRIT collaboration: it employed a bottom-up methodology whereby research organisations were responsible for designing projects; most public funding was provided by national governments; and despite the initial plan to design it as a platform for centralised and highly subsidised *Grands Projets* (French president François Mitterrand's vision in response to the Reagan administration's Strategic Defense Initiative), most projects were eventually small. Still, the initiative did incorporate large initiatives piloted by the Big 12 firms, such as the Joint European

Submicron Silicon Initiative for the next generation of micro-chips and the high-definition television project.[38]

In principle, we see that the legal and political complexities allowed the EU institutions to focus mostly on pre-competitive and blue skies R&D, where it was perhaps easier for national interests to find common ground, and more close-to-market initiatives were carried out in different international or intergovernmental formats, which managed to pool together funding equivalent to the EU Framework Programmes (at least until Horizon 2020 for 2014–2020) and provided more agile approaches than the EU institutions.[39]

Interestingly, while projects like EUREKA were led by politicians and scientists from the larger countries pushing for big R&D initiatives, by the early 1970s OECD experts were noting that the same pattern already applied to smaller diffusion-oriented countries such as Belgium, the Netherlands, Norway, Sweden and Switzerland, where institutional experimentation was the norm:

> Without any specialized commission or ministerial departments subject to close control by top levels of government, the five countries have, for example, equipped themselves with a great many institutions which act as a link between administrative, industrial and scientific circles. Generally originating from the initiative of individuals who have felt the need to meet the requirements of a particular group or sector these bodies enjoy wide autonomy.[40]

Based on these experiences, we can conjecture that different national innovation policy intermediaries (e.g. IRSIA in

Belgium, SINTEF in Norway, TNO in the Netherlands) have also been crucial in Europe for driving innovation bureaucracies forward through dynamic feedback linkages between different actors. Still, the picture of national approaches remained as diverse as the European varieties of capitalism and innovation systems in general, with hybrid diffusion models existing next to more mission-oriented systems or even emerging on top of each other. But this is classic European variety in all policy domains.

Again, Germany probably offers the most interesting and important account of how time- and context-specific innovation capabilities were built in the research and innovation arena through different layers of mission, diffusion-orientation and hybridisation. As succinctly summarised by Reger and Kuhlmann:

The first 'layer' is characterised by big technology programmes from the mid-50s onwards, showing a marked orientation towards goals similar to those of the USA, mainly in the fields of nuclear technology, aerospace and data processing, and later microelectronics. [. . .] A second research support 'layer' was developed [. . .] from the beginning of the 1970s, in order to create and support the conditions necessary for the export of technology-intensive goods. Public funding flowed into research projects of industry and institutes for applied research to promote cross-sectoral technologies (e.g. materials), key technologies (e.g. microelectronics) and technological systems (e.g. transport systems). [. . .] In the 1970s, the reform policies of the government of the Social Democrats triggered the formation of a third research support 'layer', complementing the goals of the first and second layers by research activities in the areas of environment, public health and the employment market whose aims related primarily to social policy. [. . .] From the end of the 1970s, a fourth 'layer' came into existence with the instruments of innovation policy: their aim is the diffusion of innovative or improved technologies, also among SMEs and in less developed geographical regions. This includes the support of activities in R&D as well as the building up and strengthening of an infrastructure for the support of technology transfer from the science system into industry.[41]

This pattern was to a large extent similar to the general hybridisation of innovation bureaucracies globally that resulted, by the early 1990s, in a plethora of hybrid intermediary bodies – doers and also funders that work as intermediaries as well – in the centre of the German industry-led innovation system (e.g. higher education institutes, federal and state research establishments, national research centres, Max Planck and Fraunhofer institutes).[42]

By the late 1980s, the EU also became a formally much stronger and legitimate player in the European research and innovation landscape. The 1986 Single European Act gave the EU formal competencies over research and technological development relevant for economic competitiveness, and the 1992 Maastricht Treaty explicitly recognised that research and technological development could be linked with all other community responsibilities and agreed that member states should, in cooperation with the Commission, start coordinating their research and innovation policies across the community.[43] This provided the platform for a gradual increase in the scope of EU research and innovation actions (especially under the Framework Programme mechanism) and the emergence of specific, but less visionary and political, and much more technocratic and 'rational', research and innovation strategies and organisations in the 1990s and 2000s.

Evolutionary Strengths and Weaknesses of Hybrid Innovation Bureaucracies

The global trend of hybridisation of innovation bureaucracies in the 1970s and 1980s was a response to the changing market and political feedback: the late 1960s brought into question the legitimacy of the largely military mission-oriented research and innovation policy models; the late 1960s and 1970s also brought significant changes to business models and technological development processes as the early advances in ICT and biotechnology started to bring changes into markets and corporate dynamics.

In our co-evolutionary model, it is almost inevitable that the innovation bureaucracies had to adjust their routines and build new ones. It again took a lot of political leadership and decisions to trigger the emergence of the new hybrid networks and partnership around the innovation bureaucracies. These new hybrid forms allowed innovation bureaucracies to extend the sources of their dynamic capabilities (collaboration with private actors allowed for more experimentation, risk sharing), but paradoxically, especially in the US and other Anglo-Saxon countries, also fed the market fundamentalist narratives: instead of emphasising innovation-oriented networks and the positive impact of collaboration, one could easily claim that private sector capabilities saved the government from worse and it was time to 'reinvent the government' by introducing the private sector entrepreneurial management principles at the core of the public sector as well.[44]

As we have argued in Chapter 3, these NPM initiatives placed at the core of government did not bring more dynamic capabilities, but they reduced public sector long-term capacities as well as the overall legitimacy of innovation bureaucracies to co-lead and co-design innovation processes and systems. Hence, the 1990s and 2000s were the period of the rationalisation and technocratisation of innovation policies and bureaucracies globally through the dominant rhetoric of market failures. As we show in the next chapter, these lost decades of innovation policy gave way in turn, from the late 2000s onwards, to the repoliticisation of innovation and the search for new models of societal challenge and mission-oriented policies and bureaucracies.

6

NEOLIBERALISM, INNOVATION BUREAUCRACIES AND THE REINVENTION OF MISSIONS

Globalisation, Competitiveness and the 'Technocratisation' of Innovation

The end of the Cold War marked another fundamental shift in the global patterns of innovation policy making. Given the post-Cold War lack of a coherent source of real or 'creative' insecurity,[1] as well as the discussion of 'the end of history',[2] the 1990s became one of the main periods of de-contextualised, or neoliberal, innovation policies. There was no clear mission-like narrative and directionality in innovation policies. Hence, the discourse became dominated by concerns of 'competitiveness', as opposed to, say, development, which is mostly a comparative notion that leads to international benchmarking (how well does one fare in relation to a leading economy, the US, or even Silicon Valley or Kendall Square) and technocratic policy emulations (e.g. turning the US commercialisation tools – especially the Bayh–Dole Act – into de-contextualised global best practice[3]).

In the 1990s, such shift in policy was especially based on the global spread and emulation of what has been labelled as Washington Consensus policies combined with NPM-based approaches to reform innovation bureaucracies.[4] Driven by the neoliberal desires to cut the state and pursue cost-efficiency, NPM favoured the separation of small elites tasked with policy-level decision making from routine policy implementation (hence, lengthening and fragmenting the feedback channels); privatisation of existing public organisations and the research infrastructure of the innovation bureaucracies; and much more 'horizontal' public investment practices (no picking winners, just offering level playing fields with generic market failures in mind). NPM's focus on cost-efficiency and short-term measurable impacts decentralised many innovation bureaucracies into technocratic project management organisations with respective operational capacities to disperse funding to and evaluate the short-term impacts of different projects. Perhaps most importantly, NPM ideology largely negates the possibility of both setting directions and building dynamic capabilities in the public sector, focusing rather on a reactive market-fixing role and the insourcing of capabilities from private consultants. We can go so far as to say that NPM hacked to death the dynamic capabilities of many innovation bureaucracies, particularly in the West.

This led to what we have previously labelled as the 'copying paradox':[5] the convergence of policies and administrative practices that did not lead to expected economic convergence but to divergence in actual (government) innovation capacities and eventual policy outcomes or innovation performance. Such technocratic and managerialist approaches did not engender bureaucracies providing the agile stability needed for dynamic innovation policies and resilience of innovation systems.

In the US, this period was characterised, on the one hand, by continued rethinking of the NSS dynamics through a growing focus on the commercial viability of different programmes and the growing role of the state as venture capitalist,[6] and, on the other hand, by growing criticism of the role of the state in innovation in general, as well as in many successful industry-oriented programmes, from the ATP to the DARPA-managed Technology Reinvestment Program.[7] In East Asia, the 1990s were denoted by waves of democratisation (in South Korea and Taiwan), as well as economic instabilities (from lost decade(s) in Japan to the Asian financial crisis in the late 1990s), which required rethinking the developmentalist economic, industrial and innovation policies, and this opened the doors for global/Western best practices. In Europe, the end of the Cold War, the Maastricht Treaty and the consideration of Central and Eastern European economies for EU accession changed both the domestic and Europe-wide context of public policies: competitiveness with the US (and emerging Asia) and intra-EU convergence via competitiveness became the key policy foci.

However, as we show in the second part of this chapter, the mid-2000s started to bring questions of the directionality and contextual missions of innovation policies back into the discourse. This change in discourse was mostly driven by the broader effects of the financialisation of global economies, from the dot-com bubble and the Asian financial crisis in the late 1990s to the

GFC of 2008; the external shocks from 9/11 (US terrorist attack) to 3/11 (Japanese Fukushima disaster); and increasingly the climate emergency and most recently the COVID-19 pandemic, which have laid bare some of the imbalances in the innovation and production systems of the developed countries.

The need to tackle grand societal challenges, from climate change and the UN's Sustainable Development Goals to pressing domestic wicked issues, can be seen as a new, emerging, large-scale narrative to justify more systematic and strategic innovation policies and the building of new dynamic capabilities in the public sector. Given how policies and public management reforms are normally made, this has led most countries to search for proven and legitimate successes from history and share these as best practices: for example the gradual return to mission thinking in the West and the return to some developmentalism, if not yet Confucianism, in the East. As a novel development of the digital era, the emergence of challenge-based policy thinking has been accompanied by, in some cases, changing organisational dynamics, largely driven by new types of public agencies, such as digital transformation agencies that embody some of the key aspects of digital era organisation and new routines, from design thinking to agile planning. We will return to them in the next chapter.

Global Competition, Politicisation of Innovation and Delegation of Dynamic Capabilities

Commercialisation of the US National Security State

In the context of growing anti-statism and neoliberal policies, the US NSS shifted throughout the 1990s towards deepening its commercialisation focus in two ways. First, it bought more ready-to-use (commercial, off-the-shelf) solutions. Second, rather than trying to make defence technologies commercially relevant, it attempted to steer the directionality of private technologies through large-scale public-private technology initiatives (as a continuation of the VLSI-inspired approach of the 1980s) by investing directly into the private firms as a venture capitalist. For the latter, most NSS agencies and even some federal labs introduced their own venture capital (VC) funds, as new types of dynamic funders/intermediaries. The pilot case here was the CIA's independent, non-profit hybrid – government-funded but privately operated – In-Q-Tel (originally called Peleus), which was established in 1999 because '[t]he agency needed access to the most advanced information technology to conduct its mission. The problem was that numerous advances in the ICT field were occurring among the very technology firms that traditionally did not do business with the defense sector.'[8] To achieve the goal of transferring private technologies for public purpose, In-Q-Tel and similar funds act as early stage (when technology is still in the lab) investors that make equity investments (often supported by product development funding, sometimes from DARPA, NSF, etc.) and use board of director positions to steer the direction of technology development (as in the case of one of its most famous success stories, Keyhole Technologies, which is behind the Google Earth application).[9]

Such design of VC funds allowed government to target new segments of the innovation ecosystems, free itself from bureaucratic constraints (from internal routines to financial and investment regulations) and provide new forms of agility. In essence, it amounts to delegating the dynamic capabilities function to public-private VC partnerships: government provides strategic directionality, stable funding and socialises some of the risks, while VC partnerships develop the dynamic capabilities for discovering, betting on and collaborating with firms working on interesting technologies and solutions. Further, the creation of such VC funds seems to have been a clever way of hiding the contentious role of the state in innovation behind the rhetoric of private sector management and entrepreneurship.[10] Linda Weiss provides a nice case of how similar investments, even by organisations like DARPA, did not go well with politicians and the general public:

When the George H. W. Bush administration sacked DARPA director Craig Fields, the episode made headlines. Fields was ostensibly removed for appearing to stray too far into the commercial arena, after having taken DARPA into a series of new dual-use ventures. But the final straw came when he authorised a $4 million equity investment in a company making semiconductor devices with advanced materials. In spite of what proved to be a well-judged investment, such an obvious breach of the state-market divide left the DARPA leader vulnerable to antistatist opposition, leading to his subsequent removal. By contrast, when the CIA wanted to do the same thing that DARPA had attempted but on a much larger scale, it took the safer route by creating a hybrid – a venture capital company that looks for all the world like a wholly private venture.[11]

From a more civilian tech perspective, the 1990s and early 2000s were characterised by 'incremental evolution' of the policy instruments and programmes of the 1980s, mostly through additional funding and emulation of the DARPA routines for tech development and commercialisation as well as through improving central policy coordination of the growing innovation agenda (i.e. the National Science and Technology Council (NSTC) was established in 1993, chaired by the president, to coordinate federal S&T policy efforts).[12] Still, the clout of the neoliberal mindset set selective political constraints on the policy directions: while many government programmes related to military, health, materials, SMEs, etc. benefitted from bipartisan support and growing funding, some programmes, most notably the ATP, suffered from the early 1990s onwards from Republican criticism and obstructions, because it looked too much like explicit industrial policy intervention (ATP was closed in 2007). Next to the political constraints, the managerial twin of neoliberalism, NPM, also impacted the organisation and dynamic capabilities in more legitimate domains: the clearest example here is the growing preference for market-failure driven and contracting-out routines in the core activities of NASA.[13] This has resulted in a paradoxical shift in the original moon and ghetto paradox: as with the original juxtaposition, the government has been still largely unable to solve the social problems of the ghetto but has also lost the original ability to go to the moon, at least without the help of Musk, Bezos and the likes, as well as to define the directions and speed of space exploration policies.

Competitiveness drive in Europe

Europe entered the 1990s not only with increased legitimacy to coordinate and steer innovation policies on the European Union level but also with a new understanding of its main challenges and the role of innovation in Europe's future. In 1993, the European Commission presented a White Paper, *Growth, Competitiveness, Employment*, which emphasised that the EU needs to achieve both growth and employment, with 'competitiveness' being the main instrument to achieve these dual goals. As part of the competitiveness drive, the White Paper also emphasised the need to increase investment in technological R&D, achieve more efficient exploitation of new technologies and the results of research, and improve the coordination of national activities (which accounted for 87 per cent of Europe-wide investments, while the EU covered about 13 per cent through its Framework Programmes and other joint initiatives, such as CERN and EUREKA).[14]

By 1995, these ideas were formulated into the *Green Paper on Innovation*, which emphasised that the EU's competitiveness with the US and Japan suffered because of a lower degree of investment in both high-tech and high-growth sectors, a lower presence in high-growth geographical markets, inadequate productivity and an inability to respond to changing demands, and fragmentation of R&D efforts and innovation capacities. As a result, a major conceptual shift in R&D and innovation policy was proposed: to move from the producer-oriented industrial technology policies of the 1980s to user-oriented innovation polices to enhance Europe's ability to use new technologies.[15]

While the Green Paper proposed the idea of task forces to 'condition and catalyse ambitious research projects designed to create the "car of the future" or develop new viral vaccines' (i.e. industrial missions), the emphasis in the actual follow-up was more diffusion-oriented, emphasising the fostering of 'an innovation culture' and creating 'a framework conducive to innovation' (through a focus on human resources, labour mobility, financing and other decidedly supply-sided measures suited to an increasingly horizontal policy focus). As a result, '[b]y the late 1990s, well-articulated but cross-border uncoordinated member state science and technology (S&T) programmes combined with large-scale pan-European research infrastructures and research funding schemes run on an intergovernmental basis and with the Community Framework Programmes to turn the European research landscape into a rich but largely uncoordinated patchwork.'[16]

On the level of nation states, Darius Ornston has claimed that across (Western) European nations there was no real national prioritisation of research and innovation in the 1990s as most countries did not significantly increase funding or create fundamental policy shifts.[17] Further, most Central and Eastern European economies focused either on maintaining existing industrial structures or opted for unilateral liberalisation and no-policy industrial and innovation policies.[18]

One of the more interesting European exceptions seems to have been Finland, which managed to forge in the 1980s and scale in the 1990s a unique 'creative corporatist' agreement based on increasing public investments into R&D and innovation (even in times of significant budget cuts and austerity) by shifting from legacy policies based on price-fixing cartels in sunset industries (forestry, metals) to research consortia in high-tech industries (notably ICT). As a country strongly reliant on the Soviet Union as its main export market, the politico-economic context of Finland had always been precarious and it had started to experiment with the policies and institutions for 'creative corporatism' in the 1970s and early 1980s, but the role of these policies and institutions was scaled only during the economic crisis of the 1990s.

The legacies of strong state control and coordination of economy, as well as traditions of public-private collaboration, including in R&D, allowed Finland to introduce a rather effective innovation bureaucracy composed of the national Science and Technology Policy Council (STPC) (it was turned from the bipartite Science Policy Council into the tripartite STPC in 1987); innovation agencies such as the innovation fund Sitra (this was established in 1968 with peripheral status and limited funding but grew into Finland's largest capital investor in the 1990s) and the Finnish Funding Agency for Technology and Innovation, Tekes (this was established in 1983); and national research institutes supported by a network of different private associations and actors (peak-level industry and labour associations) participating in the council and other coordination activities. In simple terms, while the STPC acted as a broad-based platform for coordinating and legitimising different priorities and initiatives (from education and scientific research to economic activities), Sitra and Tekes, which often funded the same companies in different phases of growth (Tekes covering technological innovations and Sitra venture funding), forged through and maintained the incentives for public-private research collaborations (i.e. by the 1990s, large enterprises, if interested in Tekes funding, had to collaborate with SMEs as well as with public research institutes). Furthermore, Sitra is credited with initiating and establishing, together with other government initiatives such as Finnish Industry Investments Ltd (a state-owned investment company) and Start Fund of Kera (the regional development agency), the Finnish VC industry. In 1990 Sitra founded the Finnish Venture Capital Foundation.[19]

One can argue that the Finnish model of innovation bureaucracy is an archetypical example of the European best practice towards which all systems have aspired: broad-based legitimacy of S&T investments and directions (via high-level policy councils) supported by dynamic change agents – in the form of doers, funders, intermediaries – such as Sitra to initiate novel research directions, policy paradigms and instruments to be scaled and institutionalised by larger organisations such as Tekes, Kera and others. As shown by several studies by Breznitz and Ornston,[20] this balance has been rather hard to achieve and sustain within the broader context of politicisation of innovation, which makes the specialised dynamic and peripheral Schumpeterian development agencies (such as Sitra) and their dynamic capabilities a common target for politicians, who claim their successes for political re-election campaigns and then load them with more and more wicked policy tasks. This inevitably blurs their missions and reduces the actual capacities and capabilities of the organisations to respond to expectations.

The broader EU comparisons have shown that such agencies, and the 'agencification' drive in general,[21] have been rather ineffective in other countries, particularly those dominated by neoliberal desires and expectations: a focus on cost-efficiency, market failures and non-directionality in policy interventions, along with the projectification of research and innovation, has resulted in weak policy coordination (and an inability to adjust to short-term changes in innovation ecosystems), dominance of machine or robotic bureaucracies and instrumental scientific and innovation values through counting of publications and patents, and VC funding versus achieving actual goals and delivering public value.[22]

Democratisation and competitiveness drive in East Asia

For East Asian economies, the 1990s epitomised similar important shifts of innovation policies and bureaucracies. Democratisation in South Korea and Taiwan, and administrative reform attempts in Japan, increased the political competition for resources and weakened the historically public-private developmentalist networks. Liberalisation, development of firms and their growing integration into global production, value and innovation networks increased the autonomous innovation capabilities and power of these firms vis-à-vis governments and made policy challenges even more complex.[23]

Hence, the 1990s and early 2000s were characterised by attempts to introduce Western-like, or global-mainstream, innovation policies and bureaucracies. In the mid-1990s, all three countries introduced laws and routines for drafting R&D and innovation strategies that continue to this day. In 1995, Japan adopted the S&T Basic Law and started to adopt the five-year Science and Technology Basic Plans. The third plan

(2006–2010) was further complemented by Innovation 25 as a long-term strategic guideline looking into 2025.[24] In 1997, South Korea adopted the Special Law for Science and Technology Innovation and introduced the Science and Technology Innovation Five-Year Plan. In the early 2000s, it adopted Vision 2025: Korea's Long-Term Plan for Science and Technology Development, which became the basis for subsequent five-year Science and Technology Basic Plans. Between 1997 and 2006, this led to one of the highest global growth rates of public R&D investments.[25] In Taiwan, the 1999 Fundamental Science and Technology Act requires the organisation of national broad-based S&T conferences every four years and revisions of national policies every two years, through adopting either national S&T plans or White Papers. This was complemented by a significant increase in S&T funding and the organisation of national R&D programmes, for example in telecommunications, energy and different strands of biotechnology.[26]

The first innovation strategies (until the mid-2000s) were trial-and-error-like and rather technocratic efforts to introduce new priorities to innovation policies, mimicking the global policy discourses and priorities. The first common goal was linked to global competitiveness, that is to either retake global innovation leadership (Japan) or become one among the core group of global innovation leaders (South Korea and Taiwan). The second goal was to increase the overall public funding of R&D and innovation. In addition, countries tried to define technological priorities, but this often led to 'bucket lists' of tens of overlapping and competing technologies, supported and funded by different government agencies, along with difficulties in setting clear priorities.[27]

In Japan and South Korea, these formal policies and strategies were paralleled throughout the 1990s and 2000s by several administrative reforms in line with the NPM agenda and influenced by what was seen as Western best practices. In Japan, both the 1990s and especially the early 2000s saw attempts to redesign the Japanese administrative system to formally reduce the power of bureaucracy vis-à-vis political institutions:[28] MITI was reformed into the Ministry of Economy, Trade and Industry (METI), the Ministry of Education and Science and Technology Agency were merged into the Ministry of Education, Culture, Sports, Science and Technology (conveniently shortened to MEXT), and many of the existing bureaus and agencies (such as AIST, but also research centres and universities) were reformed into arm's-length administrative agencies. It was envisioned that two high-level councils under the prime minister – the Council for Economic and Fiscal Policy and the Council for Science and Technology Policy (CSTP) – would act as 'control towers', or rulers, for S&T policy, coordinating and monitoring of the activities of different actors (especially METI and MEXT). Further, there were strong attempts to introduce rather linear and NPM-like planning mechanisms into policy making – the so-called PDCA (Plan-Do-Check-Act) cycle and key performance indicators for performance monitoring.[29]

In South Korea, the nodal planning body, the EPB, was dismantled in 1994 and since then there have been continued attempts to bring back some coordination capabilities and top-down planning under the new innovation and governance logics. Between 1998 and 2008, this was attempted through the newly established MOST and the presidential NSTC (composed of public and private sector members), which became an important coordinator of national innovation funding ceilings.[30] Between 2004 and 2008, a new administrative unit – Office of Science, Technology and Innovation – existed inside MOST to create a new policy level and a relatively dynamic change agent (staffed with 40 per cent MOST employees, 40 per cent from other ministries and 20 per cent from the private sector) supporting, together with the Science and Technology Ministers Meeting, the work of NSTC in a logic quite similar to the EPB but with a clear focus on innovation. Yet, local experts claim that such top-down planning was not very effective in the context of uncertainty of innovation.[31] In parallel, the by-default one-term presidents became more involved in S&T policy by setting their own top-down innovation agendas, that is Innovation Drive by Kim Dae-jung (1998–2003) and S&T Based Society by Roh Moo-hyun (2003–2008).

Taiwan has interestingly followed a peculiar non-Western path by not establishing classic R&D funding agencies but by coordinating funding and selection processes at the level of political coordination bodies and ministries. Over the course of the late 1990s and early 2000s, it was recognised that the National Science Council (NSC) centred coordination and control of predominantly bottom-up R&D and innovation initiatives might be insufficient, especially for pursuing nationally critical priorities, such as transition to the knowledge economy, environmental sustainability and quality of life. Hence, the early strategic documents and initiatives sought different mechanisms to improve top-down planning and coordination of R&D and innovation projects through different high-level meetings and committees in areas such as biotechnology, energy, industrial development, more proactive review of bottom-up drafted innovation programmes and budgets.[32]

In sum, the 1990s were characterised by further attempts to build Western-like technocratic or, to use Weber's terms, 'rational grounds'-based systems of innovation, policy making and bureaucracies and an increasing emphasis on market-based developments and governments limiting their roles to fixing market failures and improving framework conditions of innovation systems. Nevertheless, these reforms were pursued in the context of stronger legitimacy for high-level rulers and intermediaries (ministries and innovation councils). Yet, the outcomes of these attempts seem not to have satisfied policy makers and broader innovation communities, as in most countries the search for stability (how to draft longer-term and legitimate policy goals, how to provide systemic coordination) and agility (how to re-engage private sector counterparts in policy planning and delivery, how to design flexible policy interventions) remain important concerns.

Return of Missions as the Fear of Missing Out

As discussed in previous sections, the globalisation of innovation policy in the 1990s and 2000s brought about increasing focus on overall economic competitiveness (typically measured through increased exports) and the ability to bet (not as government but as the economy as a whole) on future technologies, such as ICT, bio and nano. The primary incentive for innovation policy makers was increasingly the fear of missing out, or FOMO. The idea that other countries could either leapfrog competitors in new technologies or create first-mover advantages created an increasing need to invest in future technologies and science and create organisations focused on future trends and deploying methodologies to decrypt these trends (e.g. through foresight exercises and futures councils). This was one of the key reasons for the return of mission in the 2000s, later to be supplemented by a more normative turn in innovation policy largely driven by the climate emergency and other societal challenges.[33]

Societal challenges and missions in the US

In the context of the 1990s anti-statism in the US, the Clinton and later Obama administrations sought to bring back a broader dual-use mission-oriented approach to innovation policy. During the Clinton administration, this was probably best represented by the presidential National Nanotechnology Initiative (NNI) of 2000 with the task to 'expedite the discovery, development, and deployment of nanotechnology in order to achieve responsible and sustainable economic benefits, to enhance the quality of life, and to promote national security'.[34] It was built as a coordinating tool for different agency-level investments by NSS agencies with a new mission of commercial diffusion through increased and more targeted and coordinated funding in the context of general federal budget constraints. The funding rose from US$500 million in 2001 to about US$14 billion in 2010, provided mostly by the NSF, DoD and DoE focusing on 'university-based research in nanoscale science, engineering, and technology development'.[35]

While it was envisioned as a presidential initiative, the organisational design has remained true to the hybrid model already discussed. Namely, '[i]t entails multiple partnerships that mobilize the resources of industry, academia, and government in dedicated research and engineering centres and industrial consortia, in this case focused on accelerating the commercialization of NNI developments.'[36]

After the GFC of the late 2000s triggered new directions for innovation policies, one of the 'grand challenges' or key mission areas for the global innovation community was the transition to sustainable energy systems. Not surprisingly, most regions/countries seem to have responded to this challenge by emulating their prior practices with some crucial differences. The shift to sustainable energy systems requires a more complex set of actors – from producers and grid operators to regulators and users – to adopt a new direction and make relevant investments and coordination of actions, and government institutions also need to have different capacities and capabilities to guide these processes.

To improve the capacities for energy transition and create an energy innovation system, the US emulated the DARPA model with ARPA-E. The story of ARPA-E fits well into the model of how agile stability in innovation systems emerges. The idea of ARPA-E was originally proposed by the National Academies, a private non-profit organisation providing independent advice on policy. It was formally created by President Bush in 2007 as part of the America COMPETES Act and was given its first formal budget by Obama's American Reinvestment and Recovery Act of 2009. It is institutionally housed, although intentionally in a separate building, in one of the largest bureaucratic behemoths of the US federal government, the DoE, which deals with the US nuclear weapons programme, nuclear waste management, nuclear reactor production for the US Navy, energy production and research, and genomics research (the Human Genome Project was initiated by the DoE). Its research and innovation budget has been around US$4–5 billion and it also oversees the system of national laboratories and other research centres. All these tasks require plans, missions and vision on a global scale that look decades if not more ahead (e.g. most net-zero scenarios plan for 2050).

ARPA-E was planted into this large and stable bureaucratic machinery with the explicit aim of emulating some of the dynamic and agile capabilities of DARPA, but keeping in mind the context. ARPA-E is about ten times smaller than DARPA (budget-wise). It also has slightly different routines to carry out the role of technology diffusion not to a single customer but across society, which requires different approaches to strategic mission, political legitimisation and diffusion/ deployment strategies (especially as the energy sector is dominated by large and powerful fossil fuel firms).[37] The key elements of this approach can be again summarised from research by Bonvillian:[38]

- For sharpening the strategic mission and technology prioritisation, ARPA-E has put key emphasis on 'technology visioning' to enable its technology development and selection process 'to fund higher risk projects that could be breakthroughs and transformational in energy areas where little work previously has been undertaken' based on a two-stage selection process that allows the applicants to respond to project/proposal reviews, providing space for technology debates. It has further reinforced the empowered project management culture of DARPA, emphasising that project managers need to have 'religion' or 'vision of where they want to take their portfolios, performing as vision champions, in order to sell their projects both inside and outside ARPA-E' as a substitute to formal personnel evaluation system.

- For strengthening political legitimacy, in addition to building internal support across the silos of the DoE (through collaboration with applied agencies and labs through technology consortia, etc.), ARPA-E also organises a public and highly visible summit to showcase its results and creates a broader community of supporters for its vision and role.

- Given that the energy sector can be characterised as a 'complex established legacy sector' with complex technology diffusion/implementation challenges, ARPA-E has employed project directors with both academic and commercial sector experience to integrate implementation concerns into projects from the start. Project directors are also supported by innovative tech-to-market teams 'working full time to promote implementation and commercial advances for ARPA-E technologies'.

While ARPA-E offers an agile approach to innovation management within the DoE, it also provides agile signalling (halo effect) for the industry outside DoE structures; according to Bonvillian, 'VCs and commercial firms pick up and move toward commercialization the technologies that are selected by ARPA-E as promising. In other words, the private sector views the ARPA-E project selection process as rigorous and sound enough that it is prepared to fund projects emerging from that process.'[39] In sum, ARPA-E fuses again in a unique way different ideal-typical organisational types – from funding to intermediating innovation processes – in a broader energy innovation system and bureaucracy.

Like the DARPA/ARPA-E similarities and contextual differences, when the In-Q-Tel-pioneered VC approach was emulated in the energy sector, the internal dynamics of the model were in some cases actually reversed. For example, when the defence and CIA venture funds transition technology from private to public sector, the DoE funds (often specifically set up for each national lab) focus on the opposite – from public to private sector – transfers via spin-offs and new startups.[40]

Overall, we see that the US template for agile stability has been largely repeated over time and domains: large-scale and stable bureaucracies are complemented by the creation of more dynamic and agile innovation engines (funders, doers, intermediaries) either inside the bureaucratic bodies or in the immediate feedback environments, and the island-bridge model has been the crucial link to maintain that agile stability.

When the 2009 Strategy for American Innovation relied on the continued 'DARPA-fication' of US innovation policy thinking (ARPA-E was established in 2009; ARPA-ED for education was proposed in 2011), the 2015 revisions to the strategy proposed to broaden the feedback arenas for innovation (with an emphasis on open innovation, citizen science and co-creation) and to introduce innovation labs at federal agencies to build a more systemic culture of innovation within government 'by empowering and equipping agency employees and members of the public to implement their promising ideas to more effectively serve the American people'.[41] Hence, it has been increasingly understood that the original close-knit island-bridge models of the military system are less fitting for today's social and climate-oriented challenges, and the innovation landscape needs to become much more open. This of course makes it more difficult to maintain the top-down mission-oriented models and requires different tools for creating mission mystique and maintaining links and coordination between the stable bureaucratic capacities and more dynamic organisations and networks.

The domain of digital transformation seems to reflect these changing contexts even better. Almost everybody interested in public policy knows how Obama failed in the rollout of the 2010 Affordable Care Act because the government ICT systems lacked capacity when HealthCare.gov was launched in 2013. This was quickly followed by what one could read as rapid learning of agile tech development and innovation routines from the startup scene: 18F and the US Digital Service (USDS) team were created as quick and agile SWAT teams to fix the bureaucracy:

In 2014, the White House established the US Digital Services team – a quick response team of IT engineers recruited from the private sector to help with presidential priority IT projects – and the General Services Administration's 18F software development teams. Engineers are recruited from technology companies, including Facebook, Twitter, Google, Microsoft, or Amazon. The so-called 'digital swat teams' of USDS and 18F are paired with public servants using agile software development methods to collaboratively work on high-priority projects, such as the digitization of the US immigration service forms which are still mostly paper-based, or the Department of Veterans' Affairs' education and health service delivery processes.[42]

Yet, the emergence of these units and their history seems more complex and layered than that. 18F was initiated by a group of people working as Presidential Innovation Fellows. Presidential Innovation Fellows was a pre-Obamacare initiative pushed in 2012 by the former US government chief technology officer (CTO), chief information officer, former White House Office of Science and Technology policy advisor and CTO of the Department of Veterans' Affairs to provide more agile methods and rotation of people from outside government to work on some complex public sector challenges. Initially named the Presidential Fellows Program, it tried to create a unique mission mystique to bring individuals on 'tour of duty' missions (similarly to prior White House Fellowships, Congressional Fellowships, etc.) or to provide a Peace Corp for Programmers.[43] This experimental network was made a permanent feature of government by Obama only in 2015.

Institutionally, the USDS was designed as an 'elite technology' unit, housed at the Executive Office of the President as an equivalent of the UK's Government Digital Service (we will come back to this organisation in the next chapter) and with the political legitimacy to push new digital standards and playbooks across government. At the same time, the more symbolic private sector-linked initiatives – Presidential Innovation Fellows and 18F – were housed in probably the most boring government agency one can think of: the General Service Administration; created in 1949, it houses more than 10,000 employees who work on federal government procurement, real estate, payroll, travel, vehicle fleet and technology services and currently manages a US$30+ billion budget. Its history with ICT goes back to the very creation of ICT: it built the US Federal Telecommunications Network in the 1960s and in 2010 was the first federal agency to move e-mail to the cloud. Its current technology initiatives – from training people to buying and providing ICT services across the government – are all crucial stable capacities on which government policies, data and services run.

Not surprisingly, the Trump administration, through political appointments, budget proposals and the simple deletion of public records and data from government websites, sought to undo most of the dynamic capabilities created in government, either to save the fossil fuel industry (all Trump's budget proposals aimed to explicitly close down ARPA-E) or to outsource to other private constituents some of the core public value-providing activities relying on both stable capacities and dynamic capabilities. For example, the latter applies to the weather and tornado forecasting services built by the National Oceanic and Atmospheric Administration through decades-long research and data gathering efforts, combined with new dynamic data analytical and service design capabilities initiated under Obama's administration.[44]

Again, not surprisingly, with the advent of the Biden administration, both industrial policy and the DARPA model gained renewed relevance. Thus, for instance, Biden has proposed a health-focused ARPA-H, housed at the NIH and with a 2022 budget of US$6.5 billion. Next to massive planned investments into infrastructure, the Biden administration aims to invest into (re-)building manufacturing capabilities broadly aligned with a green mission.

Overall, as innovation becomes more political and democratic, it becomes more challenging to maintain agile stability – both stable long-term capacities and more agile dynamic capabilities – in a coherent form. It requires rethinking the structures and routines that matter and the structuring of the public-private ecosystems.

Societal challenges and missions in Europe

By the 2000s, Europe gradually started to understand that the relatively vague coordination of national initiatives will not suffice for competing with the more dynamic US and Asia, especially in ICT, but also in future technologies. As a result, policy makers recognised the need for more proactive coordination, trying to improve the European Research Area (ERA) governance both via stronger top-down coordination of ERA initiatives (the Ljubljana Process) and, probably more successfully, via bottom-up initiatives such as the European Strategy Forum on Research Infrastructures, which created and opened up pan-European research infrastructures and the joint programming and technology initiatives between the EU, intergovernmental funding schemes (such as EUREKA), and national schemes and strategies.[45]

By the late 2000s, these attempts to coordinate research and innovation policies were complemented by more concrete steps. In 2007, the European Research Council was created as

the first strictly European scientific agency, in the sense that decisions of its council are taken exclusively on the basis of the scientific quality of the proposal without applying the principle of *juste retour*, like, for instance, in ESA, the European Space Agency, without consideration of political decisions on funding taken by the national governments, like in the many European intergovernmental scientific organisations, and without applying formal criteria of multi-nationality and multi-sectoriality – and of informal political equilibria – like in EU programmes.[46]

Further, the Seventh Framework Programme for 2007–2013 brought about a significant increase in EU-coordinated R&D funding: when the Sixth Framework Programme (2003–2006) had a budget of €17.5 billion, the Seventh Framework Programme (2007–2013) was adopted with a budget of over €50 billion, which turned 'the European Union into one of the most important financial contributors to the development of science and technology in Europe'.[47]

The rest of the innovation policy landscape evolved in the logic of 'experimentalist governance':[48] the EU sets broad targets/goals, and the member states and regions have the autonomy to develop context-based solutions that are assessed and refined through peer learning as part of an 'open method of coordination' and other softer and harder policy tools. While ideally this should lead to contextual learning and experimentation, given the legacies of the 1990s, we have seen more de-contextualised convergence of policy and governance arrangements with very little space for dynamic capabilities. The austerity policies in the wake of the 2008 financial crisis only further limited this space.

Ever since the so-called Lund Declaration of 2009, grand challenges have been placed at the heart of the EU's R&D policy. These were framed as 'societal challenges' for the 2014–2020 financial period and Horizon 2020 programme for R&D and innovation. From 2018 onwards, 'missions' are the key guidance on the policy level.[49] Between 2021 and 2027, the EU has committed to spending €5 billion across five mission areas,[50] and it encouraged member states to refocus their R&D and innovation policies according to a mission-oriented approach. And while each mission area has its own governance mechanism (so-called mission boards), it is relatively loose, without much direct impact on member state policies. The EU-level missions are essentially another R&D funding mechanism based on competitive grants.

In terms of implementation, national-level mission-oriented policies are predominantly implemented by existing R&D and innovation agencies and mostly through upgrading existing policy instruments. Thus, for instance, in 2021 the Danish Innovation Agency (DIA) received additional funding for four mission areas; the agency has launched a competitive call for consortia to bid for the funding. In Germany, the High-Tech Strategy 2025 lists twelve missions that function as a policy coordination layer on top of existing R&D policies and instruments, without significant additional funding. There are notable exceptions, though. The Swedish innovation agency, Vinnova, has created a whole new policy design process to develop missions in a wide-ranging engagement process, relying on service design approaches. Such an approach focuses on reframing existing policy and technological challenges (e.g. renewable energy) through cross-cutting issues (e.g. the food value chain) that can be formulated as missions (e.g. 'Ensure every pupil in Sweden eats a healthy, sustainable and tasty lunch in school'). Similar approaches can be found, for instance, in the Netherlands and the quadruple helix methodology – bringing together science, industry, policy and society – in health innovation. Thus, we can see a typology of mission-oriented policies and practices emerging in the EU:[51]

- Top-down coordination approach to better align existing policy mixes for incremental upgrading. Examples of such mission-oriented practices include the UK's 2017 industrial strategy and Germany's 2019 High-Tech Strategy 2025. In these cases, missions remain rather general and are understood as a means to better align a siloed policy landscape. In terms of public administration structures and agencies, missions are designed and carried out by existing ministerial hierarchies with low engagement from wider stakeholders. In its focus, this approach to missions is oriented towards stability and long-term agreements in investment strategies and other policy aspects.
- Sectoral coordination and implementation approach takes missions as a way to recharge essentially corporatist or coordinated market economy type sectoral coordination mechanisms. In this iteration, missions as an approach enable the widening of sectoral policies to include non-traditional policy goals and stakeholders. An example of such an

approach to missions is the previously mentioned Dutch quadruple helix approach in health and other areas. Missions are in this case a governance mechanism to deepen engagement practices and develop stakeholder capacities and as such are aimed at developing both long-term sectoral visions and agile capabilities in stakeholders to feed back, learn and adapt policy solutions.

- Design-led approach reframes siloed policy goals and builds deeper civic and stakeholder engagement. In this approach, missions are a tool to build new capabilities within innovation agencies (e.g. user-centric design capabilities), focused on rethinking the policy design process. In particular, this approach focuses on reframing policy goals away from quantitative goals (such as achieving carbon neutrality by year X) towards more communicative goals (such as providing healthy, sustainable food in every school). Another key focus is in experimental policy design, starting from iterative prototypes to rethinking delivery of policy instruments. Examples of such an approach are Sweden's Vinnova and its missions playbook, but also collaboration in Denmark between the DIA and the Danish Design Council. In this approach, agile and dynamic capabilities are clearly the focus of new initiatives. A sub-form of the design-led approach is emerging in urban missions focusing on technological (digital) sovereignty (such as in Barcelona) or the circular economy (such as in Amsterdam). These missions are often driven by user-focused policy practices (such as urban/living/policy labs) with pronounced aims to bring new capabilities into city organisations.

- Smart specialisation-based approach to missions is found in predominantly regional policies, building on smart specialisation policies developed during the 2010s in many European regions.[52] Key to such missions is a focus on 'just transitions', regions moving from carbon-heavy specialisation to a greener and more sustainable specialisation. Example of such missions can be found in the deep demonstration projects of Climate KIC (part of the European Institute for Technology),[53] or in Germany's coal-exit policies agreed on in 2020.[54] Such approaches to missions attempt to strengthen or renew regional policy coalitions and serve as collaborative platforms.

While European missions often target wide democratic engagement practices to build a renewed legitimacy for transformational policies, there is still little evidence that overall policy practices have in fact changed fundamentally. Rather, we see many European countries building missions incrementally into their existing policy and organisational landscapes. Thus, for instance, the Netherlands introduced the so-called Topsectoren approach in 2012 in order to strengthen coordination and collaboration between various R&D system actors. While originally the primary goal of this approach was to improve the match between the knowledge demands of innovative firms and the activities of research institutes, it gradually shifted towards more transformative goals as 'Mission-Oriented Topsector and Innovation Policy' (MTIP), now containing twenty-five missions within four themes. While much of the Topsector governance has evolved into MTIP governance, perhaps the most marked difference is the creation of mission teams: 'They are positioned as the engines for driving changes, as formally their tasks include the developing, executing and organizing – through engaging various ecosystem actors – of both the Missions and the multi-annual innovation programs.'[55] Similar incremental approaches can be found in most European countries implementing missions.

What is notably absent in the European context is a DARPA-style agency leading mission-oriented policies and financial instruments, although the French president, Emmanuel Macron, proposed in his 2017 Speech on New Initiative for Europe to establish a European DARPA (with focus on AI).[56] Over the years of classic EU muddling through in search of durable compromises, this idea resulted in the establishment of a more technocratic and VC-focused European Innovation Council as part of the Horizon Europe Framework Programme.[57] Macron's initial ideas are being pursued as part of the Joint European Disruption Initiative,[58] portrayed as the 'European ARPA'; in its current form it is rather an emergent network and movement pushing mission-oriented transformations and innovations from outside the EU traditional innovation bureaucracy. Another notable exception is the post-Brexit UK's commitment to creating an ARPA-UK agency, called the Advanced Research and Invention Agency (ARIA). This agency was expressly modelled on the early DARPA blueprint;[59] it was initially spearheaded by Prime Minister Boris Johnson's chief advisor, and now chief nemesis, Dominic Cummings. ARIA's focus is blue-sky, long-term research rather than specific socio-economic missions.

*Societal challenges and developmentalist
missions in East Asia*

In East Asia, the mid-2000s saw a shift towards policy rhetoric emphasising societal challenges – ageing of societies, debates on the contradiction between economic versus social and environmental developments – and the continued return of politician-led, top-down developmentalist ideas and initiatives, which differed from the Western patterns of continued technocratisation and rationalisation of innovation policies. Many of these ideas were jotted down already in government strategies and documents drafted in the early 2000s, but it took different external events – changes of political leadership, financial crisis, the Great East Japan Earthquake – to trigger more systemic shifts in innovation policies.

In Japan, *Innovation 25*, a vision document led by Prime Minister Abe (during his first term in office),[60] framed the main challenges for Japan for the next twenty years from domestic ageing and population decline to threats to the sustainability of earth posed by global population growth, resource and energy use patterns, climate change and environmental impacts. Furthermore, it explicitly emphasised the 'social context' of innovation, or how innovations can solve the problems of people in Japan and globally. In this context, Stenberg and Nagano show how the Cabinet Office gradually,[61] and through rather unconventional steps, took a more entrepreneurial policy ruler role. The CSTP introduced top priority policy issues (e.g. transformative and low-carbon technologies) as an additional layer of prioritisation and used the Special Coordination Fund (about 1 per cent of the total and 10 per cent of competitive science, technology and innovation funding) to initiate cross-ministerial coordination projects. It also used the more flexible processes of supplementary budget drafting – in 2009 R&D and innovation funding through the supplementary budget reached 38 per cent of annual public investments – to initiate more proactive and dynamic initiatives (i.e. the Transformative Technologies Fund, Funding Programme for World-Leading Innovative R&D on Science and Technology, FIRST) and coordinate 'all-Japan efforts' in high priority innovation projects. Overall, the political leadership became increasingly involved in the coordination and planning processes. For example, Stenberg and Nagano report that regarding the selection of the principal investigators for the FIRST programme, acting Prime Minister Aso claimed, 'I will make final decisions myself when it comes to choosing the central researchers and core research themes.'[62] While some of these initiatives were relatively short-lived due to the government change, they eventually became core innovation policy ideas of 'Abenomics'.

Between 2009 and 2013, Japan was governed by the Democratic Party of Japan that emphasised in its economic and innovation agenda a strong 'crisis' narrative regarding both global issues (resources scarcity, political and economic instability) and Japan-specific issues (ageing, declining population and birth-rate, economic stagnation).[63] The plans shifted R&D and innovation prioritisation even more towards an explicit problem-solving approach with a key focus on two areas of Japanese strengths – green innovation (developing low carbon energy sources, green social infrastructure and improving the efficiency of energy resources) and life innovation (medical and nursing care, health services) – and tried to integrate previously prioritised technology domains (environment, energy, health) and policy logics (solving societal challenges while sustaining international economic competitiveness).

The return of Prime Minister Abe to power in late 2012 resulted in the revision of most economic policies under 'Abenomics' and the growth-oriented Japan revitalisation strategy, Japan Is Back.[64] The strategy's Industrial Revitalization Plan sought to induce structural reforms (in universities, the regulatory environment for innovation etc.) to create opportunities for existing industries to find new growth paths and to pursue 'all-Japan efforts' in new innovation frontiers. The strategy's Strategic Market Creation Plan was based on the logic of creating new domestic and global markets by tackling current social issues. The Fifth S&T Basic Plan formalised these ideas and proposed a new paradigm for innovation,[65] that is 'realising a world-leading "super-smart society"' or Society 5.0, focusing on the long-term state-coordinated development of different socio-technical systems and the integration of different technologies from IoT and AI to bio- and nanotech.

Paralleling these strategic shifts, there have been several attempts to make the Cabinet Office the new strategic and dynamic 'headquarters' of Japanese innovation bureaucracy by establishing different mission-oriented and dynamic units to oversee policy initiatives. Examples range from supporting ICT diffusion and medical innovations (e.g. Office for Healthcare and Medical Strategy) to innovation policy in general.

In 2014, the CSTP was renamed the Council for Science, Technology and Innovation Policy (CSTI) and there have been attempts to increase its role in budgeting processes (e.g.

coordinating cross-ministerial priorities before these are submitted to the Ministry of Finance), initiating and over-seeing a 'new high-risk and high-return' innovation project as part of the Impulsing Paradigm Change Through Disruptive Technologies Programme (ImPACT) and in coordinating the cross-ministerial national challenge projects as part of the Strategic Innovation Programme (SIP). SIP continued the top-down cross-ministerial coordination initiatives of the CSTP (funded by the Special Coordination Fund), and ImPACT carried forward the ideas of the FIRST programme. The ImPACT programme tried to emulate the DARPA approach with a programme director-based model for investing in the 'high-risk, high-impact' topics.[66] An impor-tant difference is that under the CSTI, these programmes and projects were potentially under much stronger public and political scrutiny.

The SIP programme sought to implement specific projects in national priority areas agreed by the CSTI (e.g. energy, infrastructure development[67]) through comprehensive coordi-nation of funding, regulatory reforms and market support between different ministries to speed up the processes of inno-vation and diffusion. Both programmes seem to have been legitimised not only through high-level political participation (Cabinet Office) but also through the active advisory and managerial roles for high-level business representatives and entrepreneurs, as well as by setting the Tokyo Olympics as the symbolic deadline. In 2019, the ImPACT programme was superseded by the Moonshot programme, which followed largely similar organisational design to tackle ambitious R&D-based societal challenges (e.g. 'Realisation of a society in which humans can be free from limitations of body, brain, space and time by 2050').[68]

The late 2000s and GFC also overlapped with significant policy shifts in South Korea. President Lee Myung-bak's agenda, summed up in the National Strategy for Green Growth (2009–2050), the Five-Year Plan for Green Growth (2009–2013) and the Green New Deal stimulus package (2009), included significant commitments to green growth,[69] as well as an explicit focus on innovation as a tool for bringing about the new development paradigm. In many green growth technologies, the key policy focus was on local content and technological self-sufficiency.[70] These ambitious initiatives were complemented by significant reforms of the innovation bureaucracy. The Lee administration attempted to re-create a new EPB-type centralised change agent through the establishment of the Presidential Committee on Green Growth, which was a dynamic network bringing together policy makers and private sector experts.[71] At the same time, it lacked EPB-like control over budgeting processes, and critics of the agenda have argued that the actual implementation remained to a large extent driven by old legacies (a focus on supporting existing industries through infrastructure investments),[72] especially as the civil servants on the committee represented their own ministries.[73]

In the aftermath of the GFC, growing criticism of the 'elitist' policies of President Lee provided a further window for innovation policy changes, and 'the "social" aspect, which tended to have been overlooked in the policy sphere, began to be debated within innovation policy'.[74] The government of the incoming President Park Geun-hye (daughter of President

Park Chung-hee) soon defined its own developmentalist agenda, Creative Economy, which focused on S&T, ICT and SME-led job and market creation and paid lip service to the modern open innovation logic, the 'Park Chung-hee nostalgia',[75] and the 'Miracle of the Han River' narrative. To implement this agenda, the administration initially attempted a strongly top-down approach formalised in the Science and Technology Basic Plan 2013–2017 and 2014's Three-Year Plan for Economic Innovation. In 2013, the government tried to create a mission-oriented policy-level change agent by re-establishing the Ministry of Education and Ministry of Science, ICT and Future Planning – which had been merged into the Ministry of Education, Science and Technology under President Lee – to oversee the coordination and imple-mentation of the Creative Economy agenda.

The presidential change in 2017 brought about a new wave of both more explicit developmentalist mission-oriented policy initiatives and programmes (e.g. the Alchemist programme introduced in 2018 and the Korean New Deal programme in response to the COVID-19 pandemic), as well as attempts to improve top-down cross-ministerial policy coordination (e.g. the STI Office under the Ministry of Science and ICT has been granted stronger policy and budget coordination roles).[76]

In Taiwan, the 2009–2012 S&T Plan recognised that it will be increasingly difficult to maintain prior rates of economic growth;[77] that the unbalanced economic, environmental and societal impacts of the 'industrialisation first' strategy required rethinking the R&D and innovation strategies; and that it was necessary to shift from a 'technology-oriented' to a 'needs-oriented' model with 'sustainable development' and 'quality of life' concerns taking on more importance. This shift in policy rhetoric coincided with the return of the Kuomintang (KMT) to power in 2009 (after being in opposition since 2002) and the severe impact of the GFC on Taiwan.[78]

While the 2011 Golden Decade National Vision (integrated into the National Development Plan of 2013–2016) looked at economic, social and environmental goals from a new perspective, for example changing the growth model from efficiency to openness and innovation and substituting GDP as an indicator with GNH (Gross National Happiness), actual policies still 'picked' specific industries to prioritise, such as biotechnology, green energy, high-end agriculture, tourism, medicine and healthcare, culture and creation. Given the difficulties of recovering from the impacts of the GFC and the overall debatable performance of the innovation policies and system, the 2013 S&T Plan proposed, 'If economic growth could no longer guarantee to secure happiness, the distribution of resources should strike a balance between social welfare and economic development.'[79] The vision proposed in the 2015 White Paper on Science and Technology further departed from the 'economic growth first' narrative by proposing the vision of 'using intelligent technology to create a prosperous society and achieve sustainable growth' and discussing the new socio-technical concept of 'a low-carbon intelligent society'.[80] While the concept was not explicitly defined, it was used as an umbrella term for the strategic activities aimed at establishing Taiwan among global leaders in green technology.[81] According to local policy makers and scholars, part of this evolution was related to ongoing processes of democratisation, leading to more substantive debates over the content and direction of economic development and greater access of the public and interest groups to this deliberation and these choices.[82]

The governance reforms, while at times paying lip service to social innovation and bottom-up participatory approaches, have focused on strengthening the role of traditional innovation bureaucracy and top-down policy planning and control. In 2012, the government formed a new high-level coordinating body – the Board of Science and Technology (BOST) of the Executive Yuan – which is presided over by the Executive Yuan premier (the prime minister) and includes heads of key agencies, members of industry, academia and research organisations. In principle, BOST institutionalised (through explicit organisation, own staff, regulated tasks) prior more flexible and fluid policy coordination activities by the Science and Technology Advisory Group and other networks and intermediaries. As a body presided over by the premier, its role and tasks depend on the policy priorities of the premier and government in power. These may also overlap with the National Development Council (NDC), which was created in 2012 as a sort of 'mini-cabinet' to debate new social and infrastructure investments before formal Executive Yuan meetings (e.g. the NDC has deliberated the development of wider prospective industries, such as IoT). In 2014, MOST was established, based on the former NSC, but with additional roles and competencies regarding foresight, innovation policy and academia–university collaboration. The creation of MOST has raised the political salience of S&T and innovation policies, because the NSC was under the Executive Yuan, but

MOST is also accountable to the Legislative Yuan. With these two organisational changes, Taiwanese innovation bureaucracy has become relatively mainstream, spearheaded by political-level ruling and coordinating institutions (government meetings, BOST, NDC) and based on two key ministries and their policy advisory networks (e.g. the National Industrial Development Conference and the Science and Technology Development Advisory Conference, which has proposed new approaches to policy makers, i.e. to adopt the DARPA approach in mission-oriented projects).[83]

A noteworthy element of the Taiwanese system has been the lack of R&D and innovation funding agencies under the respective ministries. MOEA's different departments and bureaus are closely linked to public research organisations, such as ITRI. MOST funds universities, which are formally under the Ministry of Education, and Academia Sinica, which is under the Office of the President. In this context, the government has tried to introduce new policy instruments that adopt more flexible and risk-tolerating organisational principles (from selection to management and performance indicators) to foster cross-sectoral collaboration in high-risk and future-oriented domains. NSC/MOST and MOEA jointly launched the PIONEER Grants for Frontier Technologies Development by Academia–Industry Cooperation to undertake high-risk R&D projects in forward-looking technologies and as defined by industry interests.[84]

Following the fall of the KMT government in 2016, the new policy initiatives focused on the prior dual logic of seeking new growth drivers (development model 2.0) while also taking into account societal development needs/missions (e.g. happy society, people-centred sustainable development). On the one hand, subsequent national development plans have tried to select five to seven industries as priority areas for policy and for which DARPA-like initiatives have been designed (e.g. the AI Action Plan explicitly aims to develop pilot projects following the DARPA template[85]). On the other hand, this has been complemented, albeit in a traditional top-down design, by social innovation policy initiatives – that is the Social Innovation Action Plan (focusing on applying techno-logical and business innovations to solve society's issues) and presidential hackathons aimed at demonstrating government's emphasis on open-source data, data utilisation and practical innovation to address the needs of the country in social inno-vation, sustainable development and so on.[86]

This also has a political, indeed party-political, dimension: the victory of the indigenous-minded, yet Western-oriented, independence-promoting Democratic Progressive Party over the KMT has meant that non-Western, and particularly Chinese, solutions, especially when successful, plus all KMT successes, have become a target of policy reforms. This is because posi-tioning the country as more Western and less Chinese has become, by and large, more important than policy successes, especially so as regards innovation policy and especially the bureaucracy, where the abolition of one of the most successful non-Western, originally Confucian, institutions – the division of the government into five yuans (courts) rather than three branches, adding both public administration and oversight/accounting – is pursued as a goal in its own right and without much evidence-informed foundation, although it could easily be claimed that this is a more successful organisational form.[87] Stalled for now,[88] it remains to be seen how this will play out in the future.

Return of Innovation Policy to the Core of Government

A recent large-scale comparison of mission-oriented approaches by the OECD divides current mission-oriented policies into four types:[89]

1. centre of government-led missions found (and described in more detail above) in East Asian countries such as Japan and South Korea;
2. overarching and decentralised missions pursued by larger European innovation bureaucracies from Germany (as part of its High-Tech Strategy) and the Netherlands (as part of its Topsectoren policy) to the UK (as part of its Industrial Strategy);
3. thematic ministry-led missions (e.g. in Austria) where a ministry coordinates the directionality of the policy actions of its different agencies; and
4. agency-led missions in more coordinated and consensual Scandinavian countries (Norway, Sweden, Finland) where independent agencies use their broad mandates to forge new collective agreements and missions across different policy silos and sectors.

Hence, the converging global policy thinking has brought the big challenges of public policies to the centre of innovation policy (innovation policy matters!), but the politico-administrative legacies persist and innovation bureaucracies have been much slower to change. The shift of policy focus from competitiveness towards more substantive changes in society, without significant redesign of the innovation bureaucracies, seems to fit some regions better than others.

For East Asian economies, the return to developmentalism, or a developmental mindset,[90] seems to have been a logical step, together with the reintroduction of their prior models of agile stability: missions and policy coordination led by high-level political bodies (e.g. Presidential Committees in South Korea, Office of the Prime Minister in Japan), while implementation is the task of classic stability-oriented ministries and their agencies, which work in close collaboration with the time- and context-specific networks of academic and private sector organisations. Compared to the classic developmental state era, these develop-mentalist networks are more diverse and also include, next to national research institutions, public universities; and, next to key large companies, SMEs and startups (as private sector dynamic capabilities at the techno-economic frontier are much more diversified). Increasingly, they also entail bottom-up and grassroots (social) innovation practices utilising decentralised and relatively accessible digital technologies. This is a much looser, more flexible and unpredictable arrangement, but to a large extent it seems to be more effective than what the US and Europe have managed to provide. This is so partially because the East Asian countries have, if often less in rhetoric than in practice, retained a stronger Weber I type of core in their innovation bureaucracies: the focus on long-term stability and capacities remains a key characteristic, even for the cutting-edge innovation labs of digital agencies. Only in the last few years, driven by both political dynamics moving towards global-Western liberalism and a tendency to listen to one's own rhetoric, has this substance weakened, especially in Taiwan and most recently in Singapore, whereas in China and Vietnam, for instance, and to a lesser yet still noticeable degree in Korea, this is basically still true today.

Rather than providing new development-oriented visions, both the US and European innovation policies and strategies have partly become, because of their more complex webs of politico-administrative decision making, hostages to their own policy legacies and the resulting pressures to focus on competitiveness and the generic support of key enabling technologies (such as ICTs). Thus, even the charisma of leaders like Macron might not be sufficient to provide new real developmental narratives. As a result, we seem to be witnessing much more technocratic processes for setting missions and challenges than innovation (policy) should tackle. In the US, this initially took the form of the DARPA-fication of innovation policy, that is the creation of specific iterations of the DARPA model to tackle new socio-economic and techno-economic challenges in areas from energy (ARPA-E) to intelligence (IARPA) and homeland security (HSARPA),[91] and partial delegation of the steering and coordination of missions to the periphery of innovation bureaucracies. In the EU, the key label of innovation policy is often put centre stage and made fashionable by the EU institutions and their advisory networks. Many of the recent fads, from public procurement for innovation,[92] smart specialisation,[93] societal challenges,[94] and most recently mission-oriented innovation policy,[95] are brought to the attention of EU policy makers by academic communities. But these ideas, all related to attempts to make innovation policy more dynamic and responsive, tend to get blurred and confused by the EU political negotiations as well as by the unique form of the EU's 'experimental governance' model.[96] Yet, not all member states and regions have the capacities and capabilities to derive the best contextual solutions from this experimental policy space.

Thus, the EU still seems better at maintaining stability than providing agility, and accordingly is changing slowly. For instance, as we showed in the previous chapter, the first ideas for EU research and innovation policy were discussed in the 1950s and 1960s, but the first real EU organisation, the European Research Council, was established in the late 2000s. The idea that Europe should invest 3 per cent of its GDP in R&D was first discussed in the late 1960s in OECD networks and formalised into a strategic goal in the early 2000s (the Lisbon Agenda), but we are still discussing and measuring how far off we are from this goal. This means that even if the EU seems to be taking on more and more research and innovation policy tasks, this is often slow because member states are trying to push their particular competitiveness logic by focusing on specific societal challenges and missions in much more agile ways, but when they are competing with the size of the US and the East Asian economies (especially Japan and China), their limited critical mass is often their undoing.

While prior to the global pandemic, (innovation) policy makers were already increasingly seeking to rethink the foundations of innovation and perhaps also their wider economic policies in terms of organisational set-up and capabilities, the long-lasting shadow of the NPM is still strong. In East Asia, we see the relative strength of Weber I-type long-term capacities that allow innovation bureaucracies to react to crises like the COVID-19 pandemic with relatively high degree of efficiency, although for both political and fashion reasons, this is weakening in the smaller East and Southeast Asian states, if to very varied degrees.

In the global North/West, innovation bureaucracies are still happy to leave most of the actual innovation and discovery processes to the private and university sectors. Innovation bureaucracies mostly play the role of arm's-length funders, weighing up funding proposals according to their potential to rectify relatively narrowly defined market failures. This approach is based on assumptions that one can derive correct interventions from impersonal and mostly historical data, and there is little need for substantive co-discovery and co-design of futures. In essence, the innovation bureaucracies of the global North/West operate mostly in the 'old-style NPM'[97] routines of efficiency gains, creating a quagmire of ever more complex analytical tools and performance metrics without providing either stability or agility. Efficiency gains are the antidote to substantive policy accountability. This is perhaps best exemplified in the half-hearted attempts in most of Europe to implement seemingly novel challenge- or mission-oriented policies through a largely project-based logic of already existing funding mechanisms.

However, our argument in this book rests on the idea that innovation bureaucracies are in need of constant rejuvenation and in fact are in constant co-evolution with techno-economic structures. On the level of policies, the return of missions in the form of societal (grand) challenges is providing pressures for innovation bureaucracies to change, as missions require a level of capacity and capability that the shadows of dead NPM funding organisations simply cannot supply. In terms of organisational capabilities, it is, as we show in more detail in the next chapter, the increasing importance of digitalisation and digital transformation that provides impetus for change in innovation bureaucracies across the globe. Thus, many innovation bureaucracies are faced with the challenge of upgrading and rejuvenating their capacities and capabilities. As we will show in the next chapter, this has given rise to a new type of innovation agency – what we call neo-Weberian agencies that attempt to merge both Weber I and II-type capacities and capabilities.

7

SUMMING UP: WILL THE NEXT DECADES BE LED BY NEO-WEBERIAN INNOVATION AGENCIES?

Learning from COVID-19: Return of the State?

Prior to the COVID-19 pandemic, we could see a contradiction in how the new generation of mission-oriented innovation policies spread in both the US and the EU. In short, policies were becoming increasingly mission-based, but innovation bureaucracies were not; dynamic capabilities remained elusive for most innovation bureaucracies. In some cases, organisations could rely on existing capacities, for example DARPA and its clones in the US, but in most cases the diminishing and outsourcing of dynamic capabilities during the 1990s and 2000s is yet to be counteracted. In the meantime, the East Asian countries are, to some extent, able to go back to old developmentalist models, although combining growth, social equality and participation, and saving the climate may be too complex challenges even for developmentalist frameworks. Still, East Asian political leaders seem to be creating highly visible change agents with politically charged dynamic capabilities (presidential committees, headquarters and prime ministers' offices) for 'high-risk' innovations in ICT, the creative and green economy, 'super smart' society, and so on, which require a strong politico-administrative legitimacy hardly ever found in the Western hemisphere outside of wartime or a few exceptions, such as the 'creative corporatist' consensus in Finland.

In the Western context, COVID-19 was preceded by an increasing urgency in trying to tackle the climate emergency through 'green new deals' as a way to coordinate large-scale public-private collaborations. While this urgency had yet to translate into new organisational forms or capacities, COVID-19 seems to have opened up space both for bold policy innovations and for ambitious public organisations to build new dynamic capabilities. And it is becoming increasingly clear that the view and vision of the state prevalent in successful East Asian economies – namely, the state's strong legitimacy based on a fusion of Mandate of Heaven-type authority and a day-to-day delivery mentality – seems to have played a crucial role in dealing with the pandemic.

Arguably, there is a widespread consensus emerging among innovation policy makers that it is not enough to focus on quantitative growth in innovation policy outputs (from STEM graduates to high-tech exports); what matters at least as much is the direction of growth, or development more broadly.[1] There is ample evidence that policy makers are also attempting to implement this policy consensus. For instance, there is a distinct acceleration in green central banking,[2] an increased focus on better-coordinated macro-economic and innovation policies,[3] and the development of a new generation of innovation policies framed in the context of the Sustainable Development Goals.[4]

Such a 'normative turn' in policy goals had already intensified both conceptual and policy discussions globally prior to the onslaught of the pandemic. The response to the pandemic showed, however, why challenge-focused innovation matters so much, enabling historically rapid vaccine development and unprecedented policy and institutional responses.[5]

The pandemic responses also show why implementation issues are as important as policy framings. One could also argue that the crisis preparedness and pandemic plans (such as the US pandemic playbook designed by the Obama administration or the plans by EU member states[6]) are attempts at creating routines for agile stability, the latter seen through the lenses of resilience. In most developed economies this had been unfortunately contracted out or cut down for efficiency gains and never restored, even though very smart people advising the US government almost correctly predicted in 2017 that 'the global pandemic of 2023 dramatically reduces global travel in an effort to contain the spread of the disease, contributing to the slowing of global trade and decreased productivity'.[7]

Some parts of the innovation bureaucracies were prepared, and thanks to their anticipatory work on speeding up the development of vaccines (DARPA gave Moderna a grant for mRNA vaccine developments in 2013[8]), we have developed some key solutions to exit the pandemic remarkably fast. But in many other domains – from insufficient hospital equipment to launching track and trace apps and vaccination logistics chains, but also preparing society to accept new common behavioural rules and vaccines – the cracks in state capacities and capabilities have been visible globally.

Hence, the COVID-19 crisis-handling focused attention on public sector capacities and capabilities and how these are not necessarily correlated – and in various phases, not at all – with the level of development.[9] Indeed, during various periods of the pandemic, some of the countries that were least developed but had a strong public sector, like Bhutan, fared better than significantly further-developed ones like the UK and the US.

Next to the normative turn towards framing innovation policies through specific challenges, we are also increasingly witnessing an epistemic turn in innovation bureaucracies. The public sector adoption of working practices from (strategic and user-centred) design and agile software development practices has driven the emergence of new, often peripheral, public organisations (iLabs) and networks (task forces, SWAT and crisis teams, volunteer movements) in the form of public sector design, digital and innovation labs.[10] These working practices focus on agile processes such as prototyping and experimentation, relying on epistemological frameworks from action research and ethnography rather than economics or public policy analysis. These new agencies have brought experiential, experimental and techno-solutionist 'hacker' routines to public organisations,[11] in an attempt to formalise within organisations what we have called bureaucracy hacking. These new routines can also be seen as responding to the need to simplify existing, but often overly complex and technical, policy design and engagement practices, particularly in the aftermath of NPM reforms. The key challenge remains how the central government machinery is able to pick up and socialise such new emerging practices from the mostly – and often intentionally – peripheral iLabs and networks.

In our view, even if results are not yet clear, the emerging lessons from COVID-19 responses re-emphasise why experimentalism is not enough and show why both long-term capacities and dynamic capabilities matter. In other words, the successful responses to the pandemic demonstrate why and how agile stability can be a question of life and death. The creative combination of agile dynamic functions and long-term, stability-oriented functions seems to be at the heart of successful responses to the pandemic, both in the developed and developing world.[12] As the crisis has also brought to light fundamental vulnerabilities in many societies, particularly evident in the pandemic's gendered impacts, it has become clear why governments' responses should aim to build long-term resilience and stability.[13] The pandemic has shown that long-term capacities to provide the 'core government functions' are also,[14] at the same time, vital building blocks for agile crisis responses.[15] As we have argued, we should think of public sector capacities and capabilities in terms of both long-term capacities and dynamic capabilities. And while we argue throughout the book that these different capacities and capabilities have tended to emerge and reside historically in different organisations – coalescing into different formations of innovation organisations or what we call innovation bureaucracies – the normative and epistemic turns described above, and the COVID responses, indicate that the future of innovation bureaucracies is, or most certainly should be, to build agile stability into the DNA of every organisation.

Emergence of Mission-Oriented Neo-Weberian Public Agencies?

We speculate that out of the ashes, or embers, of the COVID-19 crisis, belonging to the policy space of wicked issues populated also by other super wicked challenges from climate change to biodiversity loss, which we haven't fully started to tackle, the idea of twenty-first-century innovation bureaucracies will emerge. Such organisations focus on long-term capacity building (e.g. in the form of building a professional workforce or functioning public digital infrastructure) as well as on dynamic capabilities for agile response to and active steering of contextual events (e.g. developing capabilities for agile public procurement or user-focused analytical tools for analysing the use of public services). They aim to be both dynamic and resilient by design. We can justifiably call these neo-Weberian agencies or, as alluded to earlier, Weber III-type agencies – attempting to combine Weber I and II in a single organisation.

In public administration literature, there has been a discussion of the NWS's emergence over the last decade. Conceived by Pollitt and Bouckaert since the 2000s, it has been at the forefront of debate since the explicit discussion in the 2011 edition of their paradigmatic *Public Management Reform* textbook.[16] The NWS posits that a new paradigm of the state has emerged in the era of post-NPM reforms. Starting from empirical observation of well-working public administration systems that (consciously) did not follow the NPM path and then transformed into a more normative ideal-type, the NWS emphasises the importance of public organisations in providing public services and at the same time recognises the need for more citizen engagement in the design and delivery of public services.[17]

In innovation policy, neo-Weberian agencies are characterised by the emergence of long-term societal goals (e.g. climate goals focusing on 2050) as core elements of policies and core missions (rather than the relatively short-term goals of relative competitiveness and growth prevalent in the 1990s and early 2000s). In parallel to the normative turn, we can also see an epistemic turn emerging. The latter can be seen in the incorporation of new methods and analytical tools such as strategic design, complexity economics, foresight and policy labs.[18] The neo-Weberian (innovation) agency is an ideal-typical synthesis of such conceptual discussions and empirical developments. It serves as a heuristic to understand ongoing changes in innovation policy and its implementation. Neo-Weberian agencies are engaged with tackling long-term socio-economic challenges and pursuing missions to solve them. Yet, we should not see them as super agencies solving challenges alone, quite to the contrary. The neo-Weberian agencies understand that part of their role is also to utilise the wider organisational configuration of innovation bureaucracies in developing dynamic capabilities.

In contrast to peripheral Schumpeterian agencies, introduced by Dan Breznitz and discussed in this book, neo-Weberian agencies do not rely on peripheral status. On the contrary, we can see how such agencies need strong political or public support to link up innovation policy discussions with wider socio-economic challenges (think of, e.g., urban circular economy discussions). In fact, coming back to our Weberian theory building, we argue that neo-Weberian agencies are incorporating key features of both Weber I and II-type organisations: the focus on long-term legitimacy and professionalisation is the hallmark of Weber I-type organisations – what we call expert organisations – while porosity to various stakeholder, epistemological and implementation frameworks has historically been key to Weber II-type organisations – what we call charismatic networks.

In Chapter 3, we developed a taxonomy of innovation bureaucracy organisations and argued that such organisations can go about fulfilling their tasks in quite different ways: some organisations can be involved in directly creating new technologies (e.g. government research institutes), others can support private companies (e.g. through grants) and yet others can be involved as intermediaries of knowledge (e.g. engineering or business associations, sustainability networks and movements). We proposed that there are five ideal-types of innovation bureaucracy organisations – creators, doers, funders, intermediaries and rulers – and we hold that in all these types of innovation bureaucracy organisation we have seen the evolution from Weber II to Weber I types of organisations, and sometimes back and forth movements between the types. In effect, more successful organisations under all types are converging around neo-Weberian blueprints, embodying agile stability.

Given the normative turn in innovation policy, we suggest that there are at least three core mission areas where such neo-Weberian agencies (should) focus on. In what follows, we will then take a brief look at how such neo-Weberian agencies are developing and implementing these long-term capacities and dynamic capabilities relevant for twenty-first-century innovation bureaucracies.

Missions and Modes of Neo-Weberian Innovation Bureaucracies

As we have argued throughout this book, there are a considerable variety of organisations dealing with innovation in the public sector. For instance, public banks differ significantly from public digital agencies in budget size, employee numbers and the tasks they carry out. Equally, drivers of change in public organisations can be highly diverse: changes can occur because of changes in political leadership, emergence of new actor networks pushing for change from inside or outside, or through creating new public institutions or new types of funding instruments.

Accordingly, we can expect the instrumentalisation of agile stability (long-term capacities and dynamic capabilities) to differ in public organisations. Here we propose a simple heuristic to think about the instrumentalisation of agile stability on neo-Weberian agencies through the different missions they are pursuing and the modes for creating and maintaining long-term capacities and dynamic capabilities in public organisations required for their respective missions. Mission mystique is a key feature of successful innovation bureaucracies. We propose that emerging mission-oriented neo-Weberian agencies are developing different types of mission mystique, with the latter depending on their mission.

Organisational or policy missions are about what is the main focus of an organisation (e.g. to fund or invest in tackling societal challenges) and its related capacities and capabilities. *Organisational modes* are about how and by whom the capacities and capabilities are maintained, driven and/or created; for example the creation of new organisations (or radical reform of existing organisations) can in itself be seen as a mode to create long-term capacities and capabilities.

First, there are (at least) three core missions that neo-Weberian innovation agencies (should) focus on:

- **Investment-focused missions and agencies.** These agencies rely on capacities and capabilities around devising investment and other financial instruments (e.g. financial regulations, grants) to fund public, private and third sector actors to focus on, for example, more economically, socially and ecologically important innovation activities.[19] Examples of such organisations are public financial institutions (e.g. investment banks), research and innovation funding agencies. Typically, these agencies are at arm's length from central government and enjoy relatively strong autonomy. We label them as investment-focused agencies and not just funders because we have been witnessing a shift (already as part of the hybridisation trends covered in Chapter 5) towards government organisation taking a more proactive and co-creative role in funding actions by trying to steer the actual use of funds in a more dynamic way.
- **Market-shaping-focused missions and agencies.** These agencies rely on capacities and capabilities around policy tools focusing on (re-)shaping markets, such as through regulation, procurement and labour rules.[20] Perhaps the key conceptual shift here is the conscious move beyond market

failure as the key policy rationale. The capacities and capabilities are relevant for central government ministries and local government departments directly engaging with creating and implementing market rules and legislation.

- **System change or transformation-focused missions and agencies.** These agencies rely on capacities and capabilities around new ways – from experimentation and design thinking to other novel methodologies for learning (and communicating lessons in easier ways) – to redefine and redesign sociotechnical systems (from mobility and energy systems to food) and policies and to engage with stakeholders and citizens, such as policy sandboxes and innovation labs.[21] The capacities and capabilities are typical for new types of public organisations such as digital agencies but also applicable in welfare services and across the public sector. These agencies matter more and more because we have increasingly learned that radical system change (i.e. from growth to sustainability) requires new ways of thinking, planning and acting to initiate system-wide and coordinated (top-down and bottom-up) movement towards common goals and actions.

Second, there are (at least) three modes for neo-Weberian agencies to create and maintain the long-term capacities and dynamic capabilities needed for such missions/focus areas:

- **Leadership-driven mode.** This mode is driven by political leaders supporting the development of new capacities and capabilities, often following election wins or the reshuffling of political leadership. This mode generates mission mystique around political entrepreneurship and often delivers rather quick set-up or reforms of relevant agencies but can also result in one-off drive for mission delivery.

- **Management-driven mode.** This mode is driven by changing management practices and routines or by creating new managerial posts and/or tasks within organisations. Examples include creating chief innovation/technology/design/resilience officer posts and functions or creating related teams to work systematically and persistently across the agency or agencies. Such agencies rely on managerial entrepreneurship to generate ideally more sustainable mission mystique.

- **New organisation-driven mode.** This mode is driven by purposefully creating new public organisations to break institutional inertia or bring new skills into the public sector. Examples can be relatively small scale, such as policy labs, or large scale, such as a new public bank. New organisations generate mission mystique based on what we can call structural entrepreneurship and this often combines the leadership modes (decisions on creating these organisation need to be made) and managerial modes (choices on organisational design and routines have to be made and implemented).

In actual policy practices, organisations can simultaneously exhibit different missions or focus areas and modes of long-term capacities and dynamic capabilities, and this is often the case. These combinations of missions and modes are ideally aimed at agile stability.

Let us briefly look at some examples. The Swedish innovation agency Vinnova has attempted to change its way of working over the last few years by creating the new post of strategic design director. This is an attempt to bring in new capabilities nested in human-centric design and, as a result, Vinnova's work is being reframed, from focusing primarily on technological issues to tackling socio-economic challenges and transforming related socio-technical systems. This has meant considerably enlarging the circle of key stakeholders and changing the way of working at Vinnova. For instance, one of the missions it has chosen is rethinking food systems to provide healthy, sustainable food in Swedish schools. To deliver this, Vinnova is working with the entire food delivery value chain, or food system, from producers to users (children and parents) and spurring innovations (via funding), creating markets and transforming existing systems from energy production and transportation to waste management.

Thus, it is an attempt to combine a relatively long-term view of investing into new technologies with short-term changes in day-to-day habits around eating. We would argue that what Vinnova is trying to do is to develop capacities and capabilities for agile stability; its mission mystique is based mostly on managerial entrepreneurialism but increasingly also on structural entrepreneurialism as it seeks to transform larger socio-economic systems such as food. While Vinnova is only at the beginning of its transformation, its blueprint is becoming increasingly copied by other Nordic countries and beyond.

Importantly, Vinnova – created in 2001 through a merger of seven research councils as a traditional innovation funder/ intermediary – has been always and still is part of a larger space of innovation bureaucracy organisations that provide complementary capacities and capabilities. What we are witnessing are attempts to redefine and redesign the borders of this space for delivering its more complex organisational mission ('to help to build Sweden's innovation capacity, contributing to sustainable growth'[22]) and specific policy missions: in the era of competitiveness and growth first, nobody would have thought that schools and pupils are important parts of innovation bureaucracy, but delivering sustainable food systems may depend the most on how kids and schools behave and collaborate with the likes of Vinnova. And these new forms of collaboration and co-creation, in turn, help Vinnova to learn and design new routines and capabilities for supporting new forms of sustainability innovations.

Another example comes from digital government. The UK's Government Digital Service (GDS), created in 2011,[23] has become a global gold standard in public sector digital agencies,[24] and it is in our view another fascinating example of a neo-Weberian agency and of agile stability in action. GDS as an intermediary/doer radically changed government digital transformation mindset ('strategy is delivery'[25]) and digital procurement through spending controls on procurement contracts and creating a new digital marketplace for bids.[26] This has enabled thousands of SMEs to bid and win public tenders and to break existing oligopolistic markets and create new, more open, ICT markets around government digital transformations. At the same time, GDS also radically changed the government's digital presence by creating a unified gov.uk website and through this the entire user experience of the UK government was transformed. This is based on user research and design practices to make information and services readily available and digitally usable.[27] In its initial years, GDS offered a vision and practice of a highly dynamic and agile government agency. The capabilities that GDS brought into government formed around a redefinition of value proposition (a focus on user needs and the need to diminish failure demand) that was accompanied by an influx of people who could deliver towards this new notion of value. It is worth noting that many of the people hired by GDS outside the civil service did not come from the private sector but were from the BBC and other similar public or third-sector organisations. In its initial years, GDS was managed by normative control functions, such as hiring like-minded people, that allowed it to grow quickly and scale its activities. The value system underlying GDS was inspired as much by post-war British modernism, with its focus on public space, as by the open web movement and hacking in a positive sense. GDS was a dynamic and agile organisation that was able to jump-start digital trans-formation through a single website (gov.uk) and revamp government ICT contracts through service frameworks and spend controls. Its market-shaping abilities were formidable. However, the utilitarian approach to user needs (simplicity and authenticity of transactions) also made it susceptible to market-based logic of austerity (savings as the main metrics), which, it can be argued, has undermined GDS's ability to build platforms.

In the last few years, however, GDS has become the standard-bearer for the digital and design profession within the UK government. The hackers and doers have become the new mandarins, or at least the mandarins have co-opted some of the capabilities brought in by GDS. Its initial dynamic capabilities around user-centred design have become increasingly part of the routine skills many departments and agencies have in-house, rather than relying on a central agency.

In this sense, and somewhat counterintuitively, GDS has become a victim of its own success: as other government departments have internalised its most valuable capabilities, GDS has evolved into a stability-focused agency, albeit with some dynamic capabilities routinised. The institutionalisation of its agile approach across government has, perhaps unsurprisingly, put constraints on the original dynamism and agility of the organisation. This is an example of how dynamic capabilities and agility evolve in public organisations: they become part of the wider organisational landscape, and the original sources and reasons driving the dynamic capabilities need to be renewed; Weber type-II organisations – charismatic networks – evolve towards Weber type-I, expertise-driven, organisations. Thus, GDS is an example of an agency with agile stability through new organisation and design-focused types, relying on market-shaping dynamic capabilities; its mission mystique thrives on managerial entrepreneurialism.

Importantly, in both cases, various dynamic capabilities and their development are nested in long-term capacities, such as countervailing institutional and political structures, investments into digital infrastructure and skills, and so forth. And the capabilities are developed and evolve in interactions with other public sector actors of the broader innovation bureaucracy and often also in partnerships with private actors and citizens. Indeed, as seen in the examples above, dynamic capabilities are pivotal for more direct engagement with the private sector and citizens and for reframing the purpose of such engagements. NPM-infused public organisations merely worried about the efficiency of public policies; emerging dynamic capabilities focus on shaping markets and partnerships for a common cause, from technological solutions to tackling socio-economic challenges. This indicates different relationships with stakeholders and, accordingly, changing requirements for skills and capabilities.

Where Do We Go from Here?

Today, perhaps more than ever before, public organisations are caught between what seems to be a rock and a hard place: faced with tackling intractable or grand challenges (let's remember, one of the key defining characteristic of wicked issues is that there is no common understanding of what the problem is to begin with), governments need to develop long-term solutions (no hackathon can solve climate change), yet some aspects of these challenges require an agile and dynamic response (the pandemic and its multiple effects on societies, or migration waves partially caused by climate change).[28] As we have argued throughout this book, such a paradoxical position implies that public organisations need to develop frameworks and tools for governments to become more proactive in taking on the multifaceted, long-term issues facing societies. Yet, as we demonstrated above, NPM reforms have largely outsourced the dynamic capabilities to networks of private actors, relegating public organisations to a reactive stance and routines.

Innovation policy organisations face this dilemma in a particularly disorienting way: they are tasked to fund or lead highly risky or even uncertain innovation endeavours while they are evaluated and measured by the public and politicians based on frameworks that punish risk taking. As Vinnova's director of strategic design, Dan Hill, has said, today's innovation agencies actually do not innovate, nor are they directly involved in innovation in businesses or society at large. Innovation agencies have become project managers, often stuck in a Kafkaesque loop of needing to annually show 'return on investment' to a largely disinterested ministry of finance. Such a stage show of innovation policy making lowers the willingness to develop agile and dynamic ways of working.

As we have shown in this book, building on Max Weber, modern public organisations are fundamentally oriented towards providing stability. For dynamic changes, they often rely on charismatic outsiders who bring new skills, solutions, ways of working, even new problem definitions (e.g. breaking up oligopolistic procurement markets in ICT). Yet, the success of such charismatic leaders and their solutions needs to build either on existing long-term capacities or on processes to professionalise new capabilities into public organisations (see our GDS example above). Moving fast and breaking things works in the public sector only if it is effectively accomplished by, or together with, a (post-NPM) highly motivated, high-capacity civil service.

It is not enough to attempt to face technological challenges by focusing on creating agile organisations to replace a Weberian bureaucracy – nor is it an option to retain the latter for routine, equitable deployment, but without a new emphasis on risk taking, and contemporary and future competences. In fact, we need both, and we need both at the same time – and increasingly within the confines of the same organisation. It demands high-level judgement power, resolve, tenacity and funding to develop such an innovation bureaucracy – but if this sounds difficult and expensive, the alternative is not meeting the challenges of our times.

ACKNOWLEDGEMENTS

The initial idea for this book is more than a decade old, concretely starting, if still with a different impetus, with a day of discussion in Istanbul, literally in the shadow of the Ayasofya. During these past years, we have accumulated substantial debts with a number of scholars, civil servants and students who have helped to shape the ideas that make up our argument and its narrative.

We would like to especially thank Björn Asheim, Fred Block, Geert Bouckaert, Mike Bracken, Francesca Bria, Ana Celia Castro, Alexandre de Avila Gomide, Dan Hill, Peter Ho, Veiko Lember, Siong Guan Lim, Richard Nelson, Carlota Perez, B. Guy Peters, the late Christopher Pollitt, Erik S. Reinert, Piret Tõnurist and Robert Wade for their comments, reflections and encouragement in various forms, from conference papers to op-eds.

A particular debt of gratitude goes to Mariana Mazzucato, who more than anyone has given policy-relevant life to the concepts developed herein and with whom we are professionally affiliated by now in various capacities. We are very happy that she has written the foreword to this.

We would also like to thank Aleksandrs Cepilovs and Olga Mikheeva for assistance with research for this book.

And the editors at Yale University Press for their patience.

This is the book of an almost Confucian team of scholars – the first author is the first PhD of the second, and the third author the first author's first. But this does not mean that we ever agreed on everything, neither initially nor during the book's gestation. The world has changed immensely during the last decade, and so – if perhaps less so, intellectually speaking – have we, and that means that there needed to be more compromises among ourselves than originally envisioned. Still, in spite of the fact that some chapters are more based on individual work, this is very much *our* book, and while it would really go too far to thank each other in this section, this still belongs in the acknowledgements.

Funding for our research has come from the Institute for New Economic Thinking, Estonian Academy of Sciences, Baltic-American Freedom Fund, Japanese Society for the Promotion of Science, European Commission Horizon 2020 grants LIPSE and Growinpro and the Estonian Research Council.

ENDNOTES

1 AGILE STABILITY

1. McKinsey Global Institute, *Digital Globalization: The New Era of Global Flows* (McKinsey, 2016).
2. David Cahan, *An Institute for an Empire: The Physikalisch-Technische Reichsanstalt, 1871–1918* (New York: Cambridge University Press, 1989): 154.
3. Ibid., 17.
4. On the history of such techno-economic shifts, see Carlota Perez, *Technological Revolutions and Financial Capital: The Dynamics of Bubbles and Golden Ages* (Cheltenham: Elgar, 2002).
5. Werner von Siemens, *Lebenserinnerungen*, ed. Wilfried Feldenkirchen (Munich: Piper, 2008): 430–3; Conrad Matschoss, *Werner Siemens: A Concise Biography and Selection of His Letters* (Berlin: Julius Springer, 1916); Wolfgang Drechsler, 'Herrn Eugen Dühring's remotion', *Journal of Economic Studies* 29(4/5) (2002): 262–92.
6. Cahan, *An Institute for an Empire.*
7. See https://18f.gsa.gov/2014/05/14/hacking-bureaucracy-improving-hiring-and-software/.
8. Ines Mergel, *Digital Service Teams: Challenges and Recommendations for Government*, Using Technology Series (Washington, DC: IBM Center for the Business of Government, 2017).
9. Charles T. Goodsell, 'Mission mystique: strength at the institutional center', *American Review of Public Administration* 41(5) (2011): 477–8.
10. Cahan, *An Institute for an Empire*, 31–2.
11. Reichstag, *Verhandlungen des Deutschen Reichstag. Physikalisch-Technische Reichsanstalt, Denkschrift, betreffend die Errichtung derselben*, Etat 1887/88 Beilage B zu Anlage IV (1886/7), https://www.reichstagsprotokolle.de.
12. Reichstag, *Verhandlungen des Deutschen Reichstag. Denkschrift über die Thätigkeit der Physikalisch-Technischen Reichsanstalt in den Jahren 1891 und 1892* (1890/92 and 1892/3), https://www.reichstagsprotokolle.de.

13. Cahan, *An Institute for an Empire*, 192.
14. Ibid., 72–81.
15. Ibid., 133.
16. Piero Sraffa, *Lecture Notes on Continental Banking*, unpublished (Cambridge: Trinity College, 1930).
17. Jacob Riesser, *The German Great Banks and Their Concentration in Connection with the Economic Development of Germany* (Washington, DC: Government Printing Office, 1911).
18. Charles Goodhart, *The Evolution of Central Banks*, 2nd edn (Cambridge, MA: MIT Press, 1988); Christopher Adolph, *Bankers, Bureaucrats, and Central Bank Politics: The Myth of Neutrality* (Cambridge: Cambridge University Press, 2013).
19. Gustav von Schmoller, *Grundriß der Allgemeinen Volkswirtschaftslehre*, Teil 1 (Leipzig: Duncker & Humblot, 1900): 313–15.
20. Linda Khan, 'Amazon's antitrust paradox', *Yale Law Review* 126(3) (2017): 710–805, https://www.yalelawjournal.org/note/amazons-antitrust-paradox.
21. Such organisational fluidity is in fact an established norm in business history where discussions involving Chandler, Kocka and others initially argued that the German business firms developed along more hierarchical lines but have evolved in light of new historical research to show that many leading German firms at the time – Siemens, Thyssen, Zeiss and others – had fluid yet professional managerial cultures. For a discussion, see Jeffrey Fear, 'Cartels', in *The Oxford Handbook of Business History*, ed. Geoffrey Jones and Jonathan Zeitlin (Oxford: Oxford University Press, 2008): 268–92.
22. Mariana Mazzucato, *Missions: Mission-Oriented Research and Innovation in the European Union* (Brussels: European Commission, 2018a), https://ec.europa.eu/info/sites/info/files/mazzucato_report_2018.pdf; 'Mission-oriented innovation policies: challenges and opportunities', *Industrial and Corporate Change* 27(5) (2018): 803–15.
23. Mariana Mazzucato and Rainer Kattel, 'COVID-19 and public sector capacity', *Oxford Review of Economic Policy* 36 (supplement 1) (2020): S256–69.
24. Sarah Bosley and Robert Booth, 'What is No 10's "moonshot" Covid testing plan and is it feasible?', *The Guardian*, 9 September 2020, https://www.theguardian.com/world/2020/sep/09/what-is-no-10s-moonshot-covid-testing-plan-and-is-it-feasible.
25. Charles Leadbeater, Ravi Gurumurthy and Christopher Haley, 'The COVID-19 test: what have we learnt so far? Reflections on emerging trends', Nesta blog, 1 May 2020, https://www.nesta.org.uk/blog/covid-test/.
26. Geert Bouckaert et al., 'European coronationalism? A hot spot governing a pandemic crisis', *Public Administration Review* 80(5) (2020): 765–73.
27. Mariana Mazzucato and Giulio Quaggiotto, 'The big failure of small government', Project Syndicate, 19 May 2020, https://www.project-syndicate.org/commentary/small-governments-big-failure-covid19-by-mariana-mazzucato-and-giulio-quaggiotto-2020-05.
28. Robyn Klingler-Vidra, Ba Linh Tran and Ida Uusikyla, 'Testing capacity: state capacity and COVID-19 testing', *Global Policy Opinion*, 9 April 2020, https://www.globalpolicyjournal.com/blog/09/04/2020/testing-capacity-state-capacity-and-covid-19-testing.

29. Madeline Drexler, 'The unlikeliest pandemic success story. How did a tiny, poor nation manage to suffer only one death from the coronavirus?', *The Atlantic*, 10 February 2021.

30. See Wolfgang Drechsler and Rainer Kattel, 'Debate: the developed civil servant – providing agility and stability at the same time', *Public Money & Management* 40(8) (2020): 549–51.

31. Joseph Schumpeter, *Die Krise des Steuerstaats* (Graz and Leipzig: Leuschner & Lubensky, 1918).

32. Mariana Mazzucato, *The Entrepreneurial State: Debunking the Public vs. Private Myth in Risk and Innovation* (London: Anthem, 2013); Mariana Mazzucato et al., *COVID-19 and the Need for Dynamic State Capabilities: An International Comparison*, UNDP-IIPP Working Paper (2021).

33. Arist. *Pol.*, I.2. 1252b.

34. John Kenneth Galbraith, *Economics and the Public Purpose* (Boston: Houghton Mifflin, 1973).

35. 'A Roman bathhouse still in use after 2,000 years', https://www.bbc.com/news/magazine-24493177.

36. Richard Nelson, *The Moon and the Ghetto: An Essay on Public Policy Analysis* (New York: W.W. Norton, 1977).

37. Bruno Amable, 'Institutional complementarities in the dynamic comparative analysis of capitalism', *Journal of Institutional Economics* 12(1) (2016): 79–103.

38. See the excellent case studies of the East Asian tiger economies in Joseph Wong, *Betting on Biotech: Innovation and the Limits of Asia's Developmental State* (Ithaca: Cornell University Press, 2011).

39. Mariana Mazzucato, 'From market fixing to market-creating: a new framework for innovation policy', *Industry and Innovation* 23(2) (2016): 140–56.

40. Mariana Mazzucato, *Mission-Oriented Innovation Policy: Challenges and Opportunities*, UCL Institute for Innovation and Public Purpose (2017), https://www.ucl.ac.uk/bartlett/public-purpose/publications/2017/sep/mission-oriented-innovation-policy-challenges-and-opportunities; Rainer Kattel and Mariana Mazzucato, 'Mission-oriented innovation policy and dynamic capabilities in the public sector', *Industrial and Corporate Change* 27(5) (2018): 787–801.

41. William Bonvillian and Charles Weiss, *Technological Innovation in Legacy Sectors* (Oxford: Oxford University Press, 2015); Mark Taylor, *The Politics of Innovation: Why Some Countries Are Better Than Others at Science and Technology* (Oxford: Oxford University Press, 2016).

42. See Erkki Karo, 'Mission-oriented innovation policies and bureaucracies in East Asia', *Industrial and Corporate Change* 27(5) (2018): 867–81.

43. Oswald Spengler, *Der Untergang des Abendlandes: Umrisse einer Morphologie der Weltgeschichte*, 2 vols (Vienna: Braumüller; Munich: C.H. Beck, 1918–1923).

44. Giuseppe Tomasi di Lampedusa, *The Leopard* (London: Fontana, 1963), 29.

45. Frank Geels, 'The dynamics of transitions in socio-technical systems: a multi-level analysis of the transition pathway from horse-drawn carriages to automobiles (1860–1930)', *Technology Analysis and Strategic Management* 17(4) (2005): 445–76.

46. Christopher Pollitt, *Time, Policy, Management: Governing with the Past* (Oxford: Oxford University Press, 2008).

47. See Drechsler and Kattel, 'Debate', 549–51.
48. Charles A. O'Reilly III and Michael L. Tushman, 'The ambidextrous organizations', *Harvard Business Review* 82(4) (2004): 74–81.
49. Barack Obama, Remarks by the President in State of Union Address (2011), https://obamawhitehouse.archives.gov/the-press-office/2011/01/25/remarks-president-state-union-address.

2 STATE OF THE DEBATE

1. National Economic Council and Office of Science and Technology Policy, *A Strategy for American Innovation* (Washington, DC: The White House, 2009).
2. American Reinvestment and Recovery Act of 2009, *Public Law* No. 111-5, https://www.congress.gov/bill/111th-congress/house-bill/1/text.
3. National Economic Council and Office of Science and Technology Policy, *A Strategy for American Innovation* (Washington, DC: The White House, 2015), https://obamawhitehouse.archives.gov/sites/default/files/strategy_for_american_innovation_october_2015.pdf.
4. Stian Westlake, 'The quantity theory of innovation policy (or: why you probably don't need a DARPA)', Nesta blog, 6 April 2016, https://www.nesta.org.uk/blog/the-quantity-theory-of-innovation-policy-or-why-you-probably-dont-need-a-darpa/.
5. Christopher Freeman, *Technology Policy and Economic Performance: Lessons from Japan* (London: Pinter, 1987).
6. See Government of Japan, *The Fifth Science and Technology Basic Plan 2016–2020* (Tokyo: Government of Japan, 2016).
7. European Commission, *Research and Innovation as Sources of Renewed Growth*, COM (2014) 339 final, https://ec.europa.eu/research/innovation-union/pdf/state-of-the-union/2013/research-and-innovation-as-sources-of-renewed-growth-com-2014-339-final.pdf.
8. Based largely on Mariana Mazzucato, *Missions: Mission-Oriented Research and Innovation in the European Union* (Brussels: European Commission, 2018), https://ec.europa.eu/info/sites/info/files/mazzucato_report_2018.pdf.
9. For conceptual-theoretical models, see Mariana Mazzucato, 'From market fixing to market-creating: a new framework for innovation policy', *Industry and Innovation* 23(2) (2016): 140–56, and K. Matthias Weber and Harald Rohracher, 'Legitimizing research, technology and innovation policies for transformative change: combining insights from innovation systems and multi-level perspective in a comprehensive "failures" framework', *Research Policy* 41(6) (2012): 1037–47.
10. See Elon Musk, *Making Humans a Multiplanetary Species*, video presentation (2016), http://www.spacex.com/mars, and Elon Musk, 'Making humans a multi-planetary species', *New Space* 5(2) (2017): 46–61.
11. See https://twitter.com/elonmusk/status/1296275496942972928, 20 August 2020.
12. James Bennet, 'We need an energy miracle', interview with Bill Gates, *The Atlantic*, November 2015, https://www.theatlantic.com/magazine/archive/2015/11/we-need-an-energy-miracle/407881/.

13. Inga Ulnicane, '"Grand Challenges" concept: a return of the "big ideas" in science, technology and innovation policy?', *International Journal of Foresight and Innovation Policy* 11 (2016): 5–21.
14. Erik S. Reinert, *How Rich Countries Got Rich . . . and Why Poor Countries Stay Poor* (London: Constable, 2007); Ha-Joon Chang, *Kicking Away the Ladder: Development Strategy in Historical Perspective* (London: Anthem, 2002); Kunal Sen, 'The political dynamics of economic growth', *World Development* 47 (2013): 71–86.
15. Carlota Perez, *Technological Revolutions and Financial Capital: The Dynamics of Bubbles and Golden Ages* (Cheltenham: Elgar, 2002).
16. Alice H. Amsden, *Asia's Next Giant: South Korea and Late Industrialization* (Oxford: Oxford University Press, 1989); Robert Wade, *Governing the Market: Economic Theory and the Role of Government in East Asian Industrialization* (Princeton: Princeton University Press, 1990); Joseph Wong, *Betting on Biotech: Innovation and the Limits of Asia's Developmental State* (Ithaca: Cornell University Press, 2011).
17. See Le Taxi, http://le.taxi.
18. *Innovation and the State: Political Choices and Strategies for Growth in Israel, Taiwan and Ireland* (New Haven: Yale University Press, 2007); *Innovation in Real Places: Strategies for Prosperity in an Unforgiving World* (New York: Oxford University Press, 2021); with Michael Murphree, *Run of the Red Queen: Government, Innovation, Globalization, and Economic Growth in China* (New Haven: Yale University Press, 2011).
19. *Grundriß der Allgemeinen Volkswirtschaftslehre*, Teil 1 (Leipzig: Duncker & Humblot, 1900). On the importance and relevance of Schmoller and the German historical school, see Wolfgang Drechsler, 'The German Historical School and Kathedersozialismus', in *Handbook of Alternative Theories of Economic Development*, ed. Erik S. Reinert, Jayati Ghosh and Rainer Kattel (Cheltenham: Elgar, 2016): 109–23.
20. *An Evolutionary Theory of Economic Change* (Cambridge: Harvard University Press, 1982): 384–5.
21. Keiron Flanagan and Elvira Uyarra, 'Four dangers in innovation policy studies – and how to avoid them', *Industry and Innovation* 23(2) (2016): 177–88; Jakob Edler and Jan Fagerberg, 'Innovation policy: what, why, and how', *Oxford Review of Economic Policy* 33(1) (2017): 2–23.
22. Ben Martin, *What Is Happening to Our Universities?*, SPRU Working Papers, 2016-03 (2016); Jan Fagerberg, 'Innovation policy: rationales, lessons and challenges', *Journal of Economic Surveys* 31(2) (2016): 497–512.
23. See European Commission, *Lessons from a Decade of Innovation Policy: What Can Be Learnt from the INNO Policy Trend Chart and the Innovation Union Scoreboard* (Brussels: European Commission, 2013), and Manchester Institute of Innovation Research, *Compendium of Evidence on the Effectiveness of Innovation Policy Intervention* (London: Nesta, 2012). OECD country studies of innovation policy typically describe implementing agencies but rarely go into analytical details (e.g. whether the success of a measure has anything to do with the specific features of the agency implementing it or not).
24. For innovation systems thinking of the early 1990s, see Christopher Freeman, *Technology Policy and Economic Performance: Lessons from Japan* (London:

Pinter, 1987); Bengt-Åke Lundvall, *National Systems of Innovation: An Analytical Framework* (London: Pinter, 1992); for its rethinking in the 2010s, see Jan Fagerberg, Ben R. Martin and Esben Sloth Andersen, eds, *Innovation Studies: Evolution and Future Challenges* (Oxford: Oxford University Press, 2013); for socio-technical systems and transitions thinking, see Frank Geels, 'From sectoral systems of innovation to socio-technical systems: insights about dynamics and change from sociology and institutional theory', *Research Policy* 33(6–7) (2004): 897–920; Adrian Smith, Andy Stirling and Frans Berkhout, 'The governance of sustainable socio-technical transitions', *Research Policy* 34(10) (2005): 1491–1510; and for mission-oriented innovation policy, see Mariana Mazzucato, *The Entrepreneurial State: Debunking the Public vs. Private Myth in Risk and Innovation* (London: Anthem, 2013); Mariana Mazzucato et al., *COVID-19 and the Need for Dynamic State Capabilities: An International Comparison*, UNDP-IIPP Working Paper (2021).

25. Alice Lam, 'Organizational innovations', in *The Oxford Handbook of Innovation*, ed. Jan Fagerberg, David Mowery and Richard Nelson (Oxford: Oxford University Press, 2006): 115–47.

26. Wolfgang Drechsler, 'The rise and demise of the New Public Management', *Post-autistic Economics Review* 33 (2005): 17–28.

27. *Asia's Next Giant.*

28. *Embedded Autonomy: States and Industrial Transformation* (Princeton: Princeton University Press, 1995).

29. *Pathways from the Periphery: The Politics of Growth in the Newly Industrializing Countries* (Ithaca: Cornell University Press, 1990).

30. *Governing the Market.*

31. *MITI and the Japanese Miracle: The Growth of Industrial Policy, 1925–1975* (Stanford: Stanford University Press, 1982): 305–20.

32. 'Bureaucracy and growth: a cross-national analysis of the effects of "Weberian" state structures on economic growth', *American Sociological Review* 64(5) (1999): 748–65.

33. See also James Rauch and Peter Evans, 'Bureaucratic structure and bureaucratic performance in less developed countries', *Journal of Public Economics* 75(1) (2000): 49–71; Peter Evans, 'Transferable lessons? Re-examining the institutional prerequisites of East Asian economic policies', *Journal of Development Studies* 34(6) (1998): 66–86.

34. See http://econweb.ucsd.edu/~jrauch/codebook.html.

35. Marina Nistotskaya and Luciana Cingolani, *Bureaucratic Structure, Regulatory Quality and Entrepreneurship in a Comparative Perspective*, QoG Working Paper Series 08 (2014).

36. *The Economist*, 'Mandarin lessons', 12 March 2016, https://www.economist.com/international/2016/03/10/mandarin-lessons.

37. 'The revolutionary power of peripheral agencies: explaining radical policy innovation in Finland and Israel', *Comparative Political Studies* 46(10) (2013): 1219–45; 'The politics of partial success: fostering innovation in innovation policy in an era of heightened public scrutiny', *Socio-Economic Review* 16(4) (2018): 721–41; also Dan Breznitz, Darius Ornston and Steven Samford, 'Mission critical: the ends, means, and design of innovation agencies', *Industrial and Corporate Change* 27(5) (2018): 883–96.

38. 'ARPA-E and DARPA: applying the DARPA model to energy innovation', *Journal of Technology Transfer* 36(5) (2011): 469–513.
39. 'The revolutionary power of peripheral agencies', 1219–45.
40. 'The politics of partial success', 721–41.
41. Interviews in Singapore with Wolfgang Drechsler in March 2017 and July 2019.
42. See www.planejamento.gov.br/assuntos/gestao-publica/inovacao/innovation-week/schedule.
43. See https://apolitical.co/solution_article/how-denmark-lost-its-mindlab-the-inside-story/.
44. *2022 A Radical Agenda for Design* (2021), https://ddc.dk/2022-a-radical-agenda-for-design/.
45. Johnson, *MITI and the Japanese Miracle*.
46. Tun-Jen Cheng, Stephan Haggard and David Kang, 'Institutions and growth in Korea and Taiwan: the bureaucracy', *Journal of Development Studies* 34 (1998): 87–111.
47. Evans and Rauch, 'Bureaucracy and growth', 748–65.
48. Fred Block, 'Swimming against the current: the rise of a hidden developmental state in the United States', *Politics & Society* 36(2) (2008): 169–206; Breznitz and Ornston, 'The revolutionary power of peripheral agencies', 1219–45; 'The politics of partial success', 721–41.
49. Piret Tõnurist, Rainer Kattel and Veiko Lember, 'Innovation labs in the public sector: what they are and what they do?', *Public Management Review* 19(10) (2017): 1455–79.
50. Arnold Gehlen, *Man in the Age of Technology* (New York: Columbia University Press, 1980, original publication 1957): 44.
51. For a longer historical discussion of the concept of innovation, see Benoît Godin, 'The linear model of innovation: the historical construction of an analytical framework', *Science, Technology, and Human Values* 31(6) (2006): 639–67; 'Innovation studies: the invention of a specialty', *Minerva* 50(4) (2011): 397–421.
52. We refer here to the 1848 French edition, available via Project Gutenberg and to the 1876 English translation.
53. For a comparative discussion of Tocqueville's and Weber's discussions of America, see Stephen Kalberg, 'Tocqueville and Weber on the sociological origins of citizenship: the political culture of American democracy', *Citizenship Studies* 1(2) (1997): 199–222.
54. Alexis de Tocqueville, *Democracy in America*, Vol. 1 (Boston: John Allyn, 1876): 92.
55. Ibid., 92. 'C'est ce qui ne se découvre pas au premier coup d'œil. Les gouvernants regardent comme une première concession de rendre les fonctions électives, et comme une seconde concession de soumettre le magistrat élu aux arrêts des juges. Ils redoutent également ces deux innovations.' / 'The communities therefore in which the secondary functionaries of the government are elected are perforce obliged to make great use of judicial penalties as a means of administration. This is not evident at first sight; for those in power are apt to look upon the institution of elective functionaries as one concession, and

the subjection of the elected magistrate to the judges of the land as another. They are equally averse to both these innovations.'

56. Ibid., 121.

57. Ibid., 113.

58. Ibid., 109.

59. *Wirtschaft und Gesellschaft* does not mention Tocqueville. However, Weber's wife, Marianne Weber, claimed that Weber knew the works of Tocqueville (Dorrit Freund, 'Max Weber und Alexis de Tocqueville', *Archiv für Kulturgeschichte* 56(2) (1974): 457). Weber travelled in the US for three months in 1904 – see the extensive discussion in Dirk Kaesler, *Max Weber. Preusse, Denker, Muttersohn. Eine Biographie* (Munich: Beck, 2014): 563–637.

60. Max Weber, *Wirtschaft und Gesellschaft: Die Wirtschaft und die gesellschaftlichen Ordnungen und Mächte. Nachlass 2: Religiöse Gemeinschaften*, MWS I/22 (Tübingen: Mohr Siebeck, 2008 [1922]): 156, 545–50, 561.

61. Ibid., 565.

62. Freund, 'Max Weber und Alexis de Tocqueville'.

63. *Gemeinschaft und Gesellschaft* (Leipzig: Fues's Verlag, 1887).

64. Tom Burns and G.M. Stalker, *The Management of Innovations* (London: Tavistock, 1961).

65. Robert B. Duncan, 'The ambidextrous organization: designing dual structures for innovations', in *The Management of Organization Design: Strategies and Implementation*, Vol. 1, ed. R.H. Kilmann, L.R. Pondy and D.P. Slevin (New York: North-Holland, 1976).

66. James G. March, 'Exploration and exploitation in organizational learning', *Organization Science* 2(1) (special issue) (1991): 71–87.

67. David Teece, 'Dynamic capabilities and entrepreneurial management in large organizations: toward a theory of the (entrepreneurial) firm', *European Economic Review* 86 (2016): 202–16.

68. Constance Helfat and Jeffery Martin, 'Dynamic managerial capabilities: review and assessment of managerial impact on strategic change', *Journal of Management* 41 (2015): 1281–1312.

69. Charles A. O'Reilly III and Michael L. Tushman, 'The ambidextrous organizations', *Harvard Business Review* 82(4) (2004): 74–81; 'Ambidexterity as a dynamic capability: resolving the innovator's dilemma', *Research in Organizational Behavior* 28 (2008): 185–206.

70. *Theorie der wirtschaftlichen Entwicklung* (Berlin: Duncker & Humblot, 1912): 142–57.

71. Weber, *Wirtschaft und Gesellschaft*; Eugenie Samier, 'Toward a Weberian public administration: the infinite web of history, values, and authority in administrative mentalities', *Halduskultuur* 6 (2005): 60–94.

72. Weber, *Wirtschaft und Gesellschaft*, 154–5.

73. Mazzucato, *The Entrepreneurial State*.

74. Daniel Sarewitz, 'Saving science', *New Atlantis* 49 (Spring/Summer) (2016): 4–40.

75. Johan Schot and W. Edward Steinmueller, 'Three frames for innovation policy: R&D, systems of innovation and transformative change', *Research Policy* 47(9) (2018): 1554–67; Susana Borrás and Jakob Edler, 'The roles of

the state in the governance of socio-technical systems' transformation', *Research Policy* 49 (2020): 103971.

76. More in Erkki Karo and Rainer Kattel, 'Innovation and the state: towards an evolutionary theory of policy capacity', in *Policy Capacity and Governance*, ed. Xun Wu, Michael Howlett and M. Ramesh (London: Palgrave Macmillan, 2018): 123–50.

77. Gary Pisano and David Teece, 'The dynamic capabilities of firms: an introduction', *Industrial and Corporate Change* 3(3) (1994): 537–56.

78. See https://www.wired.com/2017/01/race-pass-obamas-last-law-save-tech-dc/.

79. See https://www.politico.com/agenda/story/2017/07/01/jared-kushner-office-american-innovation-000470.

80. See https://www.theguardian.com/us-news/2018/jun/18/space-force-donald-trump-orders-new-branch-of-us-military.

81. In Brazil, President Bolsonaro has been actively dismantling existing powerful development organisations such as the public bank, BNDES, and in the UK, Theresa May's government launched a mission-oriented industrial strategy in 2017, only for it to be watered down four years later under Boris Johnson.

82. See Honorata Mazepus, 'Does political legitimacy matter for policy capacity?', in *Policy Capacity and Governance*, 229–42.

83. *Compendium of Evidence on the Effectiveness of Innovation Policy Intervention.*

84. Weber, *Wirtschaft und Gesellschaft.*

85. Ibid., 156, 545–50, 561.

86. On directionality, see Mariana Mazzucato, *Mission-Oriented Innovation Policy: Challenges and Opportunities*, UCL Institute for Innovation and Public Purpose (2017), https://www.ucl.ac.uk/bartlett/public-purpose/publications/2017/sep/mission-oriented-innovation-policy-challenges-and-opportunities.

87. See also Christopher Pollitt, *Time, Policy, Management: Governing with the Past* (Oxford: Oxford University Press, 2008); *New Perspectives on Public Services: Place and Technology* (Oxford: Oxford University Press, 2012).

88. Xinzhong Yao, *An Introduction to Confucianism*, 10th printing (Cambridge: Cambridge University Press, 2011 [2001]); Jiang Yonglin, *The Mandate of Heaven and the Great Ming Code* (Seattle: University of Washington Press, 2011).

89. Max Weber, *Die Wirtschaftsethik der Weltreligionen: Konfuzianismus und Taoismus. Schriften 1915–1920, Max Weber Gesamtausgabe* (MWG) I/19 (Tübingen: Mohr Siebeck, 1989 [1920]).

90. Wolfgang Drechsler, 'Max Weber and the Mandate of Heaven', *Max Weber Studies* 20(1) (2020): 25–56.

91. Sebastian Heilmann, 'Maximum tinkering under uncertainty: unorthodox lessons from China', *Modern China* 35(4) (2009): 450–62.

92. Breznitz and Murphree, *Run of the Red Queen.*

93. Richard Appelbaum et al., *Innovation in China: Challenging the Global Science and Technology System* (Cambridge: Polity Press, 2018).

94. Ibid.

95. Breznitz and Murphree, *Run of the Red Queen.*

96. For detailed case studies, see also Breznitz, *Innovation in Real Places.*

97. Silvia Lindtner, *Prototype Nation: China and the Contested Promise of Innovation* (Princeton: Princeton University Press, 2020).

98. Kai-Fu Lee, *AI Superpowers: China, Silicon Valley, and the New World Order* (Boston: Houghton Mifflin Harcourt, 2018).

99. Wolfgang Drechsler, 'Beyond the Western paradigm: Confucian public administration', in *Public Policy in the 'Asian Century': Concepts, Cases and Futures*, ed. Sara Bice, Avery Poole and Helen Sullivan (Basingstoke: Palgrave Macmillan, 2018): 19–40.

100. Drechsler, 'Max Weber and the Mandate of Heaven', 45–7.

101. Elizabeth Perry, 'Is the Chinese communist regime legitimate?', in *The China Questions*, ed. M. Szonyi and J. Rudolph (Cambridge, MA: Harvard University Press, 2018): 11–17.

102. Weber, *Die Wirtschaftsethik der Weltreligionen*; see Drechsler, 'Max Weber and the Mandate of Heaven'.

103. Drechsler, 'Beyond the Western paradigm'.

104. Kenneth Pomeranz, *The Great Divergence: China, Europe, and the Making of the Modern World Economy* (Princeton: Princeton University Press, 2000).

105. Wolfgang Schluchter, *Die Entwicklung des okzidentalen Rationalismus: Eine Analyse von Max Webers Gesellschaftsgeschichte* (Tübingen: Mohr Siebeck, 1979).

106. 'Max Weber and patterns of Chinese history', *Chinese Journal of Sociology* 1(2) (2015): 201–30.

107. Ragnar Nurkse, 'Problems of capital formation in underdeveloped countries' (1953), in *Ragnar Nurkse: Trade and Development*, ed. Rainer Kattel, Jan Kregel and Erik S. Reinert (London: Anthem, 2009): 99–212.

108. Kishore Mahbubani, *Has China Won? The Chinese Challenge to American Primacy* (New York: Public Affairs, 2020).

109. Weber, *Die Wirtschaftsethik der Weltreligionen*.

3 ROOTS AND TYPES OF INNOVATION BUREAUCRACIES

1. Joel Mokyr, *A Culture of Growth: The Origins of the Modern Economy* (Princeton: Princeton University Press, 2016).

2. For instance, Werner Siemens was actively involved in establishing learned societies.

3. Ludwig Haber, *The Chemical Industry During the Nineteenth Century: A Study of the Economic Aspects of Applied Chemistry in Europe and North America* (New York: Oxford University Press, 1958).

4. Peter Lundgreen ('Engineering education in Europe and the USA, 1750–1930: the rise to dominance of school culture and the engineering professions', *Annals of Science* 47(1) (1990): 33–75) argues that engineers also played a crucial role in some countries in professionalising the civil service in the early nineteenth century and helped to by-pass existing 'patrimonial' structures, but for the core countries of archetypical civil serviceness, that is Germany, the UK and the US, and also for many Eastern variants, this is clearly not the case.

5. For current purposes, it is not important whether professional managers were born in the private or public sectors (for this discussion, see Alfred D. Chandler, *The Visible Hand: The Managerial Revolution in American Business* (Cambridge, MA: Harvard University Press, 1977); Keith Hoskin and Richard Macve, 'The genesis of accountability: the West Point connections', *Accounting, Organizations and Society* 13(1) (1988): 37–73; 'Reappraising the genesis of managerialism', *Accounting, Auditing & Accountability Journal* 7(2) (1994): 4–29; and Mark Wilson, *The Business of Civil War: Military Mobilization and the State, 1861–1865* (Baltimore: Johns Hopkins University Press, 2006)); it is, however, important that in both sectors this happens around the same time, in the mid-nineteenth century.

6. For example, the Centralverband Deutscher Industrieller was established in 1876 in Germany, the National Association of Manufacturers in 1895 in the US; see Hans-Ulrich Wehler, 'Der Aufstieg des Organisierten Kapitalismus und Interventionsstaats in Deutschland', in *Organisierter Kapitalismus: Kritische Studien zur Geschichtswissenschaft, 9*, ed. H.A. Winkler (Göttingen: Vandenhoeck & Ruprecht, 1974): 36–57.

7. See only William Dalrymple, *The Anarchy: The Relentless Rise of the East India Company* (London: Bloomsbury, 2019).

8. Peter Evans and James Rauch, 'Bureaucracy and growth: a cross-national analysis of the effects of "Weberian" state structures on economic growth', *American Sociological Review* 64(5) (1999): 748–65; Marina Nistotskaya and Luciana Cingolani, *Bureaucratic Structure, Regulatory Quality and Entrepreneurship in a Comparative Perspective*, QoG Working Paper Series 08 (2014).

9. For example, Charles Edquist and Leif Hommen, eds, *Small Country Innovation Systems: Globalization, Change and Policy in Asia and Europe* (Cheltenham: Elgar, 2009).

10. Bruno Amable, *The Diversity of Modern Capitalism* (Oxford: Oxford University Press, 2003); J. Rogers Hollingsworth and Robert Boyer, eds, *Contemporary Capitalism: The Embeddedness of Institutions* (Cambridge: Cambridge University Press, 1997).

11. See also Kieron Flanagan and Elvira Uyarra, 'Four dangers in innovation policy studies – and how to avoid them', *Industry and Innovation* 23(2) (2016): 177–88.

12. We differ here from institutional entrepreneurship literature as we do not focus only on organised interests (Paul Dimaggio, 'Interest and agency in institutional theory', in *Institutional Patterns and Organizations: Culture and Environment*, ed. Lynne Zucker (Cambridge, MA: Ballinger, 1988): 3–21; Bernard Leca, Julie Battilana and Eva Boxenbaum, *Agency and Institutions: A Review of Institutional Entrepreneurship* (Cambridge, MA: Harvard Business School, 2008)); charismatic networks are indeed based on individuals.

13. Albert O. Hirschman, 'The principle of the hiding hand', *National Affairs* 6 (Winter) (1967): 10–23.

14. Henry Mintzberg, *Mintzberg on Management: Inside Our Strange World of Organizations* (New York: Simon & Schuster, 1989).

15. Ibid., 198.

16. For example, innovative (and to a lesser extent entrepreneurial) configurations – being most flexible and ad hoc – can be linked or integrated (temporarily

and before they become assimilated) into different organisational configurations. Machine bureaucracies where policy and implementation are often separated can be (temporarily) made more dynamic by shifting roles; that is, policy formulators implement and implementers formulate policies. In the same way, innovative configurations can be made to work on behalf of other organisation or policy domains; that is, operating 'adhocracies' (or operating innovative configurations) concentrate on 'contract' project work while administrative adhocracies (or administrative innovative configurations) work for their own internal projects/goals (Mintzberg, *Mintzberg on Management*).

17. Christopher Pollitt and Geert Bouckaert, *Public Management Reform: A Comparative Analysis – New Public Management, Governance, and the Neo-Weberian State* (Oxford: Oxford University Press, 2011). See also Erkki Karo and Rainer Kattel, 'Innovation and the state: towards an evolutionary theory of policy capacity', in *Policy Capacity and Governance*, ed. Xun Wu, Michael Howlett and M. Ramesh (London: Palgrave Macmillan, 2018): 123–50, where we unpack these routines in more detail.

18. Bruno Amable, 'Institutional complementarities in the dynamic comparative analysis of capitalism', *Journal of Institutional Economics* 12(1) (2016): 79–103; Martin Schneider and Mihai Paunescu, 'Changing varieties of capitalism and revealed comparative advantages from 1990 to 2005: a test of the Hall and Soskice claims', *Socio-Economic Review* 10(4) (2012): 731–53.

19. Christopher Hood, 'A public management for all seasons?', *Public Administration* 69(1) (1991): 3–19; Wolfgang Drechsler, 'The rise and demise of the New Public Management', *Post-autistic Economics Review* 33 (2005): 17–28.

20. Roy Rothwell and Walter Zegveld, *Industrial Innovation and Public Policy: Preparing for the 1980s and 1990s* (London: Pinter, 1981); Gerald Sweeney, 'Introduction', in *Innovation Policies: An International Perspective*, ed. Gerald Sweeney (London: Pinter, 1985): vii–x; Hood, 'A public management for all seasons?', 3–19.

21. Wolfgang Drechsler, 'The rise and demise of the New Public Management: lessons and opportunities for South East Europe', *Uprava – Administration* 7(3) (2009): 7–27.

22. Klaus König, 'Entrepreneurial management or executive administration: the perspective of classical public administration', in *Public Management and Administrative Reform in Western Europe*, ed. Walter Kickert (Cheltenham: Elgar, 1997): 214; Christopher Hood and Ruth Dixon, 'What we have to show for 30 years of New Public Management: higher costs, more complaints', *Governance* 28(3) (2015): 265–7.

23. Hans van Mierlo, 'Lessons from the experience of OECD countries', in *Innovations in Public Management: Perspectives from East and West Europe*, ed. Tony Verheijen and David Coombes (Cheltenham: Elgar, 1998): 401.

24. Drechsler, 'The rise and demise of the New Public Management', *Post-autistic Economics Review*, 17–28.

25. Victor Lapuente and Steven Van de Walle, 'The effects of New Public Management on the quality of public services', *Governance* 33(3) (2020): 461–75.

26. However, the problem with this statement is that these three themes are designated as the 'main' ones, although during the heyday of NPM these were not really, theoretically or practically, its core features.

27. Pollitt and Bouckaert, *Public Management Reform*; see also Wolfgang Drechsler and Rainer Kattel, 'Conclusion: towards the Neo-Weberian State? Perhaps, but certainly adieu, NPM!', *NISPAcee Journal of Public Administration and Policy* 1(2) (2009): 95–9.

28. Ernst Cassirer, 'Axel Hägerström: eine Studie zur schwedischen Philosophie der Gegenwart', *Göterborgs Högskolas Årsskrift* 45(1) (1939): 1–20; see Wolfgang Drechsler, 'On the possibility of quantitative-mathematical social science, chiefly economics: some preliminary considerations', *Journal of Economic Studies* 27(4/5) (2000): 246–59.

29. Juraj Nemec, Wolfgang Drechsler and György Hajnal, 'Public policy during COVID-19: challenges for public administration and policy research in Central and Eastern Europe', *NISPAcee Journal of Public Administration and Policy* 12(2) (2020/21): 11–22.

30. Charles A. O'Reilly III and Michael L. Tushman, 'Ambidexterity as a dynamic capability: resolving the innovator's dilemma', *Research in Organizational Behavior* 28 (2008): 185–206.

31. For the US, see Fred Block and Matthew Keller, eds, *State of Innovation: The US Government's Role in Technology Development* (London: Routledge, 2015); Linda Weiss, *America Inc.? Innovation and Enterprise in the National Security State* (Ithaca: Cornell University Press, 2014). For comparative studies, see Richard Nelson, ed., *National Innovation Systems: A Comparative Analysis* (Oxford: Oxford University Press, 1993); Charles Edquist and Leif Hommen, *Small Country Innovation Systems: Globalization, Change and Policy in Asia and Europe* (Cheltenham: Elgar, 2009).

32. See most recently Defny Holidin, 'Persistent developmental limits to devising policy innovation for innovation policies in emerging economies', *Policy & Governance Review* 6(1) (2022): 1–16.

33. Alvin M. Weinberg, *Reflections on Big Science* (Oxford: Pergamon Press, 1967).

4 AGILE STABILITY IN THE POST-SECOND WORLD WAR ERA

1. Vannevar Bush, *Science, the Endless Frontier: Report to the President on a Program for Postwar Scientific Research* (Washington, DC: Office of Scientific Research and Development, 1945).

2. Daniel Sarewitz, 'Saving science', *New Atlantis* 49 (Spring/Summer) (2016): 4–40.

3. 'Innovation and the invisible hand of government', in *State of Innovation: The US Government's Role in Technology Development*, ed. Fred Block and Matthew Keller (London: Routledge, 2015): 1–26.

4. Linda Weiss, *America Inc.? Innovation and Enterprise in the National Security State* (Ithaca: Cornell University Press, 2014): 2.

5. Richard Nelson, *The Moon and the Ghetto: An Essay on Public Policy Analysis* (New York: W.W. Norton, 1977); 'The Moon and the Ghetto revisited', *Science and Public Policy* 38(9) (2011): 681–90.

6. David C. Mowery and Nathan Rosenberg, *Paths of Innovation: Technological Change in 20th-Century America* (Cambridge: Cambridge University Press, 1999): 6.

7. Weiss, *America Inc.?*

8. Sarewitz, 'Saving science'.
9. Weiss, *America Inc.?*, 29.
10. Ibid.
11. As of 2009, there were thirty-nine of the federal labs (formally known as Federally Funded Research and Development Centers) 'deploying a budget of US$15.2 billion to develop and commercialise innovations in everything from semiconductors and specialty materials to nanotechnology, robotics, and advanced batteries' (Weiss, *America Inc.?*, 159–60). While the German Fraunhofer Society consists of public labs focusing on applied research for commercial application (including reliance on commercial co-financing), the US labs are not public institutions but hybrids that are publicly funded and privately managed with a key focus on the mission of the funding agency (mostly DoE and DoD) with growing emphasis on commercial diffusion.
12. The dichotomy was originally proposed by Henry Ergas, *Does Technology Policy Matter?* (Brussels: Centre for European Policy Studies, 1986): 1–68.
13. Weiss, *America Inc.?*, 4.
14. Ibid., 25.
15. Ibid., 28.
16. Ibid., 32.
17. Ibid., 55–7: as independently owned and run-for-profit investment companies that merge public and private resources, SBICs were, until the 1980s, the main source of US venture funding and rule setting in the industry. The industry saw an increase of private VC funds only in 1980s when the US legislation allowed pension funds to invest in venture capital.
18. Ibid.
19. Annie Jacobsen, *The Pentagon's Brain: An Uncensored History of DARPA, America's Top-Secret Military Research Agency* (Hachette UK, 2015), Kindle edition.
20. William Bonvillian, 'DARPA and its ARPA-E and IARPA clones: a unique innovation organization model', *Industrial and Corporate Change* 27(5) (2018): 897–914.
21. Jacobsen, *The Pentagon's Brain*, Kindle location 2983.
22. Ibid.
23. 'DARPA and its ARPA-E and IARPA clones', 904–5.
24. See also studies by Dan Breznitz, Darius Ornston and Steven Samford, 'Mission critical: the ends, means, and design of innovation agencies', *Industrial and Corporate Change* 27(5) (2018): 883–96; Veiko Lember, Rainer Kattel and Piret Tõnurist, 'Technological capacity in the public sector: the case of Estonia', *International Review of Administrative Sciences* 84(2) (2018): 214–30; Ines Mergel, 'Agile innovation management in government: a research agenda', *Government Information Quarterly* 33(3) (2016): 516–23.
25. Dan Breznitz and Darius Ornston, 'The politics of partial success: fostering innovation in innovation policy in an era of heightened public scrutiny', *Socio-Economic Review* 16(4) (2018): 721–41.
26. Peter Tindemans, 'Post-war research, education and innovation policy-making in Europe', in *European Science and Technology Policy: Towards Integration or Fragmentation*, ed. Henri Delanghe, Ugur Muldur and Luc Soete (Cheltenham: Elgar, 2009): 4.

27. Ibid., 22.
28. John Krige, *American Hegemony and the Postwar Reconstruction of Science in Europe* (Cambridge, MA: MIT Press, 2008).
29. Ibid., 75–76, for how the private foundations – from Rockefeller to Ford – were more flexible and generous in financing European S&T reconstruction than the Marshall Plan rules.
30. John Peterson and Margaret Sharp, *Technology Policy in the European Union* (London: Macmillan, 1998): 28.
31. Pierre Papon, 'Intergovernmental cooperation in the making of European research', in *European Science and Technology Policy: Towards Integration or Fragmentation*, ed. Henri Delanghe, Ugur Muldur and Luc Soete (Cheltenham: Elgar, 2009): 24.
32. Ibid.
33. Ergas, *Does Technology Policy Matter?*
34. Andrew Schonfield, *Modern Capitalism: The Changing Balance of Public and Private Power* (Oxford: Oxford University Press, 1966).
35. Ibid., 128.
36. Ibid., 105.
37. Ibid., 111.
38. Ibid., 98.
39. Ergas, *Does Technology Policy Matter?*
40. See Gunnar Trumbull, *Silicon and the State: French Innovation Policy in the Internet Age* (Washington, DC: Brookings Institution Press, 2004).
41. Ergas, *Does Technology Policy Matter?*, 18.
42. Guido Reger and Stefan Kuhlmann, *European Technology Policy in Germany: The Impact of European Community Policies upon Science and Technology in Germany* (Heidelberg: Physica, 1995): 14.
43. Ibid.
44. Schonfield, *Modern Capitalism*.
45. Ibid., 141, also 133.
46. Ibid., 374–5; Giovanni Dosi, *Technical Change and Survival: Europe's Semiconductor Industry*, Sussex European Papers No. 9 (1981).
47. 'The developmental state: Israel, South Korea, and Taiwan compared', *Studies in Comparative International Development* 33(1) (1998): 65–93.
48. Stephan Haggard, *Pathways from the Periphery: The Politics of Growth in the Newly Industrializing Countries* (Ithaca: Cornell University Press, 1990); Joseph Wong, *Betting on Biotech: Innovation and the Limits of Asia's Developmental State* (Ithaca: Cornell University Press, 2011); Elizabeth Thurbon, *Developmental Mindset: The Revival of Financial Activism in South Korea* (Ithaca: Cornell University Press, 2016).
49. Haggard, *Pathways from the Periphery*; Karl Fields, 'Not of a piece: developmental states, industrial policy, and evolving patterns of capitalism in Japan, Korea, and Taiwan', in *East Asian Capitalism: Diversity, Continuity, and Change*, ed. Andrew Walter and Xiaoke Zhang (Oxford: Oxford University Press, 2012): 46–67; Yin-Wah Chu, ed., *The Asian Developmental State: Reexaminations and New Departures* (New York: Palgrave Macmillan, 2016).

50. Chalmers Johnson, *MITI and the Japanese Miracle: The Growth of Industrial Policy, 1925–1975* (Stanford: Stanford University Press, 1982); Chu, *The Asian Developmental State*; Thurbon, *Developmental Mindset*.

51. In addition, Japan was the one Confucian country in which Confucianism specifically was not a label for local principles but a consciously imported cultural technique during the pre-Meiji Edo period, the Shogunate. But even then, contrary to all other Confucian systems, in spite of a Confucian academy, intellectual elite and so on, being a Confucian scholar did not make one a bureaucrat or candidate but more of a free-floating intellectual – the recruitment pools for civil servants, or civil servant elites, were the Samurai class, on the upper end the Daimyos, and even the Imperial court aristocracy in Kyoto. And while the first and last group are overrepresented in Japanese bureaucracy even today, there was and is no continuity into the Meiji and post-Meiji civil service from these positions, and, again, even if there was, this would not imply any Confucian legacy. See Wolfgang Drechsler, 'Beyond the Western paradigm: Confucian public administration', in *Public Policy in the 'Asian Century': Concepts, Cases and Futures*, ed. Sara Bice, Avery Poole and Helen Sullivan (Basingstoke: Palgrave Macmillan, 2018): 19–40.

52. Johnson, *MITI and the Japanese Miracle*; Gregory W. Noble, *Collective Action in East Asia* (Ithaca: Cornell University Press, 1999).

53. Hiroko Shimada Logie, 'The Japanese civil service: paradox of a reform driven by but ignoring emotion', *Haldduskultuur* 21(2) (2021): 64–79.

54. Thurbon, *Developmental Mindset*.

55. Yongsoo Hwang, 'Korean STI policies in the institution building phase', *STI Policy Review* 2(4) (2011): 9–18.

56. Ibid., 13.

57. Jieun Seong, 'Evolution and features of the Korean science and technology policy coordination system', *STI Policy Review* 2(1) (2011): 1–12.

58. Hwang, 'Korean STI policies in the institution building phase'; Manyong Moon, 'The creation of government-supported research institutes during the Park Chung-hee era', *STI Policy Review* 2(2) (2011): 55–67.

59. Hwang, 'Korean STI policies in the institution building phase', 13.

60. Ibid., 15

61. Moon, 'The creation of government-supported research institutes during the Park Chung-hee era', 55–65.

62. Hwang, 'Korean STI policies in the institution building phase', 15.

63. Moon, 'The creation of government-supported research institutes during the Park Chung-hee era', 57.

64. What these agencies could coordinate in terms of functions differed greatly between economies; that is Japanese and South Korean nodal agencies could use public finances (policy loans, etc.) for the purposes of industrialisation and technological development (as well as import and export controls, etc.), while the Taiwanese had experienced the political and economic backlash from macroeconomic stability, so were thus more wary of public financial instabilities and therefore insulated monetary policy institutions and instruments from industrial and innovation policy and bureaucrats.

5 HYBRIDISATION OF INNOVATION BUREAUCRACIES IN THE 1970S AND 1980S

1. OECD, *Science and Growth: A New Perspective – Report of the Secretary General's Ad Hoc Group on New Concepts of Science Policy* (Paris: OECD Publishing, 1971).
2. Ibid., 55; see also Richard Nelson, *The Moon and the Ghetto: An Essay on Public Policy Analysis* (New York: W.W. Norton, 1977).
3. B. Guy Peters and Donald Savoie, 'Civil service reform: misdiagnosing the patient', *Public Administration Review* 54(5) (1994): 418–25.
4. OECD, *Science and Growth*, 61.
5. Linda Weiss, *America Inc.? Innovation and Enterprise in the National Security State* (Ithaca: Cornell University Press, 2014).
6. Stanford Research Institute International functions as an innovation hybrid that is formally independent but strongly reliant on NSS/federal funding, as well as collaboration with universities and national labs, for implementing different contract-based research projects with specifically articulated demand and project goals (such as the DARPA-funded Cognitive Agent that Learns and Organizes, which was spun out of what is now known as the Apple iPhone SIRI application) (see Weiss, *America Inc.?*, 157–9).
7. Weiss, *America Inc.?*, 36.
8. In addition to the Offset Strategy as the key NSS narrative, Ronald Reagan came to power (in 1981) under a double squeeze to cut down government and respond to the USSR in Afghanistan (as well as the rise of Japan and the DRAM dependency crisis). Under his new mission, the Strategic Defense Initiative, which never fully materialised and was nicknamed Star Wars (as the goal was to build a shield in space to protect the US from USSR missiles), the Pentagon got its own DARPA clone. The Strategic Defense Initiative Organization focused on sensors, lasers, space propulsion, ultra-high-speed computing, advanced space materials and so on, as well as Office of Technology Applications to commercialise its products (see Weiss, *America Inc.?*, 38, 41).
9. 'Swimming against the current: the rise of a hidden developmental state in the United States', *Politics & Society* 36(2) (2008): 178.
10. Carlota Perez, *Technological Revolutions and Financial Capital: The Dynamics of Bubbles and Golden Ages* (Cheltenham: Elgar, 2002).
11. Bhaven Sampat, 'Mission-oriented biomedical research at the NIH', *Research Policy* 41(10) (2012): 1729–41.
12. 'Swimming against the current', 178.
13. Block, 'Swimming against the current', 169–206; 'Innovation and the invisible hand of government', in *State of Innovation: The US Government's Role in Technology Development,* ed. Fred Block and Matthew Keller (London: Routledge, 2015): 1–26.
14. Matthew Keller and Fred Block, 'Explaining the transformation in the US innovation system: the impact of a small government program', *Socio-Economic Review* 11(4) (2013): 640.
15. Weiss, *America Inc.?*
16. In the health domain, as the developments were somewhat further away from the commercialisation frontier, the Human Genome Project (from 1990 to

2003) was developed first as an international research collaboration funded by public agencies (in the US by the DoE and NIH).

17. Block, 'Swimming against the current', 182.
18. Scott Callon, *Divided Sun: MITI and the Breakdown of Japanese High-Tech Industrial Policy, 1975–1993* (Stanford: Stanford University Press, 1995).
19. Kiyonori Sakakibara, *From Imitation to Innovation: The Very Large Scale Integrated (VLSI) Semiconductor Project in Japan* (Cambridge, MA: MIT Press, 1983), http://hdl.handle.net/1721.1/47985.
20. Ibid.
21. Callon, *Divided Sun*.
22. Robert Wade, *Governing the Market: Economic Theory and the Role of Government in East Asian Industrialization* (Princeton: Princeton University Press, 1990).
23. Elizabeth Thurbon, *Developmental Mindset: The Revival of Financial Activism in South Korea* (Ithaca: Cornell University Press, 2016).
24. Sungjoo Hong, 'Korean STI policies in technology catching-up stage', *STI Policy Review* 2(4) (2011): 19–28.
25. Yongsuk Jang, 'Evolution of Korean STI policies', *STI Policy Review* 2(4) (2011): 1–8.
26. Hong, 'Korean STI policies in technology catching-up stage'.
27. Jang, 'Evolution of Korean STI policies'.
28. See John Mathews, 'The origins and dynamics of Taiwan's R&D consortia', *Research Policy* 31(4) (2002): 633–51.
29. Michelle Hsieh, 'Embedding the economy: the state and export-led development in Taiwan', in *The Asian Developmental State: Reexaminations and New Departures*, ed. Yin-Wah Chu (New York: Palgrave Macmillan, 2016): Kindle edition, chapter 4.
30. J. Meghan Greene, *The Origins of the Developmental State in Taiwan: Science Policy and the Quest for Modernization* (Cambridge, MA: Harvard University Press, 2008).
31. Luc Soete, 'From industrial to innovation policy', *Journal of Industry, Competition and Trade* 7(3–4) (2007): 273.
32. Peter Tindemans, 'Post-war research, education and innovation policy-making in Europe', in *European Science and Technology Policy: Towards Integration or Fragmentation*, ed. Henri Delanghe, Ugur Muldur and Luc Soete (Cheltenham: Elgar, 2009), 2.
33. *When Small States Make Big Leaps: Institutional Innovation and High-Tech Competition in Western Europe* (Ithaca: Cornell University Press, 2012).
34. John Peterson and Margaret Sharp, *Technology Policy in the European Union* (London: Macmillan, 1998); Tindemans, 'Post-war research, education and innovation policy-making in Europe'; Pierre Papon, 'Intergovernmental co-operation in the making of European research', in *European Science and Technology Policy: Towards Integration or Fragmentation*, ed. Henri Delanghe, Ugur Muldur and Luc Soete (Cheltenham: Elgar, 2009): 24–43.
35. Peterson and Sharp, *Technology Policy in the European Union*, 5–6.
36. Tindemans, 'Post-war research, education and innovation policy-making in Europe', 16–17.

37. EUREKA Secretariat (1985) cited in Peterson and Sharp, *Technology Policy in the European Union*, 7.
38. Peterson and Sharp, *Technology Policy in the European Union*, 7–8.
39. Papon, 'Intergovernmental cooperation in the making of European research', 38.
40. OECD, *The Research System: Comparative Survey of the Organization and Financing of Fundamental Research* (Paris: OECD Publishing, 1972): 18–19.
41. Guido Reger and Stefan Kuhlmann, *European Technology Policy in Germany: The Impact of European Community Policies upon Science and Technology in Germany* (Heidelberg: Physica, 1995): 14.
42. Reger and Kuhlmann, *European Technology Policy in Germany*, 13–14.
43. Luca Guzzetti, 'The "European research area" idea in the history of community policy-making', in *European Science and Technology Policy: Towards Integration or Fragmentation*, ed. Henri Delanghe, Ugur Muldur and Luc Soete (Cheltenham: Elgar, 2009): 64–77.
44. David Osborne and Ted Gaebler, *Reinventing Government: How the Entrepreneurial Spirit Is Transforming the Public Sector* (New York: Addison-Wesley, 1992).

6 NEOLIBERALISM, INNOVATION BUREAUCRACIES AND THE REINVENTION OF MISSIONS

1. Mark Taylor, *The Politics of Innovation: Why Some Countries Are Better Than Others at Science and Technology* (Oxford: Oxford University Press, 2016).
2. Francis Fukuyama, 'The end of history?', *National Interest* 16 (1989): 3–18.
3. David Mowery and Bhaven Sampat, 'Universities in national innovation systems', in *The Oxford Handbook of Innovation*, ed. Jan Fagerberg and David Mowery (Oxford: Oxford University Press, 2006).
4. Slavo Radošević, 'Policies for promoting technological catch up: a post-Washington approach', *International Journal of Institutions and Economies* 1(1) (2009): 23–52; Erkki Karo and Rainer Kattel, 'The copying paradox: why converging policies but diverging capacities for development in Eastern European innovation systems?', *International Journal of Institutions and Economies* 2(2) (2009): 167–216.
5. Ibid.
6. Linda Weiss, *America Inc.? Innovation and Enterprise in the National Security State* (Ithaca: Cornell University Press, 2014).
7. Fred Block, 'Swimming against the current: the rise of a hidden developmental state in the United States', *Politics & Society* 36(2) (2008): 169–206; 'Innovation and the invisible hand of government', in *State of Innovation: The US Government's Role in Technology Development,* ed. Fred Block and Matthew Keller (London: Routledge, 2015): 1–26.
8. Weiss, *America Inc.?*, 66.
9. Ibid., 67.
10. See also Block, 'Swimming against the current', on the idea of the 'hidden developmental state'.

11. Weiss, *America Inc.?*, 164.
12. Block, 'Innovation and the invisible hand of government', 1–26.
13. Mariana Mazzucato and Douglas Robinson, 'Co-creating and directing innovation ecosystems? NASA's changing approach to public-private partnerships in low-earth orbit', *Technological Forecasting and Social Change* 136 (2018): 166–77.
14. Luca Guzzetti, 'The "European research area" idea in the history of community policy-making', in *European Science and Technology Policy: Towards Integration or Fragmentation*, ed. Henri Delanghe, Ugur Muldur and Luc Soete (Cheltenham: Elgar, 2009): 67–8.
15. John Peterson and Margaret Sharp, *Technology Policy in the European Union* (London: Macmillan, 1998): 15.
16. Henri Delanghe, Ugur Muldur and Luc Soete, *European Science and Technology Policy: Towards Integration or Fragmentation* (Cheltenham: Elgar, 2009): 354.
17. *When Small States Make Big Leaps: Institutional Innovation and High-Tech Competition in Western Europe* (Ithaca: Cornell University Press, 2012).
18. Dorothee Bohle and Béla Greskovits, *Capitalist Diversity on Europe's Periphery* (Ithaca: Cornell University Press, 2012); Karo and Rainer, 'The copying paradox', 167; Erkki Karo, 'The evolution of innovation policy governance systems and policy capacities in the Baltic States', *Journal of Baltic Studies* 42(4) (2011): 511–36.
19. Dan Breznitz and Darius Ornston, 'The revolutionary power of peripheral agencies: explaining radical policy innovation in Finland and Israel', *Comparative Political Studies* 46(10) (2013): 1219–45.
20. Ibid.; Dan Breznitz and Darius Ornston, 'The politics of partial success: fostering innovation in innovation policy in an era of heightened public scrutiny', *Socio-Economic Review* 16(4) (2018): 721–41.
21. OECD, *Governance of Innovation Systems* (Paris: OECD Publishing, 2005).
22. Rebecca Boden et al., 'Men in white coats . . . men in grey suits', *Accounting, Auditing & Accountability Journal* 11(3) (1998): 267–91; Margit Suurna and Rainer Kattel, 'Europeanization of innovation policy in Central and Eastern Europe', *Science and Public Policy* 37(9) (2010): 646–64; Barry Bozeman and Daniel Sarewitz, 'Public value mapping and science policy evaluation', *Minerva* 49(1) (2011): 1–23; Barry Bozeman and Jan Youtie, 'Robotic bureaucracy: administrative burden and red tape in university research', *Public Administration Review* 80(1) (2020): 157–62.
23. See Gary Gereffi, 'Global value chains in a post-Washington Consensus world', *Review of International Political Economy* 21(1) (2014): 9–37.
24. Lennart Stenberg and Hiroshi Nagano, 'Priority setting in Japanese research and innovation policy', *Vinnova Analysis* 23 (2009).
25. Jeong Hyop Lee, 'Issues and policies in the STI leadership phase', *STI Policy Review* 2(4) (2011): 29–38.
26. MOST (Ministry of Science and Technology), *Policy Overview Booklet* (Taipei: Ministry of Science and Technology, 2014).
27. On Japan, see Stenberg and Nagano, 'Priority setting in Japanese research and innovation policy'; on South Korea, see Moonjung Choi and Han-Lim Choi, 'Foresight for science and technology priority setting in Korea', *Foresight and STI Governance* 9(3) (2015): 54–67.

28. Heizō Takenaka, *The Structural Reforms of the Koizumi Cabinet: An Insider's Account of the Economic Revival of Japan* (Tokyo: Nikkei Publishing, 2008).
29. See also Erkki Karo, 'Mission-oriented innovation policies and bureaucracies in East Asia', *Industrial and Corporate Change* 27(5) (2018): 867–81.
30. Sungjoo Hong, 'Korean STI policies in technology catching-up stage', *STI Policy Review* 2(4) (2011): 19–28; Jieun Seong, 'Evolution and features of the Korean science and technology policy coordination system', *STI Policy Review* 2(1) (2011): 1–12.
31. Jieun Seong and Wichin Song, 'Assessment of innovation policy coordination through Korean Office of Science, Technology and Innovation (OSTI)', *STI Policy Review* 4(2) (2014): 96–112.
32. Karo, 'Mission-oriented innovation policies and bureaucracies in East Asia', 867–81.
33. Johan Schot and W. Edward Steinmueller, 'Three frames for innovation policy: R&D, systems of innovation and transformative change', *Research Policy* 47(9) (2018): 1554–67; Susana Borrás and Jakob Edler, 'The roles of the state in the governance of socio-technical systems' transformation', *Research Policy* 49 (2020): 103971.
34. Weiss, *America Inc.?*, 125.
35. Weiss, *America Inc.?*, 126.
36. Weiss, *America Inc.?*, 127.
37. See William Bonvillian and Richard Van Atta, 'ARPA-E and DARPA: applying the DARPA model to energy innovation', *Journal of Technology Transfer* 36(5) (2011): 469–513; William Bonvillian, 'DARPA and its ARPA-E and IARPA clones: a unique innovation organization model', *Industrial and Corporate Change* 27(5) (2018): 897–914.
38. 'DARPA and its ARPA-E and IARPA clones', 897–914.
39. Bonvillian, 'DARPA and its ARPA-E and IARPA clones', 909.
40. The origins of this reverse approach in the energy sector can be traced back to 1986 when the Arch Development Corporation was established to commercialise patented inventions from the Argonne National Laboratory in collaboration with the University of Chicago. It was created in the context of the Reagan government's cut-back pressures, as well as a growing expectation that inventions and the know-how of national labs should be put to broader use (see Weiss, *America Inc.?*, 70, 71).
41. National Economic Council and Office of Science and Technology Policy, *A Strategy for American Innovation 2015* (Washington, DC: The White House, 2015), 9, https://obamawhitehouse.archives.gov/sites/default/files/strategy_for_american_innovation_october_2015.pdf.
42. Ines Mergel, 'Agile innovation management in government: a research agenda', *Government Information Quarterly* 33(3) (2016): 516–23.
43. See https://www.wired.com/2017/01/race-pass-obamas-last-law-save-tech-dc/.
44. See the excellent case studies in Michael Lewis, *The Fifth Risk: Undoing Democracy* (London: Penguin, 2018).
45. Delanghe et al., *European Science and Technology Policy*, 354.
46. Guzzetti, 'The "European research area" idea in the history of community policy-making', 75.

47. Ibid.
48. Charles F. Sabel and Jonathan Zeitlin, eds, *Experimentalist Governance in the European Union: Towards a New Architecture* (Oxford: Oxford University Press, 2010).
49. Mariana Mazzucato, 'Mission oriented innovation policies: challenges and opportunities', *Industrial and Corporate Change* 27(5) (2018): 803–15; Florian Wittmann et al., *Developing a Typology for Mission-Oriented Innovation Policies*, Working Paper No. 64 (Fraunhofer ISI Discussion Papers – Innovation Systems and Policy Analysis, 2020); OECD, *The Design and Implementation of Mission-Oriented Innovation Policies: A New Systemic Policy Approach to Address Societal Challenges*, OECD Science, Technology and Industry Policy Papers No. 100 (Paris: OECD Publishing, 2021).
50. These areas are: cancer; adaptation to climate change including societal transformation; healthy oceans, seas, coastal and inland waters; climate-neutral and smart cities; and soil health and food.
51. There have been various attempts trying to categorise missions in the European and OECD context, for example Wittmann et al., *Developing a Typology for Mission-oriented Innovation Policies*, and OECD, *The Design and Implementation of Mission-Oriented Innovation Policies*.
52. On smart specialisation as a form of mission-oriented policies in European regions, see Dominique Foray, 'Smart specialization strategies as a case of mission-oriented policy: a case study on the emergence of new policy practices', *Industrial and Corporate Change* 27(5) (2018): 817–32.
53. See https://www.climate-kic.org/programmes/deep-demonstrations/.
54. The key analytical and legislative documents can be found here: https://www.bmwi.de/Redaktion/DE/Artikel/Wirtschaft/kohleausstieg-und-strukturwandel.html.
55. Matthijs Jannsen, *Post-commencement Analysis of the Dutch 'Mission-Oriented Topsector and Innovation Policy' Strategy*, Mission-Oriented Policy Observatory, Universiteit Utrecht (2020), https://www.uu.nl/sites/default/files/Post-commencement%20analysis%20of%20the%20Dutch%20Mission-oriented%20Topsector%20and%20Innovation%20Policy.pdf.
56. https://www.elysee.fr/en/emmanuel-macron/2017/09/26/president-macron-gives-speech-on-new-initiative-for-europe.
57. https://eic.ec.europa.eu/index_en.
58. https://www.jedi.foundation.
59. The policy statement on ARIA creation is available here: https://www.gov.uk/government/publications/advanced-research-and-invention-agency-aria-statement-of-policy-intent/advanced-research-and-invention-agency-aria-policy-statement.
60. See Government of Japan, *Long-Term Strategic Guidelines 'Innovation 25'* (Tokyo: Government of Japan, 2007).
61. 'Priority setting in Japanese research and innovation policy', 23.
62. Ibid., 84.
63. See Government of Japan, *The New Growth Strategy 2010* (Tokyo: Government of Japan, 2010); *The Fourth Science and Technology Basic Plan 2011–2015* (Tokyo: Government of Japan, 2011).

64. Government of Japan, *Japan Revitalization Strategy 'Japan Is Back'* (Tokyo: Government of Japan, 2013).

65. Government of Japan, *The Fifth Science and Technology Basic Plan 2016–2020* (Tokyo: Government of Japan, 2016).

66. ImPACT, *Impulsing Paradigm Change Through Disruptive Technologies Program Booklet* (Tokyo: Government of Japan, 2016).

67. SIP, *Strategic Innovation Program Booklet* (Tokyo: Council of Science, Technology and Innovation, 2016)

68. See https://www8.cao.go.jp/cstp/english/moonshot/top.html.

69. See Jin-Gyu Jang, 'S&T policy directions for green growth in Korea', *STI Policy Review* 1(1) (2010): 1–22.

70. Sung-Young Kim and Elizabeth Thurbon, 'Developmental environmentalism: explaining South Korea's ambitious pursuit of green growth', *Politics & Society* 43(2) (2015): 213–40.

71. Ibid.

72. See Heejin Han, 'Korea's pursuit of low-carbon green growth: a middle-power state's dream of becoming a green pioneer', *Pacific Review* 28(5) (2015): 731–54; Jieun Seong, Wichin Song and Hongtak Lim, 'The rise of Korean innovation policy for social problem-solving: a policy niche for transition?' *STI Policy Review* 7(1) (2016): 1–16.

73. Jieun Seong, 'The green growth policy of the Lee Myungbak government', *STI Policy Review* 2(2) (2011): 11–24.

74. Seong et al., 'The rise of Korean innovation policy for social problem-solving', 5.

75. Kim and Thurbon, 'Developmental environmentalism', 213–40.

76. See more in OECD, *The Design and Implementation of Mission-Oriented Innovation Policies*, 77–9.

77. National Science Council, Executive Yuan, *National Science and Technology Development Plan 2009–2012* (Taipei: National Science Council, 2009).

78. See Kevin Rosier, Sean O'Connor and Rolando Cuevas, *Taiwan's Economy amid Political Transition*, Staff Research Report (Washington, DC: US-China Economic and Security Review Commission, 2016).

79. MOST (Ministry of Science and Technology), *National Science and Technology Development Plan 2013–2016* (Taipei: Ministry of Science and Technology, 2013).

80. MOST (Ministry of Science and Technology), *White Paper on Science and Technology 2015–2018* (Taipei: Ministry of Science and Technology, 2015).

81. Ibid., 166–70.

82. Rosier et al., *Taiwan's Economy amid Political Transition*.

83. MOST, *White Paper on Science and Technology 2015–2018*, 26–7.

84. Ibid., 110–14.

85. See https://ai.taiwan.gov.tw.

86. See https://presidential-hackathon.taiwan.gov.tw/en/.

87. Bryan Ying, 'Constitutional bar set too high to dissolve control & examination yuans', *Taiwan Times*, 29 July 2020, https://thetaiwantimes.com/constitutional-bar-set-too-high-to-dissolve-control-examination-yuans/; Wolfgang Drechsler, 'Beyond the Western paradigm: Confucian public

administration', in *Public Policy in the 'Asian Century': Concepts, Cases and Futures*, ed. Sara Bice, Avery Poole and Helen Sullivan (Basingstoke: Palgrave Macmillan, 2018): 19–40.

88. Ying, 'Constitutional bar set too high to dissolve control & examination yuans'.

89. Philippe Larrue, 'The design and implementation of mission-oriented innovation policies: a new systemic policy approach to address societal challenges', *OECD Science, Technology and Industry Policy Papers*, No. 100 (Paris: OECD, 2021).

90. Elizabeth Thurbon, *Developmental Mindset: The Revival of Financial Activism in South Korea* (Ithaca: Cornell University Press, 2016).

91. Bonvillian, 'DARPA and its ARPA-E and IARPA clones', 897–914.

92. Veiko Lember, Rainer Kattel and Tarmo Kalvet, eds, *Public Procurement, Innovation and Policy: International Perspectives* (Heidelberg: Springer, 2014).

93. Dominique Foray, *Smart Specialisation: Opportunities and Challenges for Regional Innovation Policy* (London: Routledge, 2014).

94. Swedish Presidency, *The Lund Declaration: Europe Must Focus on the Grand Challenges of Our Time*. Swedish EU Presidency (2009) Lund: Sweden.

95. Mariana Mazzucato, *The Value of Everything* (London: Penguin, 2018).

96. Sabel and Zeitlin, *Experimentalist Governance in the European Union*.

97. Andrew Massey, Editorial: 'The seamless web of circumstance', *Public Money & Management* 41 (1) (2021): 1-4, 1.

7 SUMMING UP: WILL THE NEXT DECADES BE LED BY NEO-WEBERIAN INNOVATION AGENCIES?

1. Mariana Mazzucato and Carlota Perez, 'Innovation as growth policy', in *The Triple Challenge: Europe in a New Age*, ed. Jan Fagerberg, Staffan Laestadius and Ben R. Martin (Oxford: Oxford University Press, 2015); Mariana Mazzucato, 'Mission oriented innovation policies: challenges and opportunities', *Industrial and Corporate Change* 27(5) (2018): 803–15.

2. Emanuele Campiglio et al., 'Climate change challenges for central banks and financial regulators', *Nature Climate Change* 8 (2018): 462–8.

3. Mario Cimoli et al., 'Choosing sides in the trilemma: international financial cycles and structural change in developing economies', *Economics of Innovation and New Technology* 29(7) (2020): 740–61.

4. Johan Schot and W. Edward Steinmueller, 'Three frames for innovation policy: R&D, systems of innovation and transformative change', *Research Policy* 47(9) (2018): 1554–67.

5. Mariana Mazzucato and Rainer Kattel, 'COVID-19 and public sector capacity', *Oxford Review of Economic Policy* 36(supplement 1) (2020): S256–69.

6. See https://www.ecdc.europa.eu/en/seasonal-influenza/preparedness/influenza-pandemic-preparedness-plans.

7. National Intelligence Council, *Global Trends: Paradox of Progress* (Washington, DC: NIC, 2017), https://www.dni.gov/index.php/features/1685-nic-releases-global-trends-paradox-of-progress.

8. See https://www.modernatx.com/ecosystem/strategic-collaborators/mrna-strategic-collaborators-government-organizations.
9. Mariana Mazzucato et al., *COVID-19 and the Need for Dynamic State Capabilities: An International Comparison*, UNDP-IIPP Working Paper (2021).
10. Dan Hill, *Dark Matter and Trojan Horses: A Strategic Design Vocabulary* (Moscow: Strelka Press, 2015); Christian Bason, *Leading Public Design: Discovering Human-Centred Governance* (Bristol: Policy Press, 2017); Piret Tõnurist, Rainer Kattel and Veiko Lember, 'Innovation labs in the public sector: what they are and what they do?', *Public Management Review* 19(10) (2017): 1455–79; Ines Mergel, 'Agile: A new way of governing', Medium, 17 April 2020, https://medium.com/@inesmergel/agile-a-new-way-of-governing-8e2c8f7efd1.
11. Arwin van Buuren et al., 'Improving public policy and administration: exploring the potential of design', *Policy & Politics* 48(1) (2020): 3–19, https://www.ingentaconnect.com/content/tpp/pap/2020/00000048/00000001/art00001.
12. Mazzucato and Kattel, 'COVID-19 and public sector capacity'.
13. UNDP, *Checklist for a Human Rights-Based Approach to Socio-economic Country Responses to COVID-19*, 28 July 2020, https://www.undp.org/content/undp/en/home/librarypage/democratic-governance/human_rights/checklist-for-a-human-rights-based-approach-to-socio-economic-co.html.
14. UNDP, *Do Fragile and Conflict-Affected Countries Prioritise Core Government Functions?*, 8 November 2019, https://www.undp.org/content/undp/en/home/librarypage/democratic-governance/conflict-prevention/do-fragile-and-conflict-affected-countries-prioritise-core-gover.html.
15. Mazzucato et al., *COVID-19 and the Need for Dynamic State Capabilities*.
16. Christopher Pollitt and Geert Bouckaert, *Public Management Reform: A Comparative Analysis – New Public Management, Governance, and the Neo-Weberian State* (Oxford: Oxford University Press, 2011). See Christopher Pollitt et al., 'A distinctive European model? The Neo-Weberian State', *NISPAcee Journal of Public Administration and Policy* 1(2) (special issue) (2008/09).
17. Wolfgang Drechsler and Rainer Kattel. 'Conclusion: towards the Neo-Weberian State? Perhaps, but certainly adieu, NPM!', *NISPAcee Journal of Public Administration and Policy* 1(2) (2009): 95–9; Pollitt and Bouckaert, *Public Management Reform*.
18. Tõnurist et al., 'Innovation labs in the public sector'.
19. Leonardo Burlamaqui and Jan Kregel, 'Innovation, competition and financial vulnerability in economic development', *Brazilian Journal of Political Economy* 25(2) (2005); Mariana Mazzucato and L. Randall Wray, *Financing the Capital Development of the Economy: A Keynes-Schumpeter-Minsky Synthesis*, SSRN Scholarly Paper No. ID 2603847 (Rochester, NY: Social Science Research Network, 2015).
20. Veiko Lember, Rainer Kattel and Tarmo Kalvet, eds, *Public Procurement, Innovation and Policy: International Perspectives* (Heidelberg: Springer, 2014); Mariana Mazzucato, 'From market fixing to market-creating: a new framework for innovation policy', *Industry and Innovation* 23(2) (2016): 140–56.

21. Hilary Cottam, *Radical Help: How We Can Remake the Relationships Between Us and Revolutionise the Welfare State* (London: Little, Brown, 2018); Rainer Kattel and Ville Takala, *Dynamic Capabilities in the Public Sector: The Case of the UK's Government Digital Service*, UCL Institute for Innovation and Public Purpose Working Paper Series (IIPP WP 2021/01) (2021), https://www.ucl.ac.uk/bartlett/public-purpose/publications/2021/jan/dynamic-capabilities-public-sector-case-uks-government-digital-service.
22. See: https://www.vinnova.se/en/about-us/.
23. See the co-created history of GDS: https://gds.blog.gov.uk/story/.
24. Amanda Clarke, 'Digital government units: what are they and what do they mean for digital era public management renewal?', *International Public Management Journal* (2019): 1–31.
25. Andrew Greenway et al., *Digital Transformation at Scale: Why the Strategy Is Delivery* (London: London Publishing Partnership, 2018).
26. Julian Birkinshaw and Scott Duncan, *The UK Government Digital Service* (London: London Business School, 2014).
27. Kattel and Takala, *Dynamic Capabilities in the Public Sector.*
28. Wolfgang Drechsler and Rainer Kattel, 'Debate: the developed civil servant – providing agility and stability at the same time', *Public Money & Management* 40(8) (2020): 549–51.

BIBLIOGRAPHY

Pure web-based information is not repeated here; all hyperlinks are valid as of 31 May 2022.

Acemoglu, Daron and James Robinson, *Why Nations Fail: The Origins of Power, Prosperity, and Poverty* (New York: Crown Publishing, 2012).

Adolph, Christopher, *Bankers, Bureaucrats, and Central Bank Politics: The Myth of Neutrality* (Cambridge: Cambridge University Press, 2013).

Ahrens, Joachim, *Governance and Economic Development: A Comparative Institutional Approach* (Cheltenham: Elgar, 2002).

Amable, Bruno, 'Institutional complementarities in the dynamic comparative analysis of capitalism', *Journal of Institutional Economics* 12(1) (2016): 79–103.

—, 'Institutional complementarity and diversity of social systems of innovation and production', *Review of International Political Economy* 7(4) (2000): 645–87.

—, *The Diversity of Modern Capitalism* (Oxford: Oxford University Press, 2003).

American Reinvestment and Recovery Act of 2009, Public Law No. 111-5, https://www.congress.gov/bill/111th-congress/house-bill/1/text.

Amsden, Alice, *Asia's Next Giant: South Korea and Late Industrialization* (Oxford: Oxford University Press, 1989).

Andersen, Esben, *Schumpeter's Evolutionary Economics: A Theoretical, Historical and Statistical Analysis of the Engine of Capitalism* (London: Anthem, 2009).

Appelbaum, Richard, Cong Cao, Xueying Han, Rachel Parker and Denis Simon, *Innovation in China: Challenging the Global Science and Technology System* (Cambridge: Polity Press, 2018).

Arthur, W. Brian, *Increasing Returns and Path Dependence in the Economy* (Ann Arbor: University of Michigan Press, 1994).

Avnimelech, Gil and Morris Teubal, 'Evolutionary targeting', *Journal of Evolutionary Economics* 18(2) (2008): 151–66.

Bason, Christian, *Leading Public Design: Discovering Human-Centred Governance* (Bristol: Policy Press, 2017).

BIBLIOGRAPHY

Becker, Markus, ed., *Handbook of Organizational Routines* (Cheltenham: Elgar, 2008).

Becker, Selwyn and Thomas Whisler, 'The innovative organization: a selective view of current theory and research', *Journal of Business* 40(4) (1967): 462–9.

Bennet, James, 'We need an energy miracle', interview with Bill Gates, *The Atlantic*, November 2015, https://www.theatlantic.com/magazine/archive/2015/11/we-need-an-energy-miracle/407881/.

Birkinshaw, Julian and Scott Duncan, *The UK Government Digital Service* (London: London Business School, 2014).

Block, Fred, 'Innovation and the invisible hand of government', in *State of Innovation: The US Government's Role in Technology Development,* ed. Fred Block and Matthew Keller (London: Routledge, 2015): 1–26.

—, 'Swimming against the current: the rise of a hidden developmental state in the United States', *Politics & Society* 36(2) (2008): 169–206.

Block, Fred and Matthew Keller, eds, *State of Innovation: The US Government's Role in Technology Development* (Boulder: Paradigm, 2011).

—, *State of Innovation: The US Government's Role in Technology Development* (London: Routledge, 2015).

Boden, Rebecca, Philip Gummett, Deborah Cox and Kate Barker, 'Men in white coats . . . men in grey suits', *Accounting, Auditing & Accountability Journal* 11(3) (1998): 267–91.

Bohle, Dorothee and Béla Greskovits, *Capitalist Diversity on Europe's Periphery* (Ithaca: Cornell University Press, 2012).

Bonvillian, William, 'DARPA and its ARPA-E and IARPA clones: a unique innovation organization model', *Industrial and Corporate Change* 27(5) (2018): 897–914.

Bonvillian, William and Charles Weiss, *Technological Innovation in Legacy Sectors* (Oxford: Oxford University Press, 2015).

Bonvillian, William and Richard Van Atta, 'ARPA-E and DARPA: applying the DARPA model to energy innovation', *Journal of Technology Transfer* 36(5) (2011): 469–513.

Borrás, Susana and Jakob Edler, 'The roles of the state in the governance of socio-technical systems' transformation', *Research Policy* 49 (2020).

Bosley, Sarah and Robert Booth, 'What is No 10's "moonshot" Covid testing plan and is it feasible?', the *Guardian*, 9 September 2020, https://www.theguardian.com/world/2020/sep/09/what-is-no-10s-moonshot-covid-testing-plan-and-is-it-feasible.

Bouckaert, Geert, Davide Galli, Sabine Kuhlmann, Renate Reiter and Steven Van Hecke, 'European coronationalism? A hot spot governing a pandemic crisis', *Public Administration Review* 80(5) (2020): 765–73.

Bozeman, Barry and Daniel Sarewitz, 'Public value mapping and science policy evaluation', *Minerva* 49(1) (2011): 1–23.

Bozeman, Barry and Jan Youtie, 'Robotic bureaucracy: administrative burden and red tape in university research', *Public Administration Review* 80(1) (2020): 157–62.

Breznitz, Dan, *Innovation and the State: Political Choices and Strategies for Growth in Israel, Taiwan and Ireland* (New Haven: Yale University Press, 2007).

—, *Innovation in Real Places: Strategies for Prosperity in an Unforgiving World* (New York: Oxford University Press, 2021).

Breznitz, Dan and Darius Ornston, 'The politics of partial success: fostering inno-vation in innovation policy in an era of heightened public scrutiny', *Socio-Economic Review* 16(4) (2018): 721–41.

—, 'The revolutionary power of peripheral agencies: explaining radical policy innovation in Finland and Israel', *Comparative Political Studies* 46(10) (2013): 1219–45.

Breznitz, Dan and Michael Murphree, *Run of the Red Queen: Government, Innovation, Globalization, and Economic Growth in China* (New Haven: Yale University Press, 2011).

Breznitz, Dan, Darius Ornston and Steven Samford, 'Mission critical: the ends, means, and design of innovation agencies', *Industrial and Corporate Change* 27(5) (2018): 883–96.

Burlamaqui, Leonardo and Jan Kregel, 'Innovation, competition and financial vulnerability in economic development', *Brazilian Journal of Political Economy* 25(2) (2005): 5–22.

Burns, Tom and G.M. Stalker, *The Management of Innovations* (London: Tavistock, 1961).

Bush, Vannevar, *Science, the Endless Frontier: Report to the President on a Program for Postwar Scientific Research* (Washington, DC: Office of Scientific Research and Development, 1945).

Cahan, David, *An Institute for an Empire: The Physikalisch-Technische Reichsanstalt, 1871–1918* (New York: Cambridge University Press, 1989).

Callon, Scott, *Divided Sun: MITI and the Breakdown of Japanese High-Tech Industrial Policy, 1975–1993* (Stanford: Stanford University Press, 1995).

Campiglio, Emanuele, Yannis Dafermos, Pierre Monnin, Josh Ryan-Collins, Guido Schotten and Misa Tanaka, 'Climate change challenges for central banks and financial regulators', *Nature Climate Change* 8 (2018): 462–8.

CAO, Moonshot Research and Development Program, 2018, https://www8.cao.go.jp/cstp/english/moonshot/top.html.

Cassirer, Ernst, 'Axel Hägerström: eine Studie zur schwedischen Philosophie der Gegenwart', *Göterborgs Högskolas Årsskrift* 45(1) (1939): 1–120.

Cha, D.-W., 'The creative economy of the Park Geun-hye administration', *Korea's Economy* 30 (2015): 34–46.

Chandler, Alfred D., *The Visible Hand: The Managerial Revolution in American Business* (Cambridge, MA: Harvard University Press, 1977).

Chang, Ha-Joon, *Kicking Away the Ladder: Development Strategy in Historical Perspective* (London: Anthem, 2002).

Chazan, Guy, 'How Germany got coronavirus right', *Financial Times*, 4 June 2020, https://www.ft.com/content/cc1f650a-91c0-4e1f-b990-ee8ceb5339ea.

Cheng, Tun-Jen, Stephan Haggard and David Kang, 'Institutions and growth in Korea and Taiwan: the bureaucracy', *Journal of Development Studies* 34(6) (1998): 87–111.

Choi, Moonjung and Han-Lim Choi, 'Foresight for science and technology priority setting in Korea', *Foresight and STI Governance* 9(3) (2015): 54–67.

Chu, Yin-Wah, ed., *The Asian Developmental State: Reexaminations and New Departures* (New York: Palgrave Macmillan, 2016).

Cimoli, Mario, Jose Antonio Ocampo, Gabriel Porcile and Nunzia Saporito, 'Choosing sides in the trilemma: international financial cycles and structural change in developing economies', *Economics of Innovation and New Technology* 29(7) (2020): 740–61.

Clarke, Amanda, 'Digital government units: what are they and what do they mean for digital era public management renewal?', *International Public Management Journal* 23(3) (2019): 1–31.

Cohen, Michael D. et al., 'Routines and other recurring action patterns of organizations: contemporary research issues', *Industrial and Corporate Change* 5(3) (1996): 653–98.

Cottam, Hilary, *Radical Help: How We Can Remake the Relationships Between Us and Revolutionise the Welfare State* (London: Little, Brown, 2018).

Crouch, Colin, *Capitalist Diversity and Change: Recombinant Governance and Institutional Entrepreneurs* (Oxford: Oxford University Press, 2005).

Dalrymple, William, *The Anarchy: The Relentless Rise of the East India Company* (London: Bloomsbury, 2019).

Delanghe, Henri, Ugur Muldur and Luc Soete, *European Science and Technology Policy: Towards Integration or Fragmentation* (Cheltenham: Elgar, 2009).

Dimaggio, Paul, 'Interest and agency in institutional theory', in *Institutional Patterns and Organizations: Culture and Environment*, ed. Lynne Zucker (Cambridge, MA: Ballinger, 1988): 3–21.

Dosi, Giovanni, *Technical Change and Survival: Europe's Semiconductor Industry*, Sussex European Papers No. 9 (1981).

Drechsler, Wolfgang, 'Beyond the Western paradigm: Confucian public administration', in *Public Policy in the 'Asian Century': Concepts, Cases and Futures*, ed. Sara Bice, Avery Poole and Helen Sullivan (Basingstoke: Palgrave Macmillan, 2018): 19–40.

—, 'Herrn Eugen Dühring's remotion', *Journal of Economic Studies* 29(4/5) (2002): 262–92.

—, 'Max Weber and the Mandate of Heaven', *Max Weber Studies* 20(1) (2020): 25–56.

—, 'On the possibility of quantitative-mathematical social science, chiefly economics: some preliminary considerations', *Journal of Economic Studies* 27(4/5) (2000): 246–59.

—, 'The German Historical School and Kathedersozialismus', in *Handbook of Alternative Theories of Economic Development*, ed. Erik S. Reinert, Jayati Ghosh and Rainer Kattel (Cheltenham: Elgar, 2016): 109–23.

—, 'The rise and demise of the New Public Management', *Post-autistic Economics Review* 33 (2005): 17–28.

—, 'The rise and demise of the New Public Management: lessons and opportunities for South East Europe', *Uprava – Administration* 7(3) (2009): 7–27.

Drechsler, Wolfgang and Rainer Kattel, 'Conclusion: towards the neo-Weberian state? Perhaps, but certainly adieu, NPM!', *NISPAcee Journal of Public Administration and Policy* 1(2) (2009): 95–9.

—, 'Debate: the developed civil servant – providing agility and stability at the same time', *Public Money & Management* 40(8) (2020): 549–51.

Drexler, Madeline, 'The unlikeliest pandemic success story. How did a tiny, poor nation manage to suffer only one death from the coronavirus?', *The Atlantic*, 10 February 2021.

Duncan, Robert B., 'The ambidextrous organization: designing dual structures for innovations', in *The Management of Organization Design: Strategies and Implementation*, Vol. 1, ed. R.H. Kilmann, L.R. Pondy and D.P. Slevin (New York: North-Holland, 1976): 167–88.

Dunleavy, Patrick, Helen Margetts, Simon Bastow and Jane Tinkler, 'New Public Management is dead – long live digital-era governance', *Journal of Public Administration Research and Theory* 16(3) (2006): 467–94.

Edler, Jakob and Jan Fagerberg, 'Innovation policy: what, why, and how', *Oxford Review of Economic Policy* 33(1) (2017): 2–23.

Edler, Jakob, Paul Cunningham and Abdullah Gök, eds, *Handbook of Innovation Policy Impact* (Cheltenham: Elgar, 2016).

Edquist, Charles, 'Design of innovation policy through diagnostic analysis: identification of systemic problems (or failures)', *Industrial and Corporate Change* 20(6) (2011): 1725–53.

Edquist, Charles and Leif Hommen, eds, *Small Country Innovation Systems: Globalization, Change and Policy in Asia and Europe* (Cheltenham: Elgar, 2009).

Ergas, Henry, *Does Technology Policy Matter?* (Brussels: Centre for European Policy Studies, 1986).

European Commission, 'Growth, competitiveness, employment: the challenges and ways forward into the 21st century', White Paper, COM_1993_ 0700_FIN (1993).

—, *Lessons from a Decade of Innovation Policy: What Can Be Learnt from the INNO Policy Trend Chart and the Innovation Union Scoreboard* (Brussels: European Commission, 2013).

—, *Research and Innovation as Sources of Renewed Growth*, COM (2014) 339 final, https://ec.europa.eu/research/innovation-union/pdf/state-of-the-union/2013/research-and-innovation-as-sources-of-renewed-growth-com-2014-339-final.pdf.

Evans, Peter, *Embedded Autonomy: States and Industrial Transformation* (Princeton: Princeton University Press, 1995).

—, 'Transferable lessons? Re-examining the institutional prerequisites of East Asian economic policies', *Journal of Development Studies* 34(6) (1998): 66–86.

Evans, Peter and James Rauch, 'Bureaucracy and growth: a cross-national analysis of the effects of "Weberian" state structures on economic growth', *American Sociological Review* 64(5) (1999): 748–65.

Fagerberg, Jan, 'Innovation policy: rationales, lessons and challenges', *Journal of Economic Surveys* 31(2) (2016): 497–512.

Fagerberg, Jan, Ben R. Martin and Esben Sloth Andersen, eds, *Innovation Studies: Evolution and Future Challenges* (Oxford: Oxford University Press, 2013).

Fear, Jeffrey, 'Cartels', in *The Oxford Handbook of Business History*, ed. Geoffrey Jones and Jonathan Zeitlin (Oxford: Oxford University Press, 2008): 268–92.

Fields, Karl, 'Not of a piece: developmental states, industrial policy, and evolving patterns of capitalism in Japan, Korea, and Taiwan', in *East Asian Capitalism: Diversity, Continuity, and Change*, ed. Andrew Walter and Xiaoke Zhang (Oxford: Oxford University Press, 2012): 46–67.

Flanagan, Keiron and Elvira Uyarra, 'Four dangers in innovation policy studies – and how to avoid them', *Industry and Innovation* 23(2) (2016): 177–88.

Foray, Dominique, *Smart Specialisation: Opportunities and Challenges for Regional Innovation Policy* (London: Routledge, 2014).

—, 'Smart specialization strategies as a case of mission-oriented policy: a case study on the emergence of new policy practices', *Industrial and Corporate Change* 27(5) (2018): 817–32.

Freeman, Christopher, *Technology Policy and Economic Performance: Lessons from Japan* (London: Pinter, 1987).

Freund, Dorrit, 'Max Weber und Alexis de Tocqueville', *Archiv für Kulturgeschichte* 56(2) (1974): 457–64.

Fukuyama, Francis, 'The end of history?', *National Interest* 16 (1989): 3–18.

Galbraith, John Kenneth, *Economics and the Public Purpose* (Boston: Houghton Mifflin, 1973).

Gaspar, Vitor, Raphael Lam and Mehdi Raissi, 'Fiscal policies to contain the damage from COVID-19', IMF blog, 15 April 2020, https://blogs.imf.org/2020/04/15/fiscal-policies-to-contain-the-damage-from-covid-19/.

Geels, Frank, 'From sectoral systems of innovation to socio-technical systems: insights about dynamics and change from sociology and institutional theory', *Research Policy* 33(6–7) (2004): 897–920.

—, 'The dynamics of transitions in socio-technical systems: a multi-level analysis of the transition pathway from horse-drawn carriages to automobiles (1860–1930)', *Technology Analysis and Strategic Management* 17(4) (2005): 445–76.

Gehlen, Arnold, *Man in the Age of Technology* (New York: Columbia University Press, 1980, original publication [1957]).

Gereffi, Gary, 'Global value chains in a post-Washington Consensus world', *Review of International Political Economy* 21(1) (2014): 9–37.

Godin, Benoît, 'Innovation studies: the invention of a specialty', *Minerva* 50(4) (2011): 397–421.

—, 'The linear model of innovation: the historical construction of an analytical framework', *Science, Technology, and Human Values* 31(6) (2006): 639–67.

Goodhart, Charles, *The Evolution of Central Banks*, 2nd edn (Cambridge, MA: MIT Press, 1988).

Goodsell, Charles T., 'Mission mystique: strength at the institutional center', *American Review of Public Administration* 41(5) (2011): 477–8.

Government of Japan, *Japan Revitalization Strategy 'Japan Is Back'* (Tokyo: Government of Japan, 2013).

—, *Long-Term Strategic Guidelines 'Innovation 25'* (Tokyo: Government of Japan, 2007).

—, *The Fifth Science and Technology Basic Plan 2016–2020* (Tokyo: Government of Japan, 2016).

—, *The Fourth Science and Technology Basic Plan 2011–2015* (Tokyo: Government of Japan, 2011).

—, *The New Growth Strategy 2010* (Tokyo: Government of Japan, 2010).

Greene, J. Meghan, *The Origins of the Developmental State in Taiwan: Science Policy and the Quest for Modernization* (Cambridge, MA: Harvard University Press, 2008).

BIBLIOGRAPHY

Greenway, Andrew, Ben Terrett, Mike Bracken and Tom Loosemore, *Digital Transformation at Scale: Why the Strategy Is Delivery* (London: London Publishing Partnership, 2018).

Guzzetti, Luca, 'The "European research area" idea in the history of community policy-making', in *European Science and Technology Policy: Towards Integration or Fragmentation*, ed. Henri Delanghe, Ugur Muldur and Luc Soete (Cheltenham: Elgar, 2009): 64–77.

Haber, Ludwig, *The Chemical Industry During the Nineteenth Century: A Study of the Economic Aspects of Applied Chemistry in Europe and North America* (New York: Oxford University Press, 1958).

Haggard, Stephan, *Pathways from the Periphery: The Politics of Growth in the Newly Industrializing Countries* (Ithaca: Cornell University Press, 1990).

Han, Heejin, 'Korea's pursuit of low-carbon green growth: a middle-power state's dream of becoming a green pioneer', *Pacific Review* 28(5) (2015): 731–54.

Hartley, Jean, 'Innovation in governance and public services: past and present', *Public Money and Management* 25(1) (2005): 27–34.

Hausmann, Ricardo, Dani Rodrik and Andrés Velasco, 'Growth diagnostics', in *The Washington Consensus Reconsidered: Towards a New Global Governance*, ed. Narcís Serra and Joseph E. Stiglitz (New York: Oxford University Press, 2008).

Heilmann, Sebastian, 'Maximum tinkering under uncertainty: unorthodox lessons from China', *Modern China* 35(4) (2009): 450–62.

Helfat, Constance and Jeffery Martin, 'Dynamic managerial capabilities: review and assessment of managerial impact on strategic change', *Journal of Management* 41(5) (2015): 1281–1312.

Helfat, Constance and Margaret Peteraf, 'Managerial cognitive capabilities and the microfoundations of dynamic capabilities', *Strategic Management Journal* 36(6) (2015): 831–50.

Hill, Dan, *Dark Matter and Trojan Horses: A Strategic Design Vocabulary* (Moscow: Strelka Press, 2015).

Hirschman, Albert O., 'The principle of the hiding hand', *National Affairs* 6(Winter) (1967): 10–23.

Hodgson, Geoffrey, 'The concept of a routine', in *Handbook of Organizational Routines*, ed. Markus Becker (Cheltenham: Elgar, 2008), 15–38.

Holidin, Defny, 'Persistent developmental limits to devising policy innovation for innovation policies in emerging economies', *Policy & Governance Review* 6(1) (2022): 1–16.

Hollingsworth, J. Rogers and Robert Boyer, eds, *Contemporary Capitalism: The Embeddedness of Institutions* (Cambridge: Cambridge University Press, 1997).

Hong, Sungjoo, 'Korean STI policies in technology catching-up stage', *STI Policy Review* 2(4) (2011): 19–28.

Hood, Christopher, 'A public management for all seasons?', *Public Administration* 69(1) (1991): 3–19.

Hood, Christopher and Ruth Dixon, 'A model of cost-cutting in government? The great management revolution in UK central government reconsidered', *Public Administration* 91(1) (2013): 114–34.

—, 'What we have to show for 30 years of New Public Management: higher costs, more complaints', *Governance* 28(3) (2015): 265–7.

BIBLIOGRAPHY

Hoskin, Keith and Richard Macve, 'Reappraising the genesis of managerialism', *Accounting, Auditing & Accountability Journal* 7(2) (1994): 4–29.

—, 'The genesis of accountability: the West Point connections', *Accounting, Organizations and Society* 13(1) (1988): 37–73.

Howlett, Michael, 'Policy analytical capacity: the supply and demand for policy analysis in government', *Policy and Society* 34(3) (2015): 173–82.

Hsieh, Michelle, 'Embedding the economy: the state and export-led development in Taiwan', in *The Asian Developmental State: Reexaminations and New Departures*, ed. Yin-Wah Chu (New York: Palgrave Macmillan, 2016): Kindle edition, chapter 4.

Hwang, Yongsoo, 'Korean STI policies in the institution building phase', *STI Policy Review* 2(4) (2011): 9–18.

ImPACT, *Impulsing Paradigm Change Through Disruptive Technologies Program Booklet* (Tokyo: Government of Japan, 2016).

Jacobsen, Annie, *The Pentagon's Brain: An Uncensored History of DARPA, America's Top-Secret Military Research Agency* (Hachette UK, 2015).

Jang, Jin-Gyu, 'S&T policy directions for green growth in Korea', *STI Policy Review* 1(1) (2010): 1–22.

Jang, Yongsuk, 'Evolution of Korean STI policies', *STI Policy Review* 2(4) (2011): 1–8.

Jannsen, Matthijs, *Post-commencement Analysis of the Dutch 'Mission-Oriented Topsector and Innovation Policy' Strategy*, Mission-Oriented Policy Observatory, Universiteit Utrecht (2020), https://www.uu.nl/sites/default/files/Post-commencement%20analysis%20of%20the%20Dutch%20Mission-oriented%20Topsector%20and%20Innovation%20Policy.pdf.

Johnson, Chalmers, *MITI and the Japanese Miracle: The Growth of Industrial Policy, 1925–1975* (Stanford: Stanford University Press, 1982).

Kaesler, Dirk, *Max Weber: Preusse, Denker, Muttersohn. Eine Biographie* (Munich: Beck, 2014).

Kalberg, Stephen, 'Tocqueville and Weber on the sociological origins of citizenship: the political culture of American democracy', *Citizenship Studies* 1(2) (1997): 199–222.

Karo, Erkki, 'Mission-oriented innovation policies and bureaucracies in East Asia', *Industrial and Corporate Change* 27(5) (2018): 867–81.

—, 'The evolution of innovation policy governance systems and policy capacities in the Baltic States', *Journal of Baltic Studies* 42(4) (2011): 511–36.

Karo, Erkki and Rainer Kattel, 'Innovation and the state: towards an evolutionary theory of policy capacity', in *Policy Capacity and Governance*, ed. Xun Wu, Michael Howlett and M. Ramesh (London: Palgrave Macmillan, 2018): 123–50.

—, 'Public management, policy capacity, innovation and development', *Brazilian Journal of Political Economy* 34(1) (2014): 80–102.

—, 'The copying paradox: why converging policies but diverging capacities for development in Eastern European innovation systems?', *International Journal of Institutions and Economies* 2(2) (2009): 167–206.

Kattel, Rainer, 'What would Max Weber say about public-sector innovation?', *NISPAcee Journal of Public Administration and Policy* 8(1) (2015): 9–19.

Kattel, Rainer and Mariana Mazzucato, 'Mission-oriented innovation policy and dynamic capabilities in the public sector', *Industrial and Corporate Change* 27(5) (2018): 787–801.

BIBLIOGRAPHY

Kattel, Rainer and Ville Takala, *Dynamic Capabilities in the Public Sector: The Case of the UK's Government Digital Service*, UCL Institute for Innovation and Public Purpose Working Paper Series (IIPP WP 2021/01) (2021), https://www.ucl. ac.uk/bartlett/public-purpose/publications/2021/jan/dynamic-capabilities-public-sector-case-uks-government-digital-service.

Kattel, Rainer, Aleksandrs Cepilovs, Wolfgang Drechsler and Tarmo Kalvet, *Can We Measure Public Sector Innovation? A Literature Review*, LIPSE Working Papers 2 (Rotterdam: Erasmus University, 2014).

Keller, Matthew and Fred Block, 'Explaining the transformation in the US innovation system: the impact of a small government program', *Socio-Economic Review* 11(4) (2013): 629–56.

Khan, Linda, 'Amazon's antitrust paradox', *Yale Law Review* 126(3) (2017): 710–805, https://www.yalelawjournal.org/note/amazons-antitrust-paradox.

Kim, Sung-Young and Elizabeth Thurbon, 'Developmental environmentalism: explaining South Korea's ambitious pursuit of green growth', *Politics & Society* 43(2) (2015): 213–40.

Klingler-Vidra, Robyn, Ba Linh Tran and Ida Uusikyla, 'Testing capacity: state capacity and COVID-19 testing', *Global Policy Opinion*, 9 April 2020, https://www.globalpolicyjournal.com/blog/09/04/2020/testing-capacity-state-capacity-and-covid-19-testing.

König, Klaus, 'Entrepreneurial management or executive administration: the perspective of classical public administration', in *Public Management and Administrative Reform in Western Europe*, ed. Walter Kickert (Cheltenham: Elgar, 1997): 213–32.

Krige, John, *American Hegemony and the Postwar Reconstruction of Science in Europe* (Cambridge, MA: MIT Press, 2008).

Lam, Alice, 'Organizational innovations', in *The Oxford Handbook of Innovation*, ed. Jan Fagerberg, David Mowery and Richard Nelson (Oxford: Oxford University Press, 2006): 115–47.

Lampedusa, Giuseppe Tomasi di, *The Leopard* (London: Fontana, 1963).

Lapuente, Victor and Steven Van de Walle, 'The effects of New Public Management on the quality of public services', *Governance* 33(3) (2020): 461–75.

Larrue, Philippe, 'The design and implementation of mission-oriented innovation policies: a new systemic policy approach to address societal challenges', *OECD Science, Technology and Industry Policy Papers*, No. 100 (Paris: OECD, 2021).

Lazonick, William and Mariana Mazzucato, 'The risk–reward nexus in the innovation–inequality relationship: who takes the risks? Who gets the rewards?', *Industrial and Corporate Change* 22(4) (2013): 1093–128.

Leadbeater, Charles, Ravi Gurumurthy and Christopher Haley, 'The COVID-19 test: what have we learnt so far? Reflections on emerging trends', Nesta blog, 1 May 2020, https://www.nesta.org.uk/blog/covid-test/.

Leca, Bernard, Julie Battilana and Eva Boxenbaum, *Agency and Institutions: A Review of Institutional Entrepreneurship* (Cambridge, MA: Harvard Business School, 2008).

Lee, Jeong Hyop, 'Issues and policies in the STI leadership phase', *STI Policy Review* 2(4) (2011): 29–38.

Lee, Kai-Fu, *AI Superpowers: China, Silicon Valley, and the New World Order* (Boston: Houghton Mifflin Harcourt, 2018).

BIBLIOGRAPHY

Lember, Veiko, Rainer Kattel and Piret Tõnurist, 'Technological capacity in the public sector: the case of Estonia', *International Review of Administrative Sciences* 84(2) (2018): 214–30.

Lember, Veiko, Rainer Kattel and Tarmo Kalvet, eds, *Public Procurement, Innovation and Policy: International Perspectives* (Heidelberg: Springer, 2014).

Levi-Faur, David, 'The developmental state: Israel, South Korea, and Taiwan compared', *Studies in Comparative International Development* 33(1) (1998): 65–93.

Lewis, Michael, *The Fifth Risk: Undoing Democracy* (London: Penguin, 2018).

Lin, Justin Yifu, *New Structural Economics: A Framework for Rethinking Development and Policy* (Washington, DC: World Bank, 2012).

Lindtner, Silvia, *Prototype Nation: China and the Contested Promise of Innovation* (Princeton: Princeton University Press, 2020).

Litwak, Eugene and Josefina Figueira, 'Technological innovation and theoretical functions of primary groups and bureaucratic structures', *American Journal of Sociology* 73(4) (1968): 468–81.

Lundgreen, Peter, 'Engineering education in Europe and the U.S.A., 1750–1930: the rise to dominance of school culture and the engineering professions', *Annals of Science* 47(1) (1990): 33–75.

Lundvall, Bengt-Åke, 'Innovation studies: a personal interpretation of "the state of the art"', in *Innovation Studies: Evolution and Future Challenges*, ed. Jan Fagerberg, Ben Martin and Esben Sloth Andersen (Cheltenham: Elgar, 2013), 21–70.

—, *National Systems of Innovation: An Analytical Framework* (London: Pinter, 1992).

Lynn, Laurence, 'Innovation and reform in public administration: one subject or two?', in *Handbook of Innovation in Public Services*, ed. Stephen Osborne and Louise Brown (Cheltenham: Elgar, 2013), 29–43.

—, 'Innovation and the public interest: insights from the private sector', in *Innovation in American Government: Challenges, Opportunities, and Dilemmas*, ed. Alan Altshuler and Robert Behn (Washington, DC: Brookings, 1997), 83–103.

Mahbubani, Kishore, *Has China Won? The Chinese Challenge to American Primacy* (New York: Public Affairs, 2020).

Manchester Institute of Innovation Research, *Compendium of Evidence on the Effectiveness of Innovation Policy Intervention* (London: Nesta, 2012).

Mann, Michael, 'The autonomous power of the state: its origins, mechanisms and results', in *States, War and Capitalism: Studies in Political Sociology*, ed. Michael Mann (Oxford: Blackwell, 1988), 109–36.

March, James G., 'Exploration and exploitation in organizational learning', *Organization Science* 2(1) (special issue) (1991): 71–87.

Martin, Ben, *What Is Happening to Our Universities?*, SPRU Working Papers, 2016-03 (2016).

Massey, Andrew, Editorial: 'The seamless web of circumstance', *Public Money & Management* 41 (1) (2021): 1–4.

Mathews, John, 'The origins and dynamics of Taiwan's R&D consortia', *Research Policy* 31(4) (2002): 633–51.

Matschoss, Conrad, *Werner Siemens: A Concise Biography and Selection of His Letters* (Berlin: Julius Springer, 1916).

Mazepus, Honorata, 'Does political legitimacy matter for policy capacity?', in *Policy Capacity and Governance*, ed. Xun Wu, Michael Howlett and M. Ramesh (London: Palgrave Macmillan, 2018), 229–42.

Mazzucato, Mariana, *A Mission-Oriented Approach to Building the Entrepreneurial State* (Swindon: Innovate UK, 2014).

—, 'From market fixing to market-creating: a new framework for innovation policy', *Industry and Innovation* 23(2) (2016): 140–56.

—, 'Mission-oriented innovation policies: challenges and opportunities', *Industrial and Corporate Change* 27(5) (2018): 803–15.

—, *Mission-Oriented Innovation Policy: Challenges and Opportunities*, UCL Institute for Innovation and Public Purpose (2017), https://www.ucl.ac.uk/bartlett/public-purpose/publications/2017/sep/mission-oriented-innovation-policy-challenges-and-opportunities.

—, *Missions: Mission-Oriented Research and Innovation in the European Union* (Brussels: European Commission, 2018), https://ec.europa.eu/info/sites/info/files/mazzucato_report_2018.pdf.

—, *The Entrepreneurial State: Debunking the Public Vs. Private Myth in Risk and Innovation* (London: Anthem, 2013).

—, *The Value of Everything* (London: Penguin, 2018).

Mazzucato, Mariana and Carlota Perez, 'Innovation as growth policy', in *The Triple Challenge: Europe in a New Age*, ed. Jan Fagerberg, Staffan Laestadius and Ben R. Martin (Oxford: Oxford University Press, 2015), 229–64.

Mazzucato, Mariana and Douglas Robinson, 'Co-creating and directing innovation ecosystems? NASA's changing approach to public-private partnerships in low-earth orbit', *Technological Forecasting and Social Change* 136 (2018): 166–77.

Mazzucato, Mariana and Giulio Quaggiotto, 'The big failure of small government', Project Syndicate, 19 May 2020, https://www.project-syndicate.org/commentary/small-governments-big-failure-covid19-by-mariana-mazzucato-and-giulio-quaggiotto-2020-05.

Mazzucato, Mariana and L. Randall Wray, *Financing the Capital Development of the Economy: A Keynes-Schumpeter-Minsky Synthesis*, SSRN Scholarly Paper No. ID 2603847 (Rochester, NY: Social Science Research Network, 2015).

Mazzucato, Mariana and Laurie Macfarlane, *A Mission-Oriented Framework for the Scottish National Investment Bank*, UCL Institute for Innovation and Public Purpose policy paper IIPP 2019-02 (2019), https://www.ucl.ac.uk/bartlett/publicpurpose/wp2019-02.

Mazzucato, Mariana and Rainer Kattel, 'COVID-19 and public sector capacity', *Oxford Review of Economic Policy* 36(supplement 1) (2020): S256–69.

Mazzucato, Mariana, Rainer Kattel and Josh Ryan-Collins, 'Challenge-driven innovation policy: towards a new policy toolkit', *Journal of Industry, Competition and Trade* 20 (2020): 421–37.

Mazzucato, Mariana, Rainer Kattel, Giulio Quaggiotto and Milica Begovic, *COVID-19 and the Need for Dynamic State Capabilities: An International Comparison*, UNDP-IIPP Working Paper (2021).

McKinsey Global Institute, *Digital Globalization: The New Era of Global Flows* (McKinsey, 2016).

Mergel, Ines, 'Agile: a new way of governing', Medium, 17 April 2020, https://medium.com/@inesmergel/agile-a-new-way-of-governing-8e2c8f7efd1.

—, 'Agile innovation management in government: a research agenda', *Government Information Quarterly* 33(3) (2016): 516–23.

—, *Digital Service Teams: Challenges and Recommendations for Government*, Using Technology Series (Washington, DC: IBM Center for the Business of Government, 2017).

Mintzberg, Henry, *Mintzberg on Management: Inside Our Strange World of Organizations* (New York: Simon & Schuster, 1989).

Mokyr, Joel, *A Culture of Growth: The Origins of the Modern Economy* (Princeton: Princeton University Press, 2016).

Moon, Manyong. 'The creation of government-supported research institutes during the Park Chung-hee era', *STI Policy Review* 2(2) (2011): 55–65.

Moore, Mark and Jean Hartley, 'Innovations in governance', *Public Management Review* 10(1) (2008): 3–20.

MOST (Ministry of Science and Technology), *National Science and Technology Development Plan 2013–2016* (Taipei: Ministry of Science and Technology, 2013).

—, *Policy Overview Booklet* (Taipei: Ministry of Science and Technology, 2014).

—, *White Paper on Science and Technology 2015–2018* (Taipei: Ministry of Science and Technology, 2015).

Mowery, David and Bhaven Sampat, 'Universities in national innovation systems', in *The Oxford Handbook of Innovation*, ed. Jan Fagerberg and David Mowery (Oxford: Oxford University Press, 2006), 209–39.

Mowery, David C. and Nathan Rosenberg, *Paths of Innovation: Technological Change in 20th-Century America* (Cambridge: Cambridge University Press, 1999).

Musk, Elon, *Making Humans a Multiplanetary Species*, video presentation (2016), http://www.spacex.com/mars.

—, 'Making humans a multi-planetary species', *New Space* 5(2) (2017): 46–61.

—, tweet, 20 August 2020, https://twitter.com/elonmusk/status/1296275496942972928.

National Economic Council and Office of Science and Technology Policy, *A Strategy for American Innovation* (Washington, DC: The White House, 2009).

—, *A Strategy for American Innovation* (Washington, DC: The White House, 2015), https://obamawhitehouse.archives.gov/sites/default/files/strategy_for_american_innovation_october_2015.pdf.

National Intelligence Council, *Global Trends: Paradox of Progress* (Washington, DC: NIC, 2017), https://www.dni.gov/index.php/features/1685-nic-releases-global-trends-paradox-of-progress.

National Science Council, Executive Yuan, *National Science and Technology Development Plan 2009–2012* (Taipei: National Science Council, 2009).

Nelson, Richard, ed., *National Innovation Systems: A Comparative Analysis* (Oxford: Oxford University Press, 1993).

—, 'The co-evolution of technology, industrial structure, and supporting institutions', *Industrial and Corporate Change* 3(1) (1994): 47–63.

—, *The Moon and the Ghetto: An Essay on Public Policy Analysis* (New York: W.W. Norton, 1977).

—, 'The moon and the ghetto revisited', *Science and Public Policy* 38(9) (2011): 681–90.

Nelson, Richard and Katherine Nelson, 'Technology, institutions, and innovation systems', *Research Policy* 31(2) (2002): 265–72.

Nelson, Richard and Sidney Winter, *An Evolutionary Theory of Economic Change* (Cambridge, MA: Harvard University Press, 1982).

Nemec, Juraj, Wolfgang Drechsler and György Hajnal, 'Public policy during COVID-19: challenges for public administration and policy research in Central and Eastern Europe', *NISPAcee Journal of Public Administration and Policy* 12(2) (2020/21): 11–22.

Nistotskaya, Marina and Luciana Cingolani, *Bureaucratic Structure, Regulatory Quality and Entrepreneurship in a Comparative Perspective*, QoG Working Paper Series 08 (2014).

Noble, Gregory W., *Collective Action in East Asia* (Ithaca: Cornell University Press, 1999).

North, Douglass, *Understanding the Process of Economic Change* (Princeton: Princeton University Press, 2005).

Nurkse, Ragnar, 'Problems of capital formation in underdeveloped countries' (1953), in *Ragnar Nurkse: Trade and Development*, ed. Rainer Kattel, Jan Kregel and Erik S. Reinert (London: Anthem, 2009): 99–212.

O'Reilly, Charles A. III and Michael L. Tushman, 'Ambidexterity as a dynamic capability: resolving the innovator's dilemma', *Research in Organizational Behavior* 28 (2008): 185–206.

—, 'The ambidextrous organizations', *Harvard Business Review* 82(4) (2004): 74–81.

Obama, Barack, Remarks by the President in the State of Union Address (2011), https://obamawhitehouse.archives.gov/the-press-office/2011/01/25/remarks-president-state-union-address.

OECD, *Governance of Innovation Systems* (Paris: OECD Publishing, 2005).

—, *Oslo Manual 2018: Guidelines for Collecting, Reporting and Using Data on Innovation*, 4th edn (Paris: OECD Publishing, 2018).

—, *Science and Growth: A New Perspective – Report of the Secretary General's Ad Hoc Group on New Concepts of Science Policy* (Paris: OECD Publishing, 1971).

—, *The Design and Implementation of Mission-Oriented Innovation Policies: A New Systemic Policy Approach to Address Societal Challenges*, OECD Science, Technology and Industry Policy Papers No. 100 (Paris: OECD Publishing, 2021).

—, *The Research System: Comparative Survey of the Organization and Financing of Fundamental Research* (Paris: OECD Publishing, 1972).

Ornston, Darius, *When Small States Make Big Leaps: Institutional Innovation and High-Tech Competition in Western Europe* (Ithaca: Cornell University Press, 2012).

Osborne, David and Ted Gaebler, *Reinventing Government: How the Entrepreneurial Spirit Is Transforming the Public Sector* (New York: Addison-Wesley, 1992).

Osborne, Stephen and Louise Brown, 'Introduction: innovation in public services', in *Handbook of Innovation in Public Services*, ed. Stephen Osborne and Louise Brown (Cheltenham: Elgar, 2013), 1–11.

Pack, Howard and Kamal Saggi, 'Is there a case for industrial policy? A critical survey', *World Bank Research Observer* 21(2) (2006): 267–97.

Painter, Martin and Guy Peters, eds, *Tradition and Public Administration* (New York: Palgrave Macmillan, 2010).

Painter, Martin and Jon Pierre, eds, *Challenges to State Policy Capacity: Global Trends and Comparative Perspectives* (Basingstoke: Palgrave Macmillan, 2005).

Papon, Pierre, 'Intergovernmental cooperation in the making of European research', in *European Science and Technology Policy: Towards Integration or Fragmentation*, ed. Henri Delanghe, Ugur Muldur and Luc Soete (Cheltenham: Elgar, 2009): 24–43.

Perez, Carlota, *Technological Revolutions and Financial Capital: The Dynamics of Bubbles and Golden Ages* (Cheltenham: Elgar, 2002).

Perry, Elizabeth, 'Is the Chinese communist regime legitimate?', in *The China Questions*, ed. M. Szonyi and J. Rudolph (Cambridge, MA: Harvard University Press, 2018): 11–17.

Peters, Guy and Donald Savoie, 'Civil service reform: misdiagnosing the patient', *Public Administration Review* 54(5) (1994): 418–25.

Peterson, John and Margaret Sharp, *Technology Policy in the European Union* (London: Macmillan, 1998).

Piening, Erk, 'Dynamic capabilities in public organizations: a literature review and research agenda', *Public Management Review* 15(2) (2015): 209–45.

Pierson, Paul, *Politics in Time: History, Institutions, and Social Analysis* (Princeton: Princeton University Press, 2004).

Pisano, Gary and David Teece, 'The dynamic capabilities of firms: an introduction', *Industrial and Corporate Change* 3(3) (1994): 537–56.

Polidano, Charles, 'Measuring public sector capacity', *World Development* 28(5) (2000): 805–22.

Pollitt, Christopher, 'Innovation in the public sector: an innovatory overview', in *Innovation in the Public Sector: Linking Capacity and Leadership*, ed. V.J.J.M. Bekkers, Jurian Edelenbos and Bram Steijn (Basingstoke: Palgrave Macmillan, 2011): 35–43.

—, *New Perspectives on Public Services: Place and Technology* (Oxford: Oxford University Press, 2012).

—, *Time, Policy, Management: Governing with the Past* (Oxford: Oxford University Press, 2008).

Pollitt, Christopher and Geert Bouckaert, *Public Management Reform: A Comparative Analysis – New Public Management, Governance, and the Neo-Weberian State* (Oxford: Oxford University Press, 2011).

Pollitt, Christopher, Geert Bouckaert, Tiina Randma-Liiv and Wolfgang Drechsler, eds, 'A distinctive European model? The Neo-Weberian State', *NISPAcee Journal of Public Administration and Policy* 1(2) (special issue) (2008/09).

Pomeranz, Kenneth, *The Great Divergence: China, Europe, and the Making of the Modern World Economy* (Princeton: Princeton University Press, 2000).

Radošević, Slavo, 'Policies for promoting technological catch up: a post-Washington approach', *International Journal of Institutions and Economies* 1(1) (2009): 23–52.

Rauch, James and Peter Evans, 'Bureaucratic structure and bureaucratic performance in less developed countries', *Journal of Public Economics* 75(1) (2000): 49–71.

BIBLIOGRAPHY

Redpath, Theodore, *Ludwig Wittgenstein: A Student's Memoir* (London: Duckworth, 1990).

Reger, Guido and Stefan Kuhlmann, *European Technology Policy in Germany: The Impact of European Community Policies upon Science and Technology in Germany* (Heidelberg: Physica, 1995).

Reichstag, *Verhandlungen des Deutschen Reichstag: Physikalisch-Technische Reichsanstalt, Denkschrift, betreffend die Errichtung derselben*, Etat 1887/88 Beilage B zu Anlage IV (1886/7), https://www.reichstagsprotokolle.de.

Reichstag, *Verhandlungen des Deutschen Reichstag: Denkschrift über die Thätigkeit der Physikalisch-Technischen Reichsanstalt in den Jahren 1891 und 1892* (1890/92 and 1892/93), https://www.reichstagsprotokolle.de.

Reinert, Erik S., *How Rich Countries Got Rich . . . and Why Poor Countries Stay Poor* (London: Constable, 2007).

Riesser, Jacob, *The German Great Banks and Their Concentration in Connection with the Economic Development of Germany* (Washington, DC: Government Printing Office, 2011).

Rodrik, Dani, 'Goodbye Washington Consensus, hello Washington confusion? A review of the World Bank's economic growth in the 1990s: learning from a decade of reform', *Journal of Economic Literature* 44(4) (2006): 973–87.

—, *One Economics, Many Recipes: Globalization, Institutions, and Economic Growth* (Princeton: Princeton University Press, 2008).

Rosier, Kevin, Sean O'Connor and Rolando Cuevas, *Taiwan's Economy amid Political Transition*, Staff Research Report (Washington, DC: US-China Economic and Security Review Commission, 2016).

Rothwell, Roy and Walter Zegveld, *Industrial Innovation and Public Policy: Preparing for the 1980s and 1990s* (London: Pinter, 1981).

Sabel, Charles F. and Jonathan Zeitlin, eds, *Experimentalist Governance in the European Union: Towards a New Architecture* (Oxford: Oxford University Press, 2010).

Sakakibara, Kiyonori, *From Imitation to Innovation: The Very Large Scale Integrated (VLSI) Semiconductor Project in Japan* (Cambridge, MA: MIT Press, 1983), http://hdl.handle.net/1721.1/47985.

Samier, Eugenie, 'Toward a Weberian public administration: the infinite web of history, values, and authority in administrative mentalities', *Halduskultuur* 6 (2005): 60–94.

Sampat, Bhaven, 'Mission-oriented biomedical research at the NIH', *Research Policy* 41(10) (2012): 1729–41.

Sarewitz, Daniel, 'Saving science', *New Atlantis* 49 (Spring/Summer) (2016): 4–40.

Schlossstein, Dominik, 'Adaptive efficiency: can it explain institutional change in Korea's upstream innovation governance?', PFH Forschungspapiere 2009/04 (Göttingen: PFH Private University of Applied Sciences, 2009).

Schluchter, Wolfgang, *Die Entwicklung des okzidentalen Rationalismus: Eine Analyse von Max Webers Gesellschaftsgeschichte* (Tübingen: Mohr Siebeck, 1979).

Schmoller, Gustav von *Grundriß der Allgemeinen Volkswirtschaftslehre*, Teil 1 (Leipzig: Duncker & Humblot, 1900).

Schneider, Martin and Mihai Paunescu, 'Changing varieties of capitalism and revealed comparative advantages from 1990 to 2005: a test of the Hall and Soskice claims', *Socio-Economic Review* 10(4) (2012): 731–53.

Schonfield, Andrew, *Modern Capitalism: The Changing Balance of Public and Private Power* (Oxford: Oxford University Press, 1966).

Schot, Johan and W. Edward Steinmueller, 'Three frames for innovation policy: R&D, systems of innovation and transformative change', *Research Policy* 47(9) (2018): 1554–67.

Schumpeter, Joseph, *Business Cycles: A Theoretical, Historical, and Statistical Analysis of the Capitalist Process*, Vol. 1 (New York: McGraw-Hill, 1939).

—, *Capitalism, Socialism and Democracy* (London and New York: Routledge, 1942).

—, *Die Krise des Steuerstaats* (Graz and Leipzig: Leuschner & Lubensky, 1918).

—, 'Sozialistische Möglichkeiten von Heute', *Archiv für Sozialwissenschaft und Sozialpolitik* 48(21) (1921): 305–36.

—, *Theorie der wirtschaftlichen Entwicklung* (Berlin: Duncker & Humblot, 1912).

Sen, Kunal, 'The Political Dynamics of Economic Growth', *World Development* 47 (2013): 71–86.

Seong, Jieun, 'Evolution and features of the Korean science and technology policy coordination system', *STI Policy Review* 2(1) (2011): 1–12.

—, 'The green growth policy of the Lee Myungbak government', *STI Policy Review* 2(2) (2011): 11–24.

Seong, Jieun and Wichin Song, 'Assessment of innovation policy coordination through Korean Office of Science, Technology and Innovation (OSTI)', *STI Policy Review* 4(2) (2014): 96–112.

Seong, Jieun, Wichin Song and Hongtak Lim, 'The rise of Korean innovation policy for social problem-solving: a policy niche for transition?', *STI Policy Review* 7(1) (2016): 1–16.

Shimada Logie, Hiroko, 'The Japanese civil service: paradox of a reform driven by but ignoring emotion', *Halduskultuur* 21(2) (2021): 64–79.

Shotter, James and Sam Jones, 'How Central and Eastern Europe contained coronavirus', *Financial Times*, 29 April 2020, https://www.ft.com/content/f9850a8d-7323-4de5-93ed-9ecda7f6de1c.

Siemens, Werner von, *Lebenserinnerungen*, ed. Wilfried Feldenkirchen (Munich: Piper, 2008).

SIP, *Strategic Innovation Program Booklet* (Tokyo: Council of Science, Technology and Innovation, 2016)

Smith, Adrian, Andy Stirling and Frans Berkhout, 'The governance of sustainable socio-technical transitions', *Research Policy* 34(10) (2005): 1491–1510.

Soete, Luc, 'From industrial to innovation policy', *Journal of Industry, Competition and Trade* 7(3–4) (2007), 273–84.

Spengler, Oswald, *Der Untergang des Abendlandes: Umrisse einer Morphologie der Weltgeschichte*, 2 vols (Vienna: Braumüller; Munich: C.H. Beck, 1918–1923).

Sraffa, Piero, *Lecture Notes on Continental Banking*, unpublished paper (Cambridge: Trinity College, 1930).

Stenberg, Lennart and Hiroshi Nagano, 'Priority setting in Japanese research and innovation policy', *Vinnova Analysis* 23 (2009), https://www.vinnova.se/contentassets/d1060bb3bcdf478ba9519956f3c775df/va-09-23.pdf.

Suurna, Margit and Rainer Kattel, 'Europeanization of innovation policy in Central and Eastern Europe', *Science and Public Policy* 37(9) (2010): 646–64.

Swedish Presidency, *The Lund Declaration: Europe Must Focus on the Grand Challenges of Our Time*. Swedish EU Presidency (2009) Lund: Sweden.

Sweeney, Gerald, 'Introduction', in *Innovation Policies: An International Perspective*, ed. Gerald Sweeney (London: Pinter, 1985): vii–x.

Takenaka, Heizō, *The Structural Reforms of the Koizumi Cabinet: An Insider's Account of the Economic Revival of Japan* (Tokyo: Nikkei Publishing, 2008).

Taylor, Frederick Winslow, *The Principles of Scientific Management* (New York: Harper & Row, 1911).

Taylor, Mark, *The Politics of Innovation: Why Some Countries Are Better Than Others at Science and Technology* (Oxford: Oxford University Press, 2016).

Te Velde, Dirk Willem, Justin Lin, Celestin Monga and Suresh D. Tendulkar, 'DPR debate: growth identification and facilitation – the role of the state in the dynamics of structural change', *Development Policy Review* 29(3) (2011): 259–310.

Teece, David, 'Dynamic capabilities and entrepreneurial management in large organizations: toward a theory of the (entrepreneurial) firm', *European Economic Review* 86 (2016): 202–16.

Thompson, Derek, 'What's behind South Korea's COVID-19 exceptionalism?', *The Atlantic*, 6 May 2020, https://www.theatlantic.com/ideas/archive/2020/05/whats-south-koreas-secret/611215/.

Thompson, Victor, 'Bureaucracy and innovation', *Administrative Science Quarterly* 10(1) (1965): 1–20.

Thurbon, Elizabeth, *Developmental Mindset: The Revival of Financial Activism in South Korea* (Ithaca: Cornell University Press, 2016).

Tindemans, Peter, 'Post-war research, education and innovation policy-making in Europe', in *European Science and Technology Policy: Towards Integration or Fragmentation*, ed. Henri Delanghe, Ugur Muldur and Luc Soete (Cheltenham: Elgar, 2009): 3–24.

Tocqueville, Alexis de, *Democracy in America*, Vol. 1 (Boston: John Allyn, 1876).

—, *The Recollections of Alexis de Tocqueville* (London: Harvill, 1948 [1893]).

Tönnies, Ferdinand, *Gemeinschaft und Gesellschaft* (Leipzig: Fues's Verlag, 1887).

Tõnurist, Piret, Rainer Kattel and Veiko Lember, 'Innovation labs in the public sector: what they are and what they do?', *Public Management Review* 19(10) (2017): 1455–79.

Trumbull, Gunnar, *Silicon and the State: French Innovation Policy in the Internet Age* (Washington, DC: Brookings Institution Press, 2004).

Ulnicane, Inga, '"Grand Challenges" concept: a return of the "big ideas" in science, technology and innovation policy?', *International Journal of Foresight and Innovation Policy* 11 (2016): 5–21.

UNDP, *Checklist for a Human Rights-Based Approach to Socio-economic Country Responses to COVID-19*, 28 July 2020, https://www.undp.org/content/undp/en/home/librarypage/democratic-governance/human_rights/checklist-for-a-human-rights-based-approach-to-socio-economic-co.html.

—, *Do Fragile and Conflict-Affected Countries Prioritise Core Government Functions?*, 8 November 2019, https://www.undp.org/content/undp/en/home/librarypage/democratic-governance/conflict-prevention/do-fragile-and-conflict-affected-countries-prioritise-core-gover.html.

van Buuren, Arwin, Jenny Lewis, B. Guy Peters and William Voorberg, 'Improving public policy and administration: exploring the potential of design', *Policy & Politics* 48(1) (2020): 3–19.

Van de Walle, Steven, 'The state of the world's bureaucracies', *Journal of Comparative Policy Analysis* 8(4) (2006): 437–48.

van Mierlo, Hans, 'Lessons from the experience of OECD countries', in *Innovations in Public Management: Perspectives from East and West Europe*, ed. Tony Verheijen and David Coombes (Cheltenham: Elgar, 1998): 388–403.

Verhoest, Koen, Bram Verschuere and Geert Bouckaert, 'Innovative Public Sector Organizations', in *Comparative Trends in Public Management: Smart Practices Toward Blending Policy and Administration*, ed. Colin Campbell (Ottawa: Canada School of Public Service, 2006), 106–18.

Wade, Robert, *Governing the Market: Economic Theory and the Role of Government in East Asian Industrialization* (Princeton: Princeton University Press, 1990).

—, 'The American paradox: ideology of free markets and the hidden practice of directional thrust', *Cambridge Journal of Economics* 41(3) (2017): 859–80.

Weber, K. Matthias and Harald Rohracher, 'Legitimizing research, technology and innovation policies for transformative change: combining insights from innovation systems and multi-level perspective in a comprehensive "failures" framework', *Research Policy* 41(6) (2012): 1037–47.

Weber, Max, *Die Wirtschaftsethik der Weltreligionen: Konfuzianismus und Taoismus. Schriften 1915–1920*, Max Weber Gesamtausgabe (MWG) I/19 (Tübingen: Mohr Siebeck, 1989 [1920]).

—, *Wirtschaft und Gesellschaft: Die Wirtschaft und die gesellschaftlichen Ordnungen und Mächte. Nachlass 2: Religiöse Gemeinschaften*, Max Weber Gesamtausgabe (MWG) I/22 (Tübingen: Mohr Siebeck, 2008 [1922]).

Wehler, Hans-Ulrich, 'Der Aufstieg des Organisierten Kapitalismus und Interventionsstaats in Deutschland', in *Organisierter Kapitalismus: Kritische Studien zur Geschichtswissenschaft*, 9, ed. H.A. Winkler (Göttingen: Vandenhoeck & Ruprecht, 1974): 36–57.

Weinberg, Alvin M., *Reflections on Big Science* (Oxford: Pergamon Press, 1967).

Weiss, Linda, *America Inc.? Innovation and Enterprise in the National Security State* (Ithaca: Cornell University Press, 2014).

—, *The Myth of the Powerless State: Governing the Economy in a Global Era* (Cambridge: Polity Press, 1998).

Weiss, Linda and John Hobson, *States and Economic Development: A Comparative Historical Analysis* (Cambridge: Polity Press, 1995).

Westlake, Stian, 'The quantity theory of innovation policy (or: why you probably don't need a DARPA)', Nesta blog, 6 April 2016, https://www.nesta.org.uk/blog/the-quantity-theory-of-innovation-policy-or-why-you-probably-dont-need-a-darpa/.

Williamson, John, *Speeches, Testimony, Papers: Did the Washington Consensus Fail?* (Washington, DC: Institute for International Economics, 2020).

Wilson, James, *Bureaucracy: What Government Agencies Do and Why They Do It* (New York: Basic Books, 1989).

Wilson, Mark, *The Business of Civil War: Military Mobilization and the State, 1861–1865* (Baltimore: Johns Hopkins University Press, 2006).

BIBLIOGRAPHY

Witt, Ulrich, 'What is specific about evolutionary economics?', *Journal of Evolutionary Economics* 18(5) (2008): 547–75.

Wittmann, Florian, Miriam Hufnagl, Ralf Lindner, Florian Roth and Jakob Edler, *Developing a Typology for Mission-Oriented Innovation Policies*, Working Paper No. 64 (Fraunhofer ISI Discussion Papers – Innovation Systems and Policy Analysis, 2020).

Wong, Joseph, *Betting on Biotech: Innovation and the Limits of Asia's Developmental State* (Ithaca: Cornell University Press, 2011).

World Bank Governance Indicators, http://info.worldbank.org/governance/wgi/#doc.

Wu, Xun, M. Ramesh and Michael Howlett, 'Policy capacity: a conceptual framework for understanding policy competences and capabilities', *Politics and Society* 34(3) (2015): 165–71.

Yao, Xinzhong, *An Introduction to Confucianism*, 10th printing (Cambridge: Cambridge University Press, 2011 [2001]).

Yes, Prime Minister, 'The Bishop's Gambit', BBC, Season 1: Episode 7, first aired 20 February 1986.

Yeung, Henry Wai-Chung, *Strategic Coupling: East Asian Industrial Transformation in the New Global Economy* (Ithaca: Cornell University Press, 2016).

Ying, Bryan, 'Constitutional bar set too high to dissolve control & examination yuans', *Taiwan Times*, 29 July 2020, https://thetaiwantimes.com/constitutional-bar-set-too-high-to-dissolve-control-examination-yuans/.

Yonglin, Jiang, *The Mandate of Heaven and the Great Ming Code* (Seattle: University of Washington Press, 2011).

Zhao, Dingxin, 'Max Weber and patterns of Chinese history', *Chinese Journal of Sociology* 1(2) (2015): 201–30.

INDEX

Page numbers in italic indicate a table; page numbers with a suffix *n* indicate an endnote with relevant number.

INDEX

Draper Laboratory (US) 127
dynamic organisations 100–2

East Asia
  agile stability 122, 161, 188–9
  competitiveness 158
  COVID-19 response 14
  crisis efficiency 190–1
  economic instabilities 148
  economic planning agencies 121–2,
    228*n64*
  high-level initiatives 187, 188, 194
  political legitimacy 194
  science and technology 157–61
  societal challenges 177–87
  US post-war aid 113
East India Company 65
Economic Planning Board (EPB)
  (South Korea) 118, 135, 159
education
  ARPA-ED (US) 25, 166
  knowledge networks 64–5
18F (digital service delivery) 4–5,
  25–6, 167–8, 169
Eisenhower, Dwight D. 99, 100
electronics industry 113, 131–3
elites of innovation 31–2
energy
  ARPA-E (US) 25, 163–6, 169, 189
  solar energy 31
  see also green technologies
engineering education 65, 222*n4*
entrepreneurial organisations 79–80,
  81–2, 104
entrepreneurial state 11–12, 15–16
environment, green technologies 28–9,
  178, 181, 183–4
Ergas, Henry 109, 111
ESPRIT (European Strategic
  Programme for Information
  Technology) 138, 139–40
Estonia, COVID-19 response 89
EUREKA initiative 138, 140–1, 153
Europe
  mission-oriented policies 109–11,
    172–6, 234*n50*
  science and technology 154–7

  support for existing industries versus
    innovation 137–8
European Commission
  Green Paper on Innovation 153–4
  Growth, Competitiveness,
    Employment 153
European Defence Agency 109
European Innovation Council 176
European Molecular Biology
  Laboratory 108
European Organization for Nuclear
  Research (CERN) 93, 108, 153
European Research Area 170
European Research Council 171, 190
European Space Agency (ESA) 108,
  171
European Strategy Forum on Research
  Infrastructures 170
European Union
  competitiveness 148, 153–4
  ESPRIT (European Strategic
    Programme for Information
    Technology) 138, 139–40
  EUREKA initiative 138, 140–1,
    153
  European Innovation Council 176
  experimentalist governance 171–2
  Framework Programmes for R&D
    139–40, 144, 153, 154, 171
  Horizon Europe programme 28,
    176
  increase in research and innovation
    143–4
  industrial collaboration 139–40
  innovation policy challenges 189
  Joint European Disruption Initiative
    176
  Joint European Submicron Silicon
    Initiative 140–1
  mission-oriented policies 172–6,
    189–90, 234*n50*
  pandemic preparedness 195
  research and innovation policies
    28–9, 107–8, 138–41, 153–4,
    191
  societal challenges 28–9, 170–6
  stability but not agility 189–90

261

INDEX

INDEX

INDEX

INDEX